High Speed Gas

An autobiography

Sir Kenneth Hutchison, FRS

Duckworth

First published in 1987 by
Gerald Duckworth & Co. Ltd.
The Old Piano Factory
43 Gloucester Crescent, London NW1

ISBN 0 7156 2200 5

British Library Cataloguing in Publication Data

Hutchison, *Sir* Kenneth, FRS
High speed gas.
1. Hutchison, *Sir* Kenneth 2.
Gas Corporation—Biography
I. Title
338.7'6657'0924 TP733.G7

ISBN 0-7156-2200-5

Photoset in North Wales by
Derek Doyle & Associates, Mold, Clwyd
Printed and bound in Great Britain by
Redwood Burn Ltd, Trowbridge

Contents

Preface

This book of mine has taken twenty years to emerge as a manuscript suitable for the ultimate test of publication. When I retired from the Gas Council in 1966 I had planned an active future for myself leaving some free time to reflect on the past and collect material for a history of the gas industry. There was no shortage of material: what I lacked was the historian's enviable skill and patience in the assembly of material out of which to create a readable, and saleable, book. The first eight chapters were available, however, in the form of four monographs written for circulation among friends and relatives: that was a good start. When I returned from the Air Ministry to my old Company in 1945 it was not long before I found myself at the centre of most of the events which in the short space of ten years before my retirement in 1966 were to create a new gas industry out of the ashes of a century and a half of history. Those ten years were fresh in my memory and, although I kept no diaries, they were well documented in articles, lectures, discourses and the like. By good fortune I met David Martin at lunch with his parents after a college gaudy. Sir John Martin was at school and at Corpus with me. David agreed to be a partner in the editing and preparation of material for publication. Besides being a good critic and arranger he is expert in the mysteries of the computer. Denis Rooke appears half way through my story and thereafter at frequent intervals, becoming Board Member for Production in the year before I retired. He is now Sir Denis Rooke FRS, Chairman of British Gas plc. He has been most helpful throughout by placing all facilities required at my disposal. To Sir Michael Milne-Watson my gratitude for many favours in the past and for continued friendship in these later years. There are many others who should be mentioned, including Ministers and senior Civil Servants, in the course of a career in which I never ceased to be astonished at the kindness and understanding of those I worked with or for. In the space at my disposal I can do no more than just say, Thank you all.

K.H.

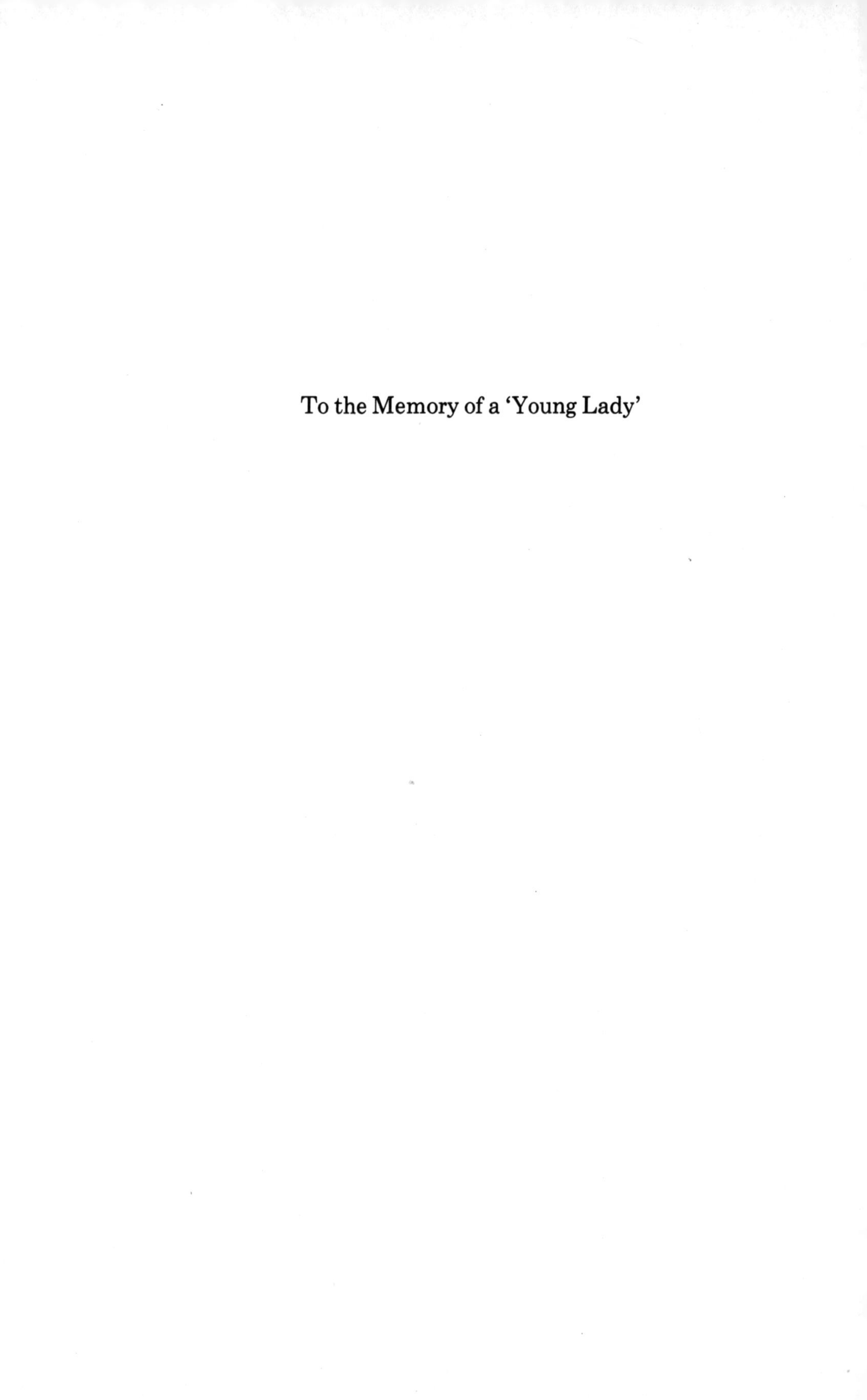

To the Memory of a 'Young Lady'

1
Corpus Christi College

> The Scholars like clever bees night and day make wax and sweet honey to the honour of God and the advantage of themselves and all Christian men.
>
> *Statutes of the Founder*

On the afternoon of Thursday 5 October 1922 the slow train that had carried me from Marylebone came to a halt at the station in down-town Oxford. Well, I can hear you say, what is so wonderful about that? In every journey that you undertake the train must stop at your destination unless of course you have been so foolish as to get on the wrong train. The importance to me of this journey was not that it had an ending but that its ending marked a beginning. Through the window on my right I had been drinking in with love and admiration the view of 'that sweet city with her dreaming spires' where I would spend the next four years and might hope to spend many more if a secret dream of an Academic future were to come true. The past was done with; here before me was ambition waiting to be fulfilled. Had I but spared a glance at something very different to be seen on the way into Oxford there would have been revealed a portent of a different future. It was the stark outline of a gasworks; no ordinary gasworks but one which, even by the lowest standards of an industry that was to employ my talents for forty years, was offensive to the eyes and the nose alike. And it was to survive for many more years against all opposition until with the coming of North Sea gas it was swept away like several hundred others. I was fresh from the Edinburgh Academy with a Scholarship in Natural Science at Corpus Christi College and was soon on my way in a taxi to the Corpus Annexe in Merton Street. It was to be the home for the next academic year of twelve freshmen, most of whom were Scholars like myself.

The *genius loci* who presided over all our doings with unquestioned authority was a college servant, or scout, called Percy Bancalari. Known to all as 'Banci' he had been tutor, confidant and stern disciplinarian in such matters as entry after midnight to many generations of Corpus freshmen. Banci met me at the door. His welcoming smile faded when I gave my name and was replaced by a look which hovered between grief and despair. 'Oh my, what are we going to do about breakfast?' What indeed, I thought, but deemed it prudent to be silent. 'You have not sent your china.' So that was it and an easy one; there was plenty of time to buy it in the town. (With that in mind and so as not to miss my first ever lunch in a smart London restaurant I had travelled by an unusual, slow and now discarded route – the timetable offered no option.) Not so, for it was early closing day, but he, Banci, had thought of that. It just so happened that a relative had a shop in the Turl nearby and was prepared to open up for any improvident freshman who cared to knock and seek admittance. It was not a very nice tea set, as I used to remind Banci when I knew him better. His reply was a laugh which in the words of Robertson-Glasgow 'bubbled up from his boots to the top of his head' (*Pelican Record*, obituary by R.C. R-G., June 1958).

I was taken to be introduced to the apartments set aside for my occupation during the coming academic year; not perhaps the best that the College had to offer, but as a mere Science Scholar in a Classical College, and the last to be elected, who was I to complain? Surely it was luxury enough to be the sole occupant of a suite comprising a sitting room and bedroom with the services of a manservant to bring and lay my breakfast and my frugal lunch of 'Commons'; consisting of a quarter loaf of crusty bread, a wedge of genuine Cheddar cheese, a generous supply of butter, and a half pint of beer – in a silver tankard – if you felt you could afford it. It was not all gracious living as I soon found out. The only baths for the entire undergraduate population, and including the one Don who used them, were three in number. They were situated in two adjoining rooms in a dark cellar under a college building, one hundred yards away on the far side of Merton Street. What these simple facilities lacked in privacy they gained in opportunities for convivial gossip, a feature shared by the place provided for another even more important daily function, rather to my astonishment at first. With no difficulty whatever I was emerging from the chrysalis of an Edinburgh day-school boy, with the burden of the 'guilt of Adam's first sin' laid on his unsuspecting shoulders at birth by the Shorter Catechism of the Presbyterian Church. Within twenty-four hours I was ready for whatever this new life had to offer, including if it were necessary or expedient, Adam's contribution, whatever that might turn out to be.

The new life began with my first awakening in a room of my very own to the sound of a fire being laid next door and the table set, and a small can of hot water placed invitingly on my wash-stand. Meanwhile Banci had been carrying our twelve breakfasts from the College kitchens, which like the baths were most of a hundred yards away, and was trying to coax congealed fried eggs and bacon back to life by the flickering flames of a newly lit fire. This I decided was the life for me: my first morning was no time for craven doubts and cowardly misgivings. I would look forward to an exciting future crowned with dazzling success. It was not the time or the place to reflect on the accidents of birth or environment which had brought me safely to that October morning in 1922. I could leave that to another self sitting at his word processor 65 years on.

Dinner in hall on the first evening of Michaelmas Term was a solemn event for the freshman; sub-fusc attire and a Scholar's gown lent a certain dignity to the occasion. Corpus had no Junior Common Room (the Dons had three!) and this was our first opportunity to meet all of our own year and cast an eye over our seniors. Scholars were privileged to sit at their own table in the centre of Hall, in strict order of seniority: the lesser orders, Exhibitioners and Commoners, had their own tables at one side. *Nos miseri et egentes homines* the Latin grace begins. Scholars were the unhappy and impecunious persons for whom it was composed and one of their number was required to recite it. The Grace goes on in some detail to tell how the good fare we were shortly to enjoy might be reconciled with our duty to that *Deus Omnipotens* who was the ultimate provider of all things here on earth: halfway through, the audience was beginning to savour the heavenly odours wafting in from the kitchens and was becoming restless. Our spokesman was not to be hurried, knowing that by ancient custom a slip of the tongue or so much as a false quantity might render him liable to a fine or 'sconce', in a silver tankard holding three pints of ale. As soon as he came to the concluding words – *alamur, foveamur, corroboremur*, the doors burst open and a dozen scouts came in bearing dishes of the excellent repast that had been foretold. Whatever our Latin grace might say it was the Manciple here on earth, in sole charge of the kitchen and himself a chef of the highest order who by skilful management and buying ensured that our meals were twice as good and half the price of anything you might find in the 'George' or any other of the taverns in current favour in the town.

The President and Fellows of Corpus

But first we must stand at our places to await the procession of Fellows to the High Table. I do not recall that the President, Thomas Case, ever appeared. He might have preferred the meals served at his own excellent table in the President's Lodge, or if still at work in his study he could have a tray of 'Commons' sent up, or simply, as we firmly believed, to avoid any risk of meeting the Chaplain, who like Case never appeared, for the converse reason we presumed. A dispute had arisen when the end of the mediaeval library was partitioned off to create a study for the President. Even if at his own expense this was going too far: Charles Plummer never forgave him.

The library and much of what it contained dated from the foundation of the College. Plummer, an authority on the mediaeval saints, was clearly justified in taking a strong line about what was being done to it. Each freshman in turn was summoned to lunch, eaten at a narrow space cleared by the scout at the end of a long book-covered table. Sharp at two he would hurry off to the Workhouse at Cowley secure in the knowledge that he had done what he could to redeem one more sinner, and go on to more congenial work among the boys at the Poor Law School. It had not always been so. Born in 1851, he won a scholarship to Corpus in 1869 and was elected to a Fellowship for life in 1873. He was appointed Chaplain while still a deacon but never proceeded to priest. His academic career was crowned with success following the publication of the two-volume edition of Bede's *Historia* in 1896. As Dean of the College he had many closely attached undergraduate friends, with sumptuous dinners in his rooms when 'the table was drawn out to its longest to receive a party of 15 or 18 friends, all delighted to be there, and their host as merry as anyone'; and there were canoe expeditions to London or Lechlade, and walking tours in the Black Forest with one or more chosen companions. Suddenly in 1902 he went into semi-retirement and it was, as I have described, a frugal lunch at one end of the long table now covered with books and a hasty retreat to his work among the boys at the Poor Law School to whom he had become a generous and friendly father figure. He lived continuously in College for 58 years, which the obituary in the *Pelican Record*, from which I have quoted freely, observes with depths of under-statement, would barely be possible again.

Lunch with the President was a more cheerful affair. There were no pauses in the flow of conversation: Thomas Case took good care of that. I cannot now recall who all the guests were: at a guess four undergraduates at a table of ten. After Grace spoken by the President, *Benedictus benedicat*, the Butler placed before our host a delicately roasted leg of well hung mutton and a single plate. We became aware of a corpulent black dog of indeterminate breed sitting expectantly beside the President's chair. Addressing Mrs Case in some such terms as 'You know, Eliza, that there is proper order in all such matters', he proceeded to carve several substantial slices. With helpings of cabbage and potatoes by the butler at the side table the heaped plateful was placed before the now impatient animal and consumed with noisy satisfaction at the far end of the room. I was questioned about my studies and unthinkingly replied 'Science'. I could not know that Case had written a letter to *The Times* some years before about 'experts who write as if all science were natural science' and still felt keenly about the matter. He was quite ready to make allowance for those denied the benefits of a classical education but he trusted that, while pursuing my studies with all the diligence to be expected of a Scholar of the College, I would always in future refer to the subject of my choice, chemistry, was it not? – as a branch of natural science: he for his part would in the years left to him continue his life long study of science in all its many manifestations, including, of course, natural science. This all in great good humour, but I was happy to observe that the table was being cleared for the sweet, a fine apple tart with large bowls of cream, and to my relief the President's attention was diverted to another guest.

Soon after this the impending retirement of Thomas Case in his eightieth year was announced. He had served the College well and several substantial legacies came to the Foundation as a result of his efforts. He wrote 78 letters to *The Times* over a span of forty years. Where he appears most reactionary, as on the admission of women to the university and the proposal to abolish Greek as a condition of entry, you can see that he was intent on preserving the Oxford he knew as one of the two centres of learning, Cambridge the other, where Greek, Latin, mathematics and mechanics, i.e. physics, would form the basis of a truly liberal education. He had no criticism to offer of the new universities for going in the opposite direction unless guilty of confusing science with natural science (*hinc illae lacrimae*). In his last seven letters (1919-1922) he tried to refute Einstein's theory of relativity by reference to the teaching of Aristotle. They were all lost causes but the letters even today make good reading. R.B. Mowat who edited them writes that 'Besides the works of Aristotle and Bacon, Case usually kept a volume of Clerk Maxwell in his bedroom'. James Clerk Maxwell was at the Edinburgh Academy in the 1840s and was somewhat of a boyhood hero of mine. Case rated him as 'one of the greatest men, thinkers and physicists of the nineteenth century'. What he would not have known was that, as reported by Eddington after a visit to Berlin, Albert Einstein had in his study just three portraits: Isaac Newton, Michael Faraday and James Clerk Maxwell. Pity is they never met, for here at last was common ground.

The procession of Fellows to the High Table was led by the Vice-President, G. Beardoe Grundy, the tutor in ancient history. He had many eccentricities of speech and manner which proved to be fertile ground for his mimics, among whom the future Lord Justice Pearce was held to be unrivalled. Born in 1860, Grundy had to leave school at 16 to earn a living as a schoolmaster, went to Blackheath as an army coach, was acting head at 24 and said later that he never again earned so much. After three years of that he had saved enough to go up to BNC, read Mods and Greats in three years and went on to study Greek history and geography. As was inevitable, he became embroiled in disputes about the sites of the battles and the tactics of the combatants which take up so much of the history of Ancient Greece. These matters he set out to resolve by the almost unprecedented step of visiting the sites. Donning hoplite armour, he was able to confound the experts by proving what men in armour carrying heavy spears could and could not do in battle. We all said it was at Marathon, but I am assured it could just as well have been at Plataea or Thermopylae. I am equally unsure about the location of the test-runs; if indeed in Greece and not at some carefully matched stretch of English countryside. But I much prefer to think of some sleepy young Greek goat herd awakened from his slumber and astonished to have one more proof if proof were needed, of the odd behaviour of mad dogs and Englishmen when exposed to the mid-day sun. Grundy excelled in sports, especially croquet; his golf it was said was effective rather than showy. The many stories attributed to him lose much of their flavour in cold print, lacking the authentic inflexions and mannerisms. There is one which is quoted in the obituary which I think stands the test, '– they murdered him under my window – I was surprised'.

Next the erect figure of F.C.S. Schiller, neatly bearded, the tutor in philosophy. He was born in 1864, one of three distinguished brothers, one a K.C., the other a banker. Like Case he went to Rugby and on to Balliol, where he took firsts in Mods and Greats. He then proceeded to Cornell where presumably he came under the influence of William James and pragmatism. He came back to England and was elected Fellow of Corpus in 1898 and began to introduce the pragmatist philosophy in the university. According to Grundy, in the world outside Oxford he was the best known teacher of philosophy in the university, 'but the mildest and most innocent reference to his philosophy exasperated the adherents of the Oxford Gospel'. As a result he never achieved his ambition to succeed to a professorship and in my time was about the only exponent of pragmatism left in Oxford. His teaching was anathema to the orthodox, among whom was a well-known tutor and Fellow of New College, H.W.B. Joseph, considered by many to be an authority on most matters. The story goes that at one guest night at the High Table in Corpus the conversation came round to the doctrine of the Virgin Birth, which Schiller declared to be 'true but not historical'. Among the guests was an earnest young man from New College who intervened to say, 'But I should like to ask Joseph about that', and could not then understand what all the laughter was about. It may have been due to the unorthodox teaching of these two Greats Tutors that, while Corpus excelled in the number of firsts in Mods, we did less well in Greats. But I found Schiller's conversation at his breakfast table and his teaching relayed by my friends most satisfying. As one recently exposed to relativity and quantum theory there was no room left for any sort of belief in the absolute.

William Phelps, the Dean, had a house in North Oxford where his mother resided, while he lived and slept in handsome rooms above the Gateway. From there he could exercise his duty of maintaining order by overseeing the goings on in the Quad when disorder erupted. He had been a Fellow and tutor in Classical Moderations all his working life and was a lonely man looking for friends, and I mean just that and no more, among the undergraduates. I was taken on a trial run through Berkshire in his aged car. As a piece of useless knowledge I had once read that the name of the pub where we lunched, the *Goat and Compasses*, was a corruption of 'God Encompasseth Us' and tried that out for size, as an opener over a tankard of ale. He thought not. That just about brought our conversation to a close and with it any ripening of our friendship. However, I might still be invited to join him for an occasional glass of wine in his room after dinner and he was happy to accept when he could our standing invitation to referee a rugger match. He was 'a man of pronounced likes and dislikes and made little effort to conceal them among his equals, which may account in part for his failure to achieve the heights which he felt were his due' (obit.) and he was openly disappointed at not being elected President in place of Livingstone. He was an incomparable tutor with a keen eye for promise in the scholarship candidates, justified by his pupils' many successes in Mods. These are the judgements of a contemporary, not mine, and at a later date. And finally, 'he liked best the clever undergraduate who was good at games and (cheerful); but who wouldn't?' The word in brackets is 'gay' in the original!

The other Mods tutor was R.W. Livingstone, later Sir Richard and President of the College. He had charm and a kindly manner set off by an impressive presence; and once arrived unheralded to visit me in the Acland Nursing Home laden with books selected to amuse and instruct in about equal numbers. Livvers must have know the cause of my being there but was careful to avoid any reference to it. I had been at a dinner in the room next to mine on the first floor of Staircase 3 where Richard Owen was celebrating his 21st, stepped out on the landing to take the air and woke up in bed at the Acland; having, so I was told, taken the whole steep flight head first in one fell swoop. My friends said I was drunk and there's an end on't, but with friends like that who needs enemies? My explanation of concussion, the result of a kick delivered to the back of my head by some ill-intentioned opponent on the rugger field that afternoon, fell on deaf ears. Livingstone may have felt that he was not yet in line to succeed Case and wisely made what I like to call the knight's move, one to the side and two ahead (just as potent in the world of business as I was to find later), so that after a spell in Belfast, where he was indeed knighted, he was recalled to be President of Corpus and became a famous man of letters and broadcaster. R.B. Mowat was a successful history tutor and a most industrious worker and researcher with 45 books in his bibliography. I only met him on a few occasions such as tea parties in his home, one such remaining in my memory bank for a chance remark by his wife in all innocence (she had been a notable hockey player) that the trouble with her Richard was that he did not put enough weight behind his stick. In 1940 he went to the USA to undertake an arduous assignment as a visiting professor lecturing to seven universities and expounding the British point of view. It was an important public service to which he sacrificed his life when the aeroplane in which he was returning crashed on a Scottish mountain.

F.B. Pidduck, the mathematical tutor, was also my moral tutor but did nothing to improve my morals or my maths. He took an instant dislike to me which I found no difficulty in reciprocating and after the first ritual breakfast I doubt if we ever spoke again. He was or had been a brilliant mathematician and might well have been interested in my fourth year research in the field of chemical kinetics but by then it was too late to mend the bridges. His failure to be elected to the Royal Society may have embittered him and like Plummer he became somewhat of a recluse towards the end of his life. The clue to our relationship is there to see in his obituary. 'He was apt to regard a man who chanced to do or say something of which he disapproved as not only weak but hateful from that moment.'

Finally and with much more pleasure I come to Professor Clark, Professor of Latin in the University and Fellow of Corpus by right. I had the good fortune to be seated next to him when I was invited to dine at High Table. I was then in my fourth year and a BA and normally sat with the other Scholars of my year. He talked at length about the France he loved, about the university and his colleagues as to whom his feelings were more mixed, and when our, or rather his, conversation came round to wine and he heard of my aversion to port, the long-enduring consequence of a fresher's indiscretion, he invited me to join him in the Senior Common Room and share his decanter of claret. When we had finished that and it was time to join the other Fellows and their guests in another common room where smoking was permitted, he waved away the case of cigars being handed round and offered instead a paper pack of French cigarettes. I had already acquired a taste for them and we both enjoyed our 'Caporals' while the stream of anecdotes continued to delight his audience.

What I first wrote about the President and Fellows of Corpus was little more than a record of undergraduate talk, imperfectly recalled after a lapse of years; in Schillerian terms, true but not historical. In justice to the memory of a body of scholarly men and dedicated teachers I sought counsel of Frank Lepper, Senior Fellow and Vice-President until he retired in 1980. He sent me some helpful notes, a few corrigenda and copies of all the obituaries from the *Pelican Record* ('Yes they are all dead, the people you speak of, and most of the writers of the obituaries are dead too'); also a copy of the privately printed volume of Thomas Case's Letters to *The Times*, 1884-1922. I have used this material to qualify but not replace some of the immature judgements of an earlier version. With the passage of the years I can look back with serenity at a period when all my mental and emotional processes were expanding towards maturity at a greater rate then ever before or since. The teaching Fellows of Corpus although divided from a new generation of undergraduates by an age gap of twenty-five or more years had much to contribute to that process.

I had confirmed at the conclusion of the scholarship examination that my tutor for the next three years would be D.Ll. Hammick, Fellow of Oriel, recently appointed and before that a schoolmaster at Winchester. His methods appeared to be easy going and not at all in the tradition of tutorial instruction at Oxford. He seldom asked for a written essay and relied on exciting our interest (I shared tutorials with the Oriel scholar, Freddie Snell) in some aspect of a subject, leaving us to read the textbooks and consult the journals and be prepared to engage in discussion at our next meeting. This suited me well enough, concentrating the mind and stretching the imagination while not making undue demands on my industry and leaving time for all those college activities which I considered essential to the full life. There was one flaw in an otherwise idyllic plan – the Scottish system of education made no provision for satisfying the examiners in two subjects. First they had to be satisfied that I was a Christian by passing an examination in Holy Scripture commonly known as Divvers; it was of no avail to plead a working knowledge of the Shorter Catechism. If you were a Muslim you could presumably demand to be examined on the Koran but the schismatic teaching of John Knox was just not on. There was nothing for it but to buy at Blackwells for a small sum a copy of *Hawkin's Guide to the Gospels and Acts* and learn by heart the answers to predictable questions such as 'Which miracles are mentioned in Luke and John but not in Matthew or Mark?' Well, I did, sitting up most of two whole nights, and passed first time, with feelings of envy of those who somewhere in the English system had qualified for exemption. After Divvers came the First Public Examination in natural science, 'Prelims' for short, which Snell and many other Scholars had been able to take from school. Hammick just did not want to know and left me to set up my own course of study, which occupied a lot of time privately earmarked for more agreeable occupations. This also I passed without too much difficulty and without interrupting the steady stream of lectures, tutorials and laboratory work designed to culminate in Final Schools at the end of the third year.

The Front Quad was our Common Room

These two obstacles surmounted, there was time to take an interest in what was happening in college, where life centred on the quadrangle famous for its sundial surmounted by a pelican in its piety feeding its young with drops of blood from its breast. Corpus was the smallest college in the university, with just over seventy undergraduates, half of whom were Scholars, and they are not necessarily the kind to shine on the playing fields of Eton or wherever, even supposing they have the time to spare. Two kinds of football and hockey in winter and cricket and tennis in summer and rowing all the year round made heavy inroads on the available workforce. Captains and secretaries vied with each other to capture unsuspecting freshmen with kind words and a warm welcome on the first few evenings of term. Unless you were strong-minded, and I was not, you might find yourself, as I did, tugging on an oar down on the Isis on a cold foggy afternoon in November in a form of torture known as 'tubbing', on fixed, not sliding, seats. The resulting wear and tear led to a condition described in a well known advertisement of the period as 'the distressing and almost universal'. Aristophanes had said it all long before in *The Frogs*. I was like Dionysius, weary of rowing across a bottomless lake on his way to the Underworld:

> What a sweat I'm all wet! What a bore!
> I'm so raw! I'm so sore! and what's more,
> The blisters have come
> On my delicate bum,
> Where I've never had blisters before.*

My condition was confirmed by 'Doggins', actually Dr H.E. Counsell, a notable character over many years of the Oxford scene and a good friend to many undergraduates. So I opted out and confined my participation to admiring, from the river bank or the College barge, the courage, skill and endurance of others.

At school distinction in the prescribed athletic pursuits had passed me by. For some real or, as I came to think, imagined weakness ('Now cough' said the doctor), it had been decreed that I should substitute gymnastics and swimming for the compulsory games which the Edinburgh Academy had been first

* Penguin Classics. Translated by David Barrett

among the day-schools to introduce. When finally I decided that this was all nonsense it was too late to catch up and I never rose above the Third XV. Corpus however welcomed me into its First (and only) XV, and I played regularly all my four years and even rose to be Captain, with the modest distinction of a Seniors Trial at Iffley Road.

Summer term so called, 'Trinity' in the academic calendar, is over by the second week of June just when, if ever, the English Summer is about to make its first brief appearance. It was never too cold to enjoy the pleasures of the river, in a well-cushioned punt on the Cherwell, not an eight-oared slave galley on the Isis. It might even be warm enough to swim at Parson's Pleasure where the young and some not so young could display themselves in a vain simulacrum of the Greek Ideals of male beauty. On passage in a punt through this sacred grove it was required that any young ladies should be disembarked and make their way behind barricades to rejoin their escorts on the other side, lest they be overcome by the bare sight of so much male nudity. When co-education has run its course and the Spartan regime, where boys and girls trained together for athletic pursuits, has replaced the Athenian, where they definitely were not, such precautions will be unnecessary.

Summer term was a time for loitering in the front quad where internees from Banci's Annexe could meet and make friends of those others who, also in their first year, but not being Scholars, had been accommodated in attics and lesser suites around the College; and receive invitations from those of two or three years seniority and still in residence in College to take coffee and a glass of port in their rooms and play a dignified rubber or two of bridge; or, more to my taste, be included in some informal gathering whose main purpose was the consumption of great quantities of beer supplied in gallon stoneware jars, as a means of promoting the pleasures of conversation:

> 'The range of subjects covered is extensive; the State of Europe: of Eton: morality among boys: bigotry among masters: the difference between Christianity professed and real: the relative merits of Eton and Association Football: the chances of a Freshman on first arriving here: the possibility of a criterion in art criticism: the way to realise the Deity: I have discussed all these merrily in the last four days.'*

The place Cambridge, the date 1877, the writer Edward Lyttelton fresh from Eton and later to be Headmaster there; but replace

* From a letter to George Nathaniel Curzon who had gone down at the end of the previous year. Quoted in *Superior Person* by Kenneth Rose.

Eton by any other Public School and you have a very fair description of how we filled in time at Corpus fifty years on.

The front quad was our Common Room and I made every use of it and resolved that when the time came to put my name down for rooms for the next two years it would be for a room in that Quad with a window providing a prospect of all that was going on there and with the priority accorded to a Scholar my wish was granted.

An announcement in the *Corpus Record* that the Governing Body had resolved that 'after due amendment of the Statutes men and women alike will be admitted to the College from October 1979 to study for all the University Examinations' passed without comment and I cannot recall that anyone felt strongly enough to write to *The Times*. Most saw it as the inevitable ending of a process begun as recently as 1974 and sanctified now by the Sex Discrimination Act (1975). The Gods thought otherwise and judged the matter to be of sufficient moment to send their Messenger to the Elysian Fields where Thomas Case was debating with Newton and Einstein a hypothesis that would prove that the General, like the Special, Theory of Relativity was no more than a restatement of principles already established by the Greek philosophers. 'Sire,' said the Messenger addressing himself first to Case, 'I come the bearer of grievous news.' For he knew of the many letters to *The Times* by which the one-time President of Corpus had sought to prevent the entry of women into the university. All three listened attentively and went their several ways with sorrowful looks and heavy hearts to ponder the consequences of a matriarchal society which they foresaw as the certain outcome of a dangerous precedent; and not before Aristotle had reminded his friends of how the Amazons, excluding all males from their company except for purposes of procreation, had become so proficient in the arts of war as nearly to overthrow Greek civilization.

Corpus had changed remarkably little in the four hundred years of its existence. It remained as it had always been, an all-male society; a married undergraduate was unthinkable, and the Fellows had been debarred by statute from matrimony until the reforms of the nineteenth century. Even so, five out of the eight remained unmarried in my time and could and did live in College, and they died unmarried with the sole exception of Schiller who married late in life and then only after he had left to live and work in America. You would hardly ever see a woman in the Quad except in Eights Week when they arrived to lend colour to our scene. An undergraduate could indeed entertain a lady in his rooms provided she left by the appointed hour of 9 pm when the gates closed and the rule was strictly enforced. The most convenient hunting ground for amorous males, the Ladies' Colleges, had their own strict rules governing all such brief encounters, and one at least insisted that no member of their flock might enter a man's rooms unless accompanied by a sort of Duenna. No wonder then that most of us decided that the whole thing was not worth the trouble it entailed and settled for a life of 'light flirtations during the vacation and deep friendships during the term' which is how Evelyn Waugh sums it up in *A Little Learning*, the first and only volume of an autobiography that he was never able to complete.

Readers of the 'Staircase in Surrey' series will recall a different scene, when Young Pattullo and his close friend Tony Mumford (later to appear as Lord Marchpane and a Cabinet Minister) delighted in spying from a corner window in the quad on the active celebration of the joys of sex by J.P. Killiecrankie (later Prebendary of Tolly Tumble) shamelessly in his room in daylight, but I never saw anything like that in Corpus. The author of the series, J.I.M. Stewart, was at the Edinburgh Academy and came up to Oriel the year before I went down. He returned to Christ Church in 1949 as University Reader in English Literature and the 'House' is where it all happens in the book, after the Second World War. But I like to place Young Pattullo where I think he properly belongs, as an undergraduate of the mid-twenties in one of the not so grand colleges.

At Corpus we were about equally divided in numbers and life style between public (boarding) schools and 'others', with public (day) schools somewhere in between. Young Pattullo found his college a friendly place as I did mine. Most of my friends were from the traditional public schools; the two friends most close to me an Etonian and a Wykehamist. I was astonished at first and slightly shocked at the freedom of talk about such matters as those on which the Etonian, Stumpe, questions Young Pattullo late one evening during the Scholarship examination. Such matters, the young Edinburgh schoolboy reflects, could not have been discussed even in their closest moments with his elder brother Ninian. A certain warmth and intimacy is established; still there is no vice in it and he hears a word of which he can only guess the meaning. When masturbation came up in casual conversation I had to keep silence and wait for a clue. It was not in the Shorter Catechism among things that 'thou shalt not do' and if our family copy of the 1900 edition of Chambers Dictionary had been to hand

I would have found myself directed to something called 'Onanism'. At that point the lexicographer hands over with the instruction 'see Genesis 38 verse 9', and leaves the rest to the reader. It was a passage already familiar to schoolboys of an enquiring frame of mind but seemed in no way relevant to a practice which most had experienced at some time or other with varying degrees of regularity and, so far as was known, without being slain by the Lord. Besides that which Onan was up before the Lord for was all to do with a woman and no one I knew had ever practised *coitus interruptus*, which appeared to be Onan's grave sin. There being no enlightenment in these matters, I continued to live as nature dictated, freed from any sense of sin; and if that suggests a thoroughly dissipated young man, bedding with whoever came along, I can only say that on those few occasions when Nature took charge the physical contact that ensued was not repeated. It was as if, curiosity satisfied, the act itself was no longer necessary as part of a deep and abiding friendship, which is also love. Oxford in the mid-twenties was not for us the Oxford of *Brideshead Revisited* – we had more in common with the Oxford of *A Little Learning* where Waugh writes of life as a Scholar and freshman at Hertford, then a small and undistinguished College, and had lunch of 'Commons', bread and butter and cheese with beer from the cask in priceless silver tankards with friends for company and conversation, and dined in Hall because it was cheaper. That was before his introduction to the notorious and short-lived Hypocrites' Club where he gained the friendship of many of the intellectual elite. Their acknowledged leader was Harold Acton, with John Sutro, founder of the famous Railway Club, Robert Byron of *Road to Oxiana* fame, Brian Howard, most decorative of all and overtly homosexual, and many others. They were to be transformed and resynthesized into the characters of his entertaining and perceptive novel with its account of an Oxford that most of us knew only by hearsay.

One benefit of life in the smallest of the colleges was the ability to recognize and know by name each one of the undergraduates; it did not mean that you wanted them all for friends. I suppose that the number of those whom I came to know well enough to do more than pass the time of day with or discuss some college matter was not above a dozen and a half. My work took me into another world and I found special pleasure and satisfaction in returning to the company of those reading humanities. I could leave all thoughts of natural science behind in the lecture theatres and laboratory and felt no urge to look for friends in other colleges. Scholars in their fourth year and Commoners in their third were out in digs and we saw less of them. In one way these seniors represented the last bastion of public school and pre-war custom by their use of surnames as a form of address except between the closest of friends and then not always in public. There were two who left the strongest impression on us freshmen. Pearce I have mentioned earlier. He was red-headed and enthusiastic about work and sport equally and very articulate and was confidently tipped for the honours that were to come his way in a career at the Bar. I can now happily acknowledge an occasion when he delivered a speech of such sparkling wit and classical splendour as to have his audience, as they say, rolling in the aisles. Not me, however, I was busy with menu card and pencil making notes for use in a forthcoming year of office as president of an engineering institution with speeches to be made to groups up and down the country, and anything from Pearce was certain to be fresh from the mint. I treasure his definition of a Pin-up Girl as Virgo Tintacta. Robertson-Glasgow, always known as R-G, was an outstanding cricketer and a blue and played for his county, Somerset. He was a famous raconteur with a fund of stories about players on and off the field and a special store of what umpires had said or done not usually intended for the record, I feel sure. He was unable for reasons of health to take the Finals for Greats and found his true vocation later as about the best and wittiest writer on cricket that the game has known. His account of the Scout, Banci, was a model of what such things should be, and I have not hesitated to borrow from it.

The third-year men were solemn by comparison, bowed down by the weight of responsibility that they carried as captains of most of our sporting activities. They were quick off the mark to visit the freshmen, Partridge for rugger and Smith for rowing, in order to sign us up for the good name of the College. I have related earlier how I had to disappoint their hopes as regards the river, although I trust I redeemed myself in their eyes on the rugger field.

We made many friends among the second-year men after the move into College and could now exchange visits at any time without the tiresome formality of booking in and out of the main gate for every transit after 9 pm. Miles Clauson was an undergraduate of that year and became my closest friend. At Eton he had been Captain of Boats and President of 'Pop'. In spite of many ties of friendship in the university, his first loyalty was to our small and socially insignificant College where he took part in all its activities, social and sporting. He had a debonair and charming manner which gained the affection of a host of friends in whatever circle he moved. Yet there was another side to his character; he could be as hard and as tough as was necessary when it came to dealing with a crisis in the fortunes of Corpus rowing. I felt privileged to be one of those admitted to the intimacy of his friendship and to share his appreciation of the good things of this earth which he knew so well how to enjoy. Arthur Couratin had a different kind of influence on my outlook on life. He was always destined for the Church, not my Presbyterian kind, and moved in the mainstream of the extreme High Church movement about the dangers of which Aunt Harriet had warned me before I left to go to Oxford. My curiosity aroused, I took to visiting such temples of near-Popery as Pusey House and the Cowley Fathers and learned to enjoy the ritual of the High Mass, the vestments, the candles, and the incense, without concerning myself too deeply about what it all meant; that came a few years later. Meanwhile since

> 'The rather rathers
> Worship at the Cowley Fathers
> But the whole hoggers
> Go to Saint Alywoggers.'

I felt compelled to visit also (O Lord of my Presbyterian Fathers, forgive me, for I am certain John Knox will not!) Saint Aloysius where I could participate in authentic Popish practices; but briefly – the Scarlet Woman was not to be allowed to ensnare yet another innocent young victim.

The Scholars of my year, confined to Banci's Annexe, had got to know each other well enough to be sure of those we would want to know better. The Senior Scholar and the one I first knew well was Herbert Rees, a day boy like myself but from Birmingham. He was devoted to music and the theatre and claimed (he may not care to be reminded of it) to have sat through twenty-five performances of *The Immortal Hour*, an opera by Rutland Boughton. The haunting melody of 'How beautiful they are, the Lordly Ones' on a composite record in the 'These you have loved' category remained for long the only survivor; until last year, when the complete opera was recorded on two 12 in. discs and I fell for it. Possibly Herbert was right after all. He soon drifted away from our small circle into the orbit of the OUDS and the Union but whenever seen in College he was good for a laugh, and still is when we meet from time to time. Lionel Barnaby had a sad and solemn face which belied his fund of stories culled from Herodotus and others of his classical studies – all rude and funny and the choicer ones outright scabrous. The solemnity of his visage was accentuated on occasions when, consumed by a yearning for affection, he could find solace only in the muted tones of his beloved trombone. One night his grief overflowed and he emerged into the front Quad at an hour well past midnight and gave the whole college, including the Dean, the benefit of a soulful rendering, fortissimo, of Bach's 'Sleepers Wake'. Even the Dean was moved, for I never heard that Lionel earned so much as a reprimand. The History Scholar of our year was John Brooks; at Winchester he had been called 'Frog' for no good reason that I could see. He had a most happy disposition and a zest for living that made him instantly welcome in any company and he had a very wide circle of friends both in Oxford and outside. We came to know each other intimately after moving into College, where he had chosen rooms adjacent to mine but on the next staircase. Any similarity ended there; his tea service was a delicate Wedgwood blue and the loose covers that concealed the unattractive College furniture were in excellent taste. It would not have been difficult to be a leader of fashion in Corpus and John never tried to be that, but his trouser bottoms were among the first to break the 20 in. barrier and came in subtle shades of blue or pink from Hall, the Tailor in the High. Does anyone now remember the Oxford bags of the 20s? John was devoted to the Turf and gave useful advice to one needy follower of form, with winners of the Derbys of 1924 and 1925.*

In our third year we both seemed to have a little more time on our hands. I think he had settled for something less than a First and could get by without too much or too intensive study. As for me, I was cruising along quite comfortably with a good prospect of a first if I could put in a satisfactory fourth year of research, and I had hopes that Hinshelwood would take me. In what racing men would call trial stakes I had managed a 'mention' in my second year and a 'place' in my third, in the Gibbs Scholarship Examination, and that seemed good enough unless something dreadful happened in my last term. I went with John on several visits to rooms, mostly in Balliol as I seem to recollect, where the company was amusing and some of the notable characters of the period were to be seen. There was also gambling. I knew the rules of poker from family sessions at penny stakes and three-penny raises, and here was a chance to test my skill on a more serious plane. Of course there is luck, long runs of it, good or bad, and this is where the poor man can fall into a trap – if he starts too high he

* For the record, Sansovino 9-2 and Manna 8-1

may not be able to lose for long enough. I was a beginner at the stakes but knew enough to keep my head down when the cards were running against me, leaving the well-heeled to battle it out until there was something in my hand worth going for. There is a scene in Canto VIII of Gilbert Frankau's epic poem of high life in the 1900s which should be obligatory reading for aspiring poker players. The hero, Jack, has been playing all night, and losing, with three rich Americans on their luxurious yacht. Dawn breaks and with it the final consolation pot; he stakes his all on a traitor Ace-Flush dealt him cold. Hogg, the opener, has drawn one card. Many raises later it is Hogg's four tens that spell ruin to our hero and the Canto ends:

> Yet when thy cards seem fair and bets are steep
> With tutored eyes the danger point discerning
> Heed thou the solemn warning of the bard:
> 'Beware of him who draws the single card.'*

There was also roulette, which is a silly game in spite of all that systems experts say and write. The bank is bound to win, even if only a small proportion of the stakes, so long as it only pays 35-1 on a number with the zero as a catch-all. I will confess that, even knowing all that, I cannot resist a visit to a respectable casino, where I enjoy the scene and like to play secure in the knowledge that no skill of mine can influence the final result, and if I have lost the money I have taken to play with I stop; somehow or other more often than not I seem to win.

As a History Scholar, John went down after three years, and stayed up just long enough after schools to do Ascot in style and Commem, during which I joined his party at the Balliol ball, an experience not to be missed but which I never again felt rich enough to repeat. He went on to a family firm of stockbrokers and a year later I joined him at 94 Grosvenor Road. But that only lasted a year; he was restless and bored with the City and gave it all up and the secure prospects it offered, and went to Western Australia in a pioneering spirit. He breeds racehorses for sale to the trainers, and I feel sure he will always be as good as ever at the business of picking winners.

The undergraduates of our following year when they emerged from Banci's Annexe and took up residence in College impressed me as being men of stern purpose and high principles, or possibly it was just that we were slipping. Several fulfilled their early promise in careers in Government service that were crowned with

* *One of us* by Gilbert Frankau. Chatto and Windus 1912

the highest honours. George Abell resumed the tradition of combining blues with firsts and service to the empire and rose to be Private Secretary to the Viceroy of India and Advisor during the years of crisis. John Martin was Dux of the whole school at the Edinburgh Academy and Dux of most of the classes in which we travelled up together, with myself content to be second. He has reminded me that when I came from nowhere (i.e. 1B) to join him in 2A, as related in Chapter 4, I scared him into a new burst of activity by being declared Dux of 2A for that one glorious year. He was in Winston Churchill's private office for virtually the whole of his wartime administration until after VE Day, as Principal Private Secretary for most of the time, and I can well believe that as a son of the manse a stern Presbyterian background may have helped him to stand the 'heat of the kitchen' which they all had to bear. The Scholars of the year after that had not come into residence in College by the time I went out to live in digs. John Aldridge took over the rooms that John Brooks had occupied, of which I had so many pleasant memories. He hung in it his own paintings, and left no doubt that he was already quite a mature artist. He went on to be RA, the only one so far as I know that Corpus can claim. He was also a hearty athlete giving powerful support to all the team in which he played, in the highest Corpus tradition. Charles Hutton, as a Commoner, was in College in my third year. He was at Fettes, against whose supposed boarding-school airs we at the Academy exercised a ritual hatred. He became a very good friend, moved freely in our third-year circle and was a pillar of the XV, which badly needed support. You can pick and you can choose in the storehouse of memory, and it is when you are trying hardest that the truth you are seeking evades all attempts to tie it up in a neat tidy parcel. And so to those whom I may have misjudged and to those whom I have failed to recall, usually because I could not present them as genuine living figures in the round and not pasteboard figures on the backcloth of memory, I will excuse myself in the terms used by dealers in any other commodity – E&OE.

Remembrance of things past

Years later when I began to read Marcel Proust's incomparable work I recalled having heard it praised by those who were engaged in reading *Du Côté de Chez Swann* and claimed they could unravel the meaning of page-long sentences written in a style as to which, so it was said, even the French were having difficulty, and preferred to await those masterly translations by C.K. Scott Moncrieff which opened the magic door to me. It is central to Proust's theme that voluntary memory is valueless as an instrument of evocation, capable only of 'reproducing for our gratified inspection those impressions of the past that were consciously and intelligently formed'; it is through the agency of involuntary memory that we recover the past, but it 'chooses its own time and place for the performance of its miracle'. So the whole magic world of Combray seen through the eyes of a child and its two ways, Swann's Way and the Guermantes Way, came from the magic of a madeleine dipped in a cup of tea. Years ago in a bookshop in Gray's Inn Road I noticed a slim volume, hardly more than an essay, entitled simply, *Proust* by Samuel Beckett. Thinking it might help to an understanding of *Remembrance of Things Past*, of whose twelve volumes I was then in about the third, I bought it for one shilling and ninepence. I found Beckett even more difficult than Proust and I put it away. Forty years on and I read by chance that a book of that title had just been sold at Sothebys for £100. Anxious search confirmed that I did indeed have a copy of the book in question. Now impelled by curiosity I began to read and could not put it down until finished and now I have not the heart to sell it, and will here acknowledge with gratitude the several quotations appearing on this and the following page.

Time regained

The last part of *A la Recherche du Temps Perdu* is both a beginning and an end. The narrator attends an afternoon reception given by the Princesse de Guermantes, one-time Mme. Verdurin, self-appointed arbiter of taste in all things artistic and musical, from the security of her 'small circle' into which no member of the Guermantes clan had ever been admitted, except arrogant and intolerant M. de Charlus in pursuit of the young pianist Charles Morel, and that did not last long before he was expelled for lack of obedience to the precepts of the 'Mistress'. While the narrator waits in the library for an interval in the music, the shape of the book to come takes form as a consequence of incidents, trivial in themselves, which have annihilated time and brought past scenes intact into present consciousness. The doors open and he enters the salon where he encounters the spectacle of time made flesh. They pass before him, characters who will fill the twelve volumes of his great work but now in the disguise of old age, through which he must penetrate before he can make his identifications. I will leave the last word to that same Baron Palamède de Charlus whom the narrator had encountered on his way to the reception, escorted by the faithful Jupien, once servitor and pander, now guardian, of an aged and fallen King Lear. He enumerates triumphantly the names of many friends now dead: Hannibal de Bréauté – dead! Charles Swann – dead! Baron de Talleyrand – dead! And each time the word 'dead' seemed to fall on the defunct like a shovelful of earth. (But cf. Beckett – 'and the dirge of his sepulchral whisper falls like clay from the spade of a gravedigger'.) I will not, like the Baron, invoke the names of those no longer living, nor like the narrator recall the mutual disbelief with which at some reunion or casual encounter we have tried, each of us, to discern in that other septuagenarian the youthful figure and features of some Adonis that we knew and perhaps loved for a while. Better far to recall the life we lived in great contentment and how hard we tried to fill every minute and every hour of every day with the enjoyment of it. This was our Lyonesse which, when our time came, we left with magic in our eyes, and by the magic of memory it is peopled by youths who will never grow older.

Ave atque vale

The last few days of the Trinity term in the summer of 1925 brought to an end the enjoyment of life in the front quad of Corpus; that and the friends I had made was the part of my Oxford experience that I treasure most of all. Many of them were going down, among their number two of my closest friends; most of those that remained would be scattered about in lodgings all over Oxford. I was fortunate in being able to join Arthur Gott, a Commoner of our year, in his comfortable digs at the far end of St. Giles; most convenient as it happened for the place where I would be working.

It was a time for regrets but I was to find out quite soon that there would be little time left over to regret anything in my fourth year. A few of us celebrated by escaping from college and following a route that led to Christ Church meadows, made our uncertain way down to the river. Here we enjoyed a ritual swim at midnight in the Isis from a barge that was conveniently open and, thus purified, climbed back to resume our sorrowful libations on a night of memories and sighs. By morning it was all back to normal and everyone busy with packing and details of travel to go their several ways; some to take up chosen careers, others to prepare for yet further examinations for the Home or Colonial or Indian Civil Service.

I was left to make my arrangements for the following year which would be dedicated to research. The results of examinations in the Honours School of Chemistry are announced only as a list of names of those 'Qualified for an Honours Degree'. A year later the 'class' is awarded and takes into account a thesis presented by the candidate, recording the results of his year's research. I would have had to be very thick not to be able to interpret the hints that Hammick was dropping and I knew I was safe for a First, all things being equal. Some are more equal than others and I had the great good fortune to be taken on by Cyril Hinshelwood for Part 2. He was the brightest star of the post-war generation of Oxford chemists and was to fulfil that early promise by a Nobel Prize and the Presidency of the Royal Society and many other honours besides. He was then a Fellow of Trinity and it so happened that he had no Scholar coming on to take Part 2 that year; my good fortune continued and I was to be his personal research assistant and not just one of the supervised. Hinsh wanted me to stay up for a week or more and to get acquainted with the laboratory where we would be working and the apparatus that we would be using. He wanted everything to be ready for a flying start at the beginning of September, and it was. But all this belongs to another and very different part of my Oxford experience; more so indeed than I could ever have guessed. On a golfing holiday in what was left of the Long Vac I met a Young Lady. My intentions were serious and so too were hers, as witness our Golden Wedding celebrated in 1979. Henceforth it was a case of 'Now your days of philandering are over.'

2
In Pursuit of Science

> Whoever in the pursuit of Science seeks after immediate practical utility may generally rest assured he will seek in vain.
>
> von Helmholtz

When Fairgrieve, my science master at the Edinburgh Academy, advised me to try for Oxford if it was chemistry that I really wanted to study, he must have been watching the march of events there during the past decade; and had made a shrewd assessment of a change – amounting to a revolution – in the study of science at a university which prided itself on its classical traditions. (These traditions were fiercely defended by Thomas Case, President of Corpus, during most of the sixty years of his residence in the university, as I have related earlier.) That decade had witnessed the final stages of what had been a painfully slow process. It began with the foundation of a few university professorships in the early part of the nineteenth century. The lectures which the professors gave were outside the College system, and since the colleges alone were responsible for determining the qualifications for graduation there was no obligation on anyone to attend them. The professors were poorly paid and some, like Buckland of Corpus, the acknowledged founder of British geology, had to find a career in the Church. But reform was in the air and gradually in the face of bitter opposition the university was persuaded to set up an Honours School of Natural Science in 1850 and to agree in 1853 to build a central museum where all the branches of natural science would come together and find accommodation. Sir Henry Acland, the Regius Professor of Medicine, led the movement for reform, another significant outcome of which was the decision in 1855 to establish a properly endowed Waynflete Chair of Chemistry with a Fellowship at Magdalen College.

A site for the new museum was found in a corner of the University Parks area, the first of many encroachments on the meadows surrounding that most pleasant of all cricket grounds. We viewed it with amusement in my time; it can now be restored to favour for what it is, an expression of John Ruskin's architectural fantasies. To this unlikely building were attached two even more improbable laboratories, one of which was for chemistry. This the architect, under the influence of Ruskin no doubt, designed as a larger-scale but otherwise faithful copy of the Abbot's Kitchen at Glastonbury. Ruskin declared that the Gothic style was just the thing for this new and exciting world of science. There is a delightful purple passage in a letter from Ruskin to Acland about the use of Gothic for the new building, quoted in *A History of the Oxford Museum* by Vernon and Vernon (Clarendon Press 1909).

> Here was the architecture which I had learned to know and love in pensive ruins. No other architecture, as I felt in an instant, could thus have adapted itself to a new and strange office ... but these old vaultings and strong buttresses – ready always to do service to man, whatever his bidding – he had but to ask it of them, and they entered at once into the lowliest ministries of the arts of healing, and the sternest and clearest offices in the service of science.

The Vernons conclude that whatever views might be held as to the suitability of Gothic architecture for a museum of scientific collections there could be no doubt as to its unsuitability for laboratories; a sentiment echoed by all who worked there for the next hundred years. The only obvious concession to its new purpose was the provision of chimneys at the four corners to carry off noxious fumes where the single one in the centre was all that the Abbot required.

The first Waynflete Professor of Chemistry was (Sir) Benjamin Brodie, appointed in 1855; he was an active and successful research worker. Among his pupils was Vernon Harcourt, who was to become an expert on gas industry matters, and wrote of Brodie. 'Nor did his devotion to research interfere with his interest in his pupils. He would come round the laboratory from time to time, and talk or lend a hand to those who were working.' He was succeeded in 1872 by (Sir) William Odling, who was appointed for life under the old statutes and held on until 1912 when he was 83. During all those forty years he contributed as far as can be seen almost nothing to the advancement of chemistry at Oxford. The Royal Society memoir quotes him as inclined to the view that 'it was not etiquette for the Professor to enter the Chemical Laboratory'. We may suppose that Ruskin's not so ancient stones also had something to say and that it was unseemly for an abbot to be found consorting with monks and lay-brethren.

The great change came when the electors appointed W.H.

Perkin to succeed Odling in the Waynflete Chair in 1912. He was the oldest of the three sons of Sir William Perkin FRS, the discoverer of aniline dyes, himself a talented scientist and very successful entrepreneur. The new Professor lost no time in persuading the university to grant funds for a new laboratory and finally secured a large benefaction from C.W. Dyson Perrins. C.W. was the son of J. Dyson Perrins who had made a fortune out of the sale, world wide, of Lea and Perrins Worcestershire Sauce. In an earlier career he had become an authority on the structure of the alkaloid berberine; the families were probably acquainted. From his experience at Edinburgh, Leeds and Manchester the new Professor knew just what was wanted and how to get it, and if his plain walls had any message to give to aspirants for Honours in the School of Chemistry it should have been 'Get on with your work and don't waste your time and mine'. Perkin was known to be a very fast worker, and the story is told how:

> Beginning at one end of a bench stocked with newly washed and dry apparatus (he always kept a washing boy busy) he gradually accumulated the soiled beakers and test tubes at the other end until there was little working space left and then he went home. But within the space of four hours he contrived to get through more work than any of his collaborators could accomplish in twice the time.

He was a brilliant and convincing lecturer at our undergraduate level, although his heart was not in it; he grudged every hour spent away from the bench and his research workers. He would enter the well-filled lecture theatre sharp on the hour and deliver to a hushed and expectant audience what could now be called a 'punch line', for example, 'As I was passing through my laboratory on my way here I tried a little experiment', or more frequently – 'On my way here I called in at the Library and read what —— had to say about ——', each leading up to a carefully rehearsed dissertation and a demonstration at the bench which never failed to draw a round of applause when as always, it came to a successful conclusion. It was a truly great professional performance.

The success of the new laboratory, named 'Dyson Perrins' after its benefactor, encouraged Oxford to try again. Funds were made available to upgrade the Dr Lee's Readership at Christ Church to a Professorship and the electors sent for Frederick Soddy, an Oxford man and the most prominent atomic chemist of the day. He had taken a first in Natural Science in 1895 and later went out to Canada where he met Ernest Rutherford at McGill and there made a valuable contribution to the interpretation of the results of the atomic physicists. Back at Glasgow he continued this work with the able collaboration of a one-time laboratory attendant and future Chairman of ICI in the person of Alexander Fleck. He formulated the Group Displacement Law and coined the word isotope, for all of which he was awarded the Nobel Prize for Chemistry in 1921. But his appointment as Professor at Aberdeen in 1914 and many trivial investigations in aid of the war effort seemed to break the continuity of his thinking, and most of the rest of his life's work consisted of social, monetary and economic theorizing of no lasting value. At Oxford he just disappeared into the Abbot's Kitchen and for all I knew he might never have existed. An efficient group of College Fellows carried on teaching inorganic chemistry. With no inspiration from above, research could not flourish in that arid climate.

During the forty years of Odling's tenure of the Chair of Chemistry the initiative passed to the College laboratories. There were in my time six of these: at Christ Church, Magdalen, Queen's, Jesus, Balliol and Trinity. These last two were fortunate in their location and in the Fellows the Colleges appointed, Nagel at Trinity, and Conroy followed by Harold Hartley at Balliol. When they joined forces to build a new laboratory inside Balliol, but right on the boundary with Trinity (into whose territory it later overflowed), it soon became pre-eminent among the College laboratories. Under the inspired leadership of Hartley, later Sir Harold, CH, CVO, FRS, Balliol-Trinity became the university centre for instruction and research in physical chemistry and so remained until the new laboratory donated by Lord Nuffield was ready for occupation at the beginning of World War Two. The arrival of two Balliol Scholars, Hinshelwood and Bowen, from their war service and the return of Hartley, still in the uniform of a Brigadier-General in the Chemical Defence Section, gave new impetus to research. From 1920 on, papers began to issue in increasing numbers to appear in the scientific journals and supplement the already considerable output of the Dyson Perrins under Professor Perkin. Oxford was now in the top bracket of the English universities as measured by the number of chemical papers published. This did not pass unobserved, and the 1925 Presidential Address to the Chemical Society included the table on p. 28.

Naturally I knew nothing of all this when I went up in 1922: the past is of no concern to the young and I had my sights firmly set on my main objective – a good degree and a good job to follow, hopefully academic. A foretaste of what might be involved in my

Chemical papers emanating from the Universities of Oxford, Cambridge and Manchester and Imperial College London in three six year periods from 1901 to 1924.

	1901-06	1908-13	1919-24
Oxford University	18	89	140
Cambridge University	82	122	142
Manchester University	91	139	82
Imperial College	101	114	143

pursuit of these aims was the confusing and formidable list of lectures posted on the notice boards in the College porch. My first visit to Hammick in his rooms in Oriel, with Freddie Snell the Oriel Scholar, made all clear. I was to disregard all lectures leading up to the First Public Examination, Prelims for short (which Snell was able to take direct from Winchester and had already passed), and of the rest half were discarded as of no account. Professor Perkin on organic chemistry and M.P. Appleby on inorganic chemistry were mandatory. Perkin's lectures I have already mentioned. Intended mainly for research workers, their great value to the undergraduate lay in their ability to arouse our interest and direct us to the original sources in textbooks and published papers. Appleby's were of a more routine character and less dramatic in their presentation. They were nevertheless of more immediate consequence in the all important matter of examination success. Inorganic chemistry was suffering a decline in public esteem; there was not a great deal of research activity and there was a lack of really good up-to-date textbooks. These were possibly the last of such courses that either lecturer gave. Appleby went to ICI to head up research at Billingham. Professor Perkin was able to reduce his lecturing commitments and devote more time to research. He died relatively young in 1929; it is conjectured that his work on strychnine which involved sodium amalgam as a reducing agent in boiling solutions had exposed him to dangerous concentrations of mercury vapour, a risk not fully comprehended at the time. One very important change that he instituted soon after the end of hostilities was the introduction of the Part 2 – research year in the Honours School of Chemistry – to which I owed the immense privilege of working with Cyril Hinshelwood in my last year at Oxford.

The prescribed working day, which included Saturday, consisted of two one-hour lectures followed by two hours' practical work, with a further two hours in the afternoon or evening. Prelims was my immediate concern with a choice of two out of three subjects, chemistry, physics or mathematics. Chemistry would have to look after itself; no way could I see how to fit in the practical work for physics. So it was a case of back to the mathematical textbooks and burn the midnight oil. All this and Divvers too made for a very busy first two terms, as to which I have already made complaint.

During my second term there were indications of some financial stringency at home and there was talk of shares having to be sold. Many of the boys from the English schools could get grants from County Education Authorities but nothing like that was to be had from Scotland. I took my problem to Hammick who thought I should try for one of the Goldsmiths Company Scholarships. I did, and succeeded, and so doubled the £80 of the Corpus Scholarship and have been most grateful ever since to the generosity of one City Livery Company at a critical time in my young life. Emboldened by success I decided to enter for the newly-founded Gibbs Scholarship, and to my surprise achieved a 'mention' but of course no money. Still there was honour and glory and a chance to try again next year. It was more than ever necessary to make sure of a good class in the Honours School – nothing less than a first for an academic career and a good second for industry and the scientific side of the Civil Service. Hammick was beginning to feel certain that he had material for two firsts and was planning accordingly. As every trainer knows it is far from easy to keep up the momentum throughout a three-year course; be it training for the Derby or an Olympic Gold Medal or the Honours Schools at Oxford. Our tutor's plan was to spend the first two years building up the equivalent of muscle by a thorough grounding in all three of the prescribed branches of chemistry. This would provide the mental stamina needed to take the candidate safely over at least two-thirds of the questions required to be answered on the Day. Aspirants for first class honours could now put on a burst of speed and dazzle the examiners by a sparkling display of depth of knowledge and understanding of the problem (spiked with several references to the literature) in answers to questions for which they had prepared by reading advanced text books and by time spent among the journals in the Radcliffe Science Library.

That as I see it was the plan, but I had found many more agreeable ways of spending my time and the grand design was in danger of foundering without entering the home straight or reaching the last lap, whichever metaphor you prefer. Hammick was undeterred and specified an old-fashioned reading party for two in the long vacation, well away from all distractions, for not less than two and preferably a full three months. We had to agree and settled for Austria where the rate of exchange remained very favourable even after recovering from the post-war astronomic inflation when you could have bought a million kroner for one pound sterling. We could enjoy real comfort in the Tyrol for five pounds a week and slum it in just bearable circumstances for a little over two. The *Kaisergebirge* were close by for week-end breaks and simple rock climbing with no call for a guide. I seem to remember making £40 last ten weeks, starting at the top in Kufstein and working our way down market to Rattenberg on the river Inn where our hostelry was devoid of any form of mod.con. and we had to take to the woods with our books on the day when a sinister cart would arrive to empty the (built in) cesspit. Even so we cut it fine and travelled home third class on hard slatted seats. The plan worked, with the aid of a hundredweight of books in a stout trunk and a determination to spend never less than forty hours a week reading and writing and cross-examining each other. We were almost always the only English speakers in any company we kept and had every opportunity to learn and practise (albeit with strong Viennese accents) German – still, in spite of the war, the language of science.

On returning to Oxford for the third, critical, year it was agreed all round that the grand design had been rescued from peril, and as a reward for good behaviour we were offered a piece of research to be carried out in the Balliol-Trinity laboratory. What strings were pulled to make that possible I never knew; Hammick had his office and laboratory in the Dyson Perrins, and Corpus and Oriel had no claim on the Balliol-Trinity *Lebensraum*. But I was overjoyed at this unexpected opportunity to work in the place where physical chemistry had found a home in Oxford and where research was being actively pursued with results that were beginning to receive recognition world wide. The problem set before us was to elucidate the nature of the reaction between bromine and formic acid in aqueous solution. First the literature search to make sure that we had not been forestalled, and to confirm that the reaction goes to completion to produce only hydrobromic acid and carbon dioxide, or

$$Br_2 + HCOOH = 2HBr + CO_2$$

in the shorthand of chemistry. Next the assembling of apparatus which had to be whatever was generally available in a teaching laboratory. And so to work. By varying the concentration of each of the reactants individually we showed that the reaction was bimolecular but that the rate was greatly diminished by the hydrobromic acid formed. We then went on to show that both the hydrogen and the bromide ions were active in this respect, but in a manner which was consistent with the hypothesis that it is the formyl ion which reacts but then only with free bromine molecules, and not with bromine that is associated with bromide ions as tri-bromide, Br_3^-. Not world-shattering indeed, but a source of great satisfaction and some inward pride when our paper was accepted for publication by the Chemical Society.

Whatever its merits, our effort could have claimed to have satisfied the von Helmholtz criterion of having no practical utility, either immediate or in any foreseeable future. But I had learned a lesson which was to remain valid for the rest of my working life: if you want to find out what is going on under almost any conceivable set of circumstances, be it in the laboratory or on a gasworks, it is always best to alter only one variable at a time.

Somewhere at the back of Queen's was a brewery, still active and renowned for its 'audit ale'. The secret, I was told by A.S. Miller, the lab. assistant, who was also the brewer, was to fill the vat with good ordinary ale and start from there. Close by stood a small building, the Queen's College Laboratory, presided over by a brilliant and irascible Fellow of Queen's called Chattaway. He was renowned for his skill in the preparation of new and rare organic chemicals and for his merciless castigation of anyone having the misfortune to spill anything on the spotlessly clean bench tops or to allow any evil smell to escape during a preparation. Those who erred in these matters were required to remove the offending vessel with all possible speed into the yard outside and wait there until it, and Chattaway, had both cooled down. Thither was I dispatched for the good of my soul (great wrath descending on any who skipped a session) and for the increase of my skill. By the end of two terms the magic had worked; preparations which had resulted in a tarry residue, inviting only the scorn of a Demonstrator at the Dyson Perrins, were producing crops of beautiful crystals, worthy of the great Perkin himself. I could face the prospect of that most severe of all trials, the seven-hour practical, with something like confidence, justified in the event as it turned out.

The ever watchful Hammick had detected a similar weakness in my grasp of the theoretical side of organic chemistry and prescribed a course of tutorials from Dr E.W. Hope, Teddy to all, the chemistry Fellow and tutor of Magdalen. This was a totally new, to me, manifestation of the tutorial system, so different from what I had become accustomed to, but most effective in its results. Each weekly essay was expected to be delivered in the style of an answer to a question in an examination paper and was closely probed for errors as if it had been just that. Discussion of some new discovery or theory followed and then back to earth with another subject for next week's essay. The system worked and when the day came for Final Schools, in the obligatory dark suit, white tie and gown, I felt totally at home with the two 'Organic' papers and became rather unstuck through excess of enthusiasm and desire to show off in the physical chemistry papers. Hammick was reassuring, without breaching the confidentiality surrounding the results. As soon as the practicals were safely past, I was able to go to meet Hinshelwood and received my instructions for the ensuing year. So began a whole new way of life and an unforgettable experience.

Hinsh, as he was known to all, was only six years older than I, but such was the respect in which he was held by the undergraduate body that it was only by an effort of will that I avoided calling him Sir. He had won a scholarship to Balliol but was unable to take it up on account of the war. He went to the Queensferry Ordnance Factory in 1916 and by 1918 when he left to come up to Oxford he had been appointed Deputy Chief Chemist at one laboratory and had developed a keen interest in the rate of chemical change, appropriately enough in solids at first. He was, and remained, a tremendously fast worker and during my three undergraduate years he published 21 original papers, alone or with several collaborators. I called on him in his rooms looking out on the great gardens of Trinity, into which we rapidly decanted; during three circuits at a brisk pace I was given a concise appreciation of the state of the art and an indication of the directions in which our research might advance the knowledge and understanding of gas reactions. It was now time for tea with toast and Fuller's cake in the company of a well-fed but to my practised eye clearly pregnant tabby cat, his faithful companion for many years. He went on; much of his work had been directed towards the identification of a substance which would react in gaseous form at temperatures and pressures such as could conveniently be used and controlled in his laboratory, and not be catalysed by the walls of the containing vessel. So far only two examples had been identified and studied; they were both inorganic and he thought the time had come for a foray into the territory of the organic chemist.

I should here explain, for it was no part of our conversation, being a subject which he had dealt with at length in his lectures and about which I had written at all too great length in Final Schools, that gas reactions like Caesar's Gaul could conveniently be divided in three parts:

First order, in which the rate of reaction is independent of pressure. They are deemed therefore not to originate in collisions between molecules, hence *Unimolecular*.

Second order, where the rate of reaction varies as the square of the pressure. They are deemed therefore to originate in collisions between two molecules, hence *Bimolecular*.

Third order, where the rate of reaction varies as the cube of the pressure. They were deemed to originate in collisions between three molecules, hence *Termolecular*.

The temperature dependence of rates of reaction had been interpreted by Arrhenius on the hypothesis that only those molecules will react which have acquired by collision or otherwise a certain minimum energy called the *heat of activation*. For all the known bimolecular reactions there was reasonable agreement between the number of molecules reacting in unit time and the number that could acquire the energy represented by this heat of activation by normal collisional process in terms of the Clerk Maxwell distribution law. There was only one unimolecular reaction on record, and here the number of molecules reacting exceeded by several orders of magnitude the number that could have acquired the heat of activation by normal collisional process.

Hinsh continued; he thought we might find suitable reactants among the family of ketones and aldehydes which might prove less prone to react catalytically than, for example, organic acids like formic acid. In proposing that we start on acetone he had another objective in view: the continuing search for a first-order reaction. He claimed, less than seriously, that the idea had come to him when, reading Dante's *Inferno*, he came across the sad fate of Paolo and Francesca, who had been condemned for all time to blow about like leaves in a great wind:

> The stormy blast of Hell
> With restless fury drives the Spirits on
> Whirled around and dashed amain with some annoy.

was such that energy acquired by collision might accumulate in the molecule at a level sufficient to part the bonds and provide an example of a first-order reaction. But it was not in his character to speculate too far in advance of the observation of facts, and we left his rooms and walked a short distance round to a back yard where stood a small inconspicuous building, clearly converted from some baser function. The evidence of this was to be seen in the marks left by the fixing of seats to the wall, according to E.J. Bowen, and the fact that the College carpenter always referred to it as 'the old Fellows' W's.' It measured I suppose about 10 ft. by 20 ft., and could accommodate at most three workers. The apparatus and equipment we used was extremely simple, primitive by today's standards, and it sufficed. Hinshelwood, visiting Max Bodenstein in Berlin, had remarked on the excellence of his laboratory, to which the great man replied '*Ja, aber Ihr Institut ist doch schrecklich*'. While pleased to have his rather meagre work-place raised to the dignity of an 'Institut', it was amusing also to reflect on this elevation, in Ruskinian terms, of the lowliest ministries of the needs of man into the sternest and clearest offices in the service of science. I was shown our newest acquisition with pride; it was a delicate instrument by which to measure the temperature in our 600°C furnace with an accuracy of 1°C. There was one small drawback; the needle which recorded the millivolts generated by a platinum-rhodium thermocouple was suspended by a filament so fine that anyone treading the ancient timbers of 'Das Institut' could generate shock-waves representing several tens of degrees centigrade. The other occupant of my part of the building was a substantial man and heavy of foot, so that agonized cries of 'Stand Still, Green!', would puncture the cloistered calm at frequent intervals when a run was progressing.

Hinsh left it to me to gather up all the pieces of equipment required for the experiments; it needed a mixture of tact and diplomacy to winkle out four mercury-sealed glass taps from a secret store jealously guarded by James Warrell. James was appointed lab boy in 1889 and round him all activities now revolved. It needed flattery and a great deal of patience to get four silica joints made for the reaction bulbs by the university glass-blower over at the Clarendon Laboratory, and to persuade him to repair our only mercury vapour vacuum pump; and another week with the hand blow-lamp putting the whole assembly together and testing for tightness under high vacuum, before I could report all ready for the planned start in September. Meanwhile Hinsh was proof-reading his soon to be published masterpiece, *The Kinetics of Chemical Change in Gaseous Systems*, and entrusted to me the final verification of some 200 references by tracing each one back to its original source. I wonder how many references copied from paper to paper and sanctified finally by inclusion in some learned tome would survive the test of a search in the original source quoted.

It seems that with only the six years difference in our ages it should have been possible to be at once on easy terms, but there had been a war in between and on his side there was a daunting intellect which manifested itself in so many directions, to name only two, mathematics and languages. He would read Dante, often aloud, to while away the time during some protracted experimental run that might take an hour or two to complete; in the original of course, while I had to make do with a 'crib'. With Bodenstein he had exchanged stories of the kind that are current among students all over the world. All through his life he took every opportunity to master yet another foreign language and to perfect those in which he was proficient. I think he relished the friendly intimacy that can develop in the most serious scientific circles if one can speak and be understood in colloquial exchange in the language of another scientist. Should all this sound like making heavy weather of small matters, it did indeed take most of one term to accustom myself to calling him 'Hinsh', and I was soon delighting in his impish humour and sardonic tales of those in high places. I heard many stories of the eccentricities of the President of Trinity, the Rev. H.E.D. Blakiston, known to all as 'Blinks'. Like Thomas Case, the President of Corpus, his life was dedicated to the classics, and he was somewhat suspicious of the pretentions of this new breed, the scientists. The best story in the repertoire is about something that happened in the year after I went down and appears in Biographical Memoirs of the Royal Society. It is by Sir Harold Thompson FRS.

> In 1927 Hinshelwood had an acute attack of appendicitis and recounted afterwards of how Blinks had visited him just before he was to be taken off to hospital, and remarked, 'Hinshelwood, this is most unfortunate, most unfortunate; our last Science Tutor died of this.' Yet in later years the two men, each having discovered the great qualities of the other, became very close friends.

It was all in character that in 1959 Hinsh had the unique distinction of being at the same time President of the Classical Association and President of the Royal Society. He was accustomed to spend a large part of the vacations in Oxford, sometimes alone in College, working in the laboratory with an assistant or in his rooms on papers and books. His other home was in London where his widowed mother lived and once a year he would take time off to accompany her on a visit to some civilized resort, like Cannes as it then was, where the air was warm and the sun could be relied on to shine. We were to start work in earnest immediately after his return, which would be at the beginning of September, and it was then that I came to know him better. Unlike many of the unmarried dons he appeared never to have any one close friend among the undergraduates to the exclusion of others. Of course he preferred them to be goodlooking and if intellectual so much the better, and if athletic and a blue as well better still. I was late on the scene but knew of his high repute as a tutor and of the hospitality of his rooms where undergraduates of all disciplines would gather for conversation and the delight of his company. His slight figure gave a suggestion almost of frailty, altogether belied by a toughness capable of testing the stamina of any selected for an afternoon walk of several miles while discussing some problem in research that was currently engaging his attention. Hinsh had a slightly distant manner which some, including myself, found rather daunting at first. I believe it stemmed from a certain shyness and he liked time in which to establish a proper rapport with any newcomer or casual acquaintance. It could also be a signal of intense concentration on any problem which was engaging his attention and which would never be far from the forefront of his mind until he could see a way clear to its solution.

Work started punctually in September, and Hinsh was present at the first few test runs, after which he entrusted me with the conduct of the experiments. He kept in close touch with the results by frequent visits to the laboratory and my reports to him in person in his rooms. I noticed how he liked to be present when some specially critical experiment was to be performed so that he could watch results emerging as temperature pressure and time were read off and recorded. It was a mental stimulus to be at the unwrapping of yet another layer of cover over the unknown and see revealed evidence for or against a hypothesis waiting hopefully on the side lines to declare itself a valid theory, which is what research is all about. At other times he came for relaxation and while one of the longer runs was in progress would be reading the *Divine Comedy* with occasional glances at the mercury column to see how things were going. And just once or twice he declared it close of play, locked up the laboratory and took me off to the theatre where, after term was over, music hall of the genuine old-fashioned brand reigned supreme.

Acetone was proving to be a good choice for his first venture into the decomposition of organic compounds but there were quite serious complications: the products of reaction were a mixed lot and it was a time-consuming process before we could be satisfied that the pressure increase was a reasonable measure of the rate of reaction. In its favour, results were reproducible and we established before long that:

(a) The decomposition of acetone vapour was a homogeneous reaction, the rate being unchanged with the bulb one third full of coarsely ground silica powder.

(b) The reaction satisfied the criterion of a unimolecular mechanism in that the velocity constant was independent of the pressure of the reactant.

This was excitement enough, for the only unimolecular reaction recorded hitherto was the decomposition of nitrogen pentoxide in 1921, and I felt like rushing out into the Broad with a shout of *Eureka!* But duty called and I must now establish the relation between reaction rate and temperature with all possible speed. Hinshelwood's reputation was growing fast and there was the risk that someone somewhere could have followed the same line of reasoning as had led to acetone. The first we would know of it might be a letter to *Nature* anticipating our result. The Arrhenius theory states that molecules in order to react must have energy in excess of a certain critical value called the Energy of Activation E. Clerk Maxwell's law of the distribution of energy in gases leads to the following relation between the velocity constant k and the temperature T:

$$\ln k = C - \frac{E}{RT}$$

where R is the gas constant and C is a constant characteristic of the reaction in question. The result came out, E = 68,500 Cals. Kinetic theory allows us to calculate the number of molecules that can acquire energy E in unit time at any given temperature.

$$\text{Result } 0.54 \times 10^{11}$$

The number of molecules actually reacting under these same conditions was:

$$1.33 \times 10^{16}$$

a discrepancy of 2×10^5, or 200,000, whereas with bimolecular reactions there had always been good agreement between the two numbers. Our results for acetone fell neatly into line with those for nitrogen pentoxide, the only other recorded case of a unimolecular reaction, so here was a quandary; kinetic theory and collisions between high-energy molecules explained bimolecular reactions, and probably termolecular also, but failed by a large margin to account for the manner in which single molecules could acquire by collision the energy required to react. Hinsh pondered long and deeply before committing our paper to the Royal Society, weighing up the alternative solutions of chain reactions (Semenov in Russia) and some form of radiation (Perrin in France), before postulating the latter but without much conviction. So he decided to present the paper in person in the hope of promoting useful discussion (it did not) and in the expectation of confronting some of his critics in the 'establishment' of the Royal Society (they did not appear). The meeting was in the old rooms in Burlington House with the President, Rutherford, in the chair and J.J. Jeans of kinetic theory renown, the Physical Secretary, at his side. I dined with Hinsh at his club and we returned, disappointed after spoiling for a fight and receiving only kind words, on that late train which delivers undergraduates just in time to reach their Colleges before midnight: a train inappropriately known, in view of the serious purpose of our mission, as the Fornicator.

Meanwhile I had been investigating the thermal decomposition of acetaldehyde, a junior member of the acetone family with a simpler structure and straightforward reaction products:

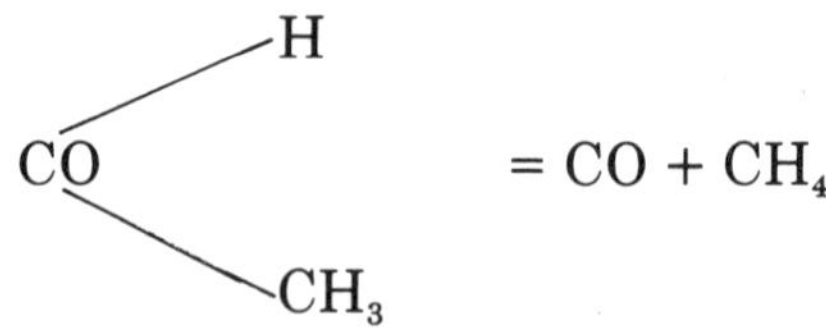

It appeared to be a bimolecular reaction and in contrast with acetone there was agreement within a factor of two between the number of molecules reacting and the number calculated from kinetic considerations. Our paper was submitted in March; about then I began to think, from talks I had with Hinsh, that he was just beginning to feel his way out of the impasse. The full revelation came in the vacation or the summer term, during a discussion with F.A. Lindemann (Lord Cherwell). He had earlier made a valuable contribution to the theory of unimolecular reactions, and now suggested that Hinshelwood should consider the energy that might be stored up in the numerous internal degrees of freedom inherent in the structure of complex molecules such as acetone. I will not try to describe all that followed from this, except to say that the calculations gave results for the number of degrees of freedom required which are entirely plausible in relation to the structure of acetone.

I had noticed and occasionally passed the time of day with a curly-headed freshman called Thompson, a pupil of Hinsh in Trinity. He was known of course as Tommy and became a Soccer blue and Sir Harold FRS, a one-time Foreign Secretary of the Royal Society, Professor Emeritus of Chemistry at Oxford and Chairman of the Football Association. Hinsh put him to work in the long vacation following my departure, on the decomposition of propionaldehyde which has affinities both with acetaldehyde and with acetone, as their formulas indicate:

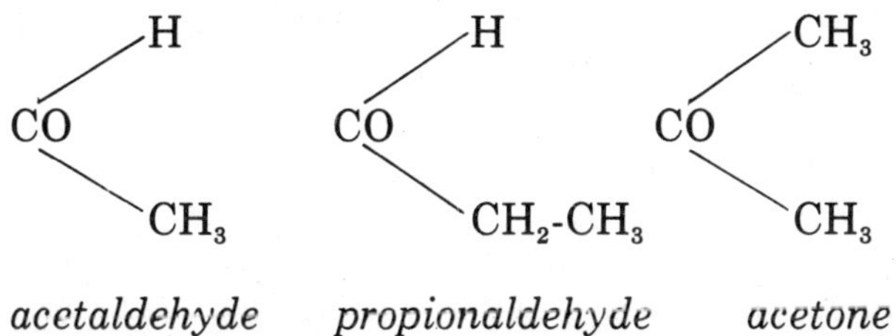

acetaldehyde *propionaldehyde* *acetone*

and it behaved accordingly, at high pressure unimolecular like acetone, at low pressure bimolecular like acetaldehyde. Just how all this was to be reconciled with all that had gone before is no part of my story. Sir Cyril Hinshelwood said it all in his Presidential Address to the Royal Society in 1957, where he describes the three stages of scientific theory:

> ... the first is that of gross oversimplification reflecting partly the need for practical working rules and even more a too enthusiastic aspiration after elegance of form. In the second stage, the symmetry of the hypothetical systems is distorted and the neatness marred as recalcitrant facts increasingly rebel against conformity. In the third stage ... a new order

> emerges, more intricately contrived, less obvious and with its parts more subtly interwoven, since it is of nature's not of man's conception.

I was putting the final touches to my Part 2 thesis as the country was getting ready to grind to a stop under the shadow of an impending General Strike. All its eighty pages had been typed by me on my £8 second-hand German typewriter (it would have cost £30 or more to have it done professionally) and with accompanying diagrams were assembled in a handsome spring binder and delivered at the appointed place on the day the strike started. The Corpus front quad was already empty as volunteers departed to man the trains, the trams, the buses and the docks and a very few went off to undisclosed Socialist assignments. I was free to do my bit for King and Country and found Hinsh assembling a party to go up to London to print the *British Gazette*. F.A. Lindemann had some part in this enterprise, which was dear to the heart of Winston Churchill, who would appear late at night behind a large cigar to watch the presses rolling. It was dull work and thankfully soon over, and I returned to Oxford at first light in an open tourer with Humphrey Raikes, the Chemistry don of Exeter at the wheel. He was a fast driver and it did little to raise morale when he told how once he had fallen asleep at the wheel and woke up unharmed in a deep ditch, from which nothing at all could be seen and for some time he thought he was dead. I watched him anxiously after that, ready to pinch hard if he showed any sign of repeating the exploit.

While waiting for my viva I prepared two other pieces of research for publication. The viva when it came was brief and formal, with some discussion of my thesis, on which I was duly awarded a BSc to add to my BA (1st. Cl. Hons. Chemistry). My immediate future was assured by an appointment as a research chemist in the new laboratory of the Gas Light and Coke Company, the appointment and the laboratory both in part the work of Harold Hartley. Early aspirations to an academic career had retreated, as I came to work with Hinshelwood and began to realize the wide gap that exists between genius and a mere talent to excel and I felt no vocation in me for the teaching profession, be it in school or university. No way could I find the money to support me in a further two years of research, the least that a Doctorate required. Practical considerations had transformed me from an intellectual idealist into a young man in a hurry to make enough money to get married, for the reason that I have already mentioned very briefly, and this ruled out all options of junior appointments at Oxford or at any of the provincial universities. So I went down towards the end of June 1926 with no regrets at all; only the happy memories of many friendships cemented during three years in College and the unique experience of working with one of the great scientific intellectuals of our generation and a very wise and friendly man.

Hinshelwood went on, as we all expected, to receive honours and recognition world wide for his achievements. The Nobel Prize, of course: it amused him to wake up and find that suddenly he was a capitalist in a small way. I believe that what he valued most was to be President of the Royal Society in its tercentenary year. President of the Chemical Society in its centenary year, of the Faraday Society, of the British Association and of the Classical Association; these were all honours but each entailed a heavy burden of work in the preparation of addresses and lectures. Sir Harold Thompson has noted how they enabled him 'to display his remarkable captivating eloquence and literary style; his insight into the place and development of science in current affairs; the depth of his natural philosophy; and his blend of the romantic and the practical.' When Frederick Soddy retired in 1937 Hinshelwood was elected to succeed him as Dr Lee's Professor of Inorganic and Physical Chemistry and was soon to be installed in a handsome new Laboratory, the gift of Lord Nuffield. He was now responsible for two large laboratories and 'in the 50s there were nine Fellows of the Royal Society working in his departments, carrying out research programmes in different fields'. He confided in me, and others have confirmed, that he found the administrative side to be a heavy burden, perhaps because he insisted on doing so much himself most conscientiously. When I wrote to congratulate him on his election as President of the Royal Society in 1955, he replied:

> It was nice of you to write and I am grateful for your good wishes. I need hardly say how much more they mean in view of the fact that you are able to evoke the good far off, old days of Dante, acetone (and Green). How impossible our present seems viewed from the perspective of then and the 'old Fellows' W's' of Trinity, as the College carpenter called them. It is all very strange.

James Warrell, who has made a brief appearance in these pages as the laboratory assistant at Balliol-Trinity, went with Hinsh to the new laboratory and stayed at his side until 1952, the last four years part-time. He had been appointed by Sir James Conroy in 1889 as lab boy at 5 shillings a week, making a total of 63 years with hardly a day off for illness. So far as he was able (or allowed to) he took on much of the burden of running the sub-structure of the new Physical Chemistry Laboratory.

E.J. Bowen FRS who returned from war service at the same time as Hinshelwood, specialized in photochemistry. I have quoted from his article on the Balliol/Trinity laboratory in *Notes and Records of the Royal Society* and his (unpublished) *Chemistry at Oxford*. I was most grateful for his help and advice throughout.

N.V. Sidgwick FRS, Fellow of Lincoln, was one of the most astute brains and polished intellects in the scientific hierarchy. He took a First in Chemistry in 1895, a distinction greeted with derision by his Classical relatives. So he studied for a further two years and took a First in Greats, and then went on to polish up his chemistry in three years at two great German universities. He returned to Oxford in 1901 and became a leading figure in organic chemistry and produced his masterpiece *The Organic Chemistry of Nitrogen*. His attitude to chemistry underwent a fundamental change after the war. Disillusioned by the traditional approach of the organic chemist, as taught by Professor Perkin, he began to think more about the structure of the atom and the work of Rutherford at Cambridge and Niels Bohr in Denmark. The electron was the key that would open the door to an understanding of valency and molecular structure and the Bohr atom was the model by which to be guided. He had been joined by Hammick in 1921 and together they formed the nucleus of a 'cell' on the ground floor of the Dyson Perrins, having more to do with physical chemistry than the Professor up above thought fitting. Hammick claimed to have found a way to allay suspicion: 'We could fool the old man that we were doing organic work if he occasionally got a whiff of pyridine from our labs.' Sidgwick was not a skilled experimenter, but he did fulfil most admirably the function of bridging the gap between modern physics and organic chemistry. He kept his Oxford colleagues up to date at informal dissertations round the tea-table and the world in general by papers and books in the inter-war years.

3
Ruthwell Revisited

As I drove up to the Kirklands Hotel on a fine evening in mid July 1985, I realised that this was indeed Ruthwell Manse, in appearance quite unchanged. My brother Pat and I had stayed there some seventy years before with Noel Dinwiddie, a school friend at the Dumfries Academy, and a son of the minister of Ruthwell. I had been talking with Noel recently on the telephone about a plan to spend three days visiting places in the south west connected with my forebears going back several centuries. There were also places which I wanted to refresh my mind about connected with the first ten years of my life before we left to live in Edinburgh, long before my departure for Oxford. Noel suggested that I should use Ruthwell as a quiet stopover after three hectic days, before picking up the motorail at Carlisle.

I walked across to the church to see again the runic cross rescued and reconstructed by earlier ministers from the demolition of the Iconoclasts. My mind went back to the 'killing years' when the Hutchisons of Dalgig were so often in danger from King Charles II's dragoons, looking for itinerant preachers and members of their congregations or any bibles that anyone might have about his person. Then there was the 'Virginian Connection' which brought romance into life at the manse of New Abbey. It was quiet at the hotel and I spent the rest of the evening recalling past events and wondering how best to assemble them in a readable form and that done what to call this chapter. The result may not be very original; there is even a suspicion of plagiarism, but it expresses my intention and the place where the chapter was conceived. For the rest read on.

The Virginian Connection

Aunt Harriet had brought up our family of three boys and twin sisters with a proper respect for the Deity and a firm belief in the superiority of the Hutchisons of Dalgig over all other families in the south west of Scotland. Her consuming interest was in the multiple relationships generated by the marriages of the three daughters of her great-grandfather Hugh, the last of our name to have lived at Dalgig and the three daughters of her grandfather Thomas, the last to be born there. We used to giggle helplessly in corners when overhearing conversations about who was who's cousin or second cousin or, yet more screamingly funny, first or second cousin once or twice removed; as members of the families of Gemmells, Cringans and Blackwoods and Greigs, Smiths and Nicholsons already into the third generation of him who begat them were fearlessly thrown into the ring and retrieved without aid of pencil or paper. But nothing was ever said about the relatives on the other side of the family represented by our grandmother's parents, the Reverend James and Mrs Hamilton, who had been Miss Harriet Smith born in Saint Augusta (now in Florida) before her marriage to the minister of New Abbey.

Enlightenment came with the discovery of two letters, which had passed between my Uncle Jim and his mother Mary Louisa, my grandmother. It was in 1907 and he was then secretary of the Calcutta Turf Club and she was a frail old lady of 84, living with her unmarried daughter in the turmoil of a family of five orphaned children not long arrived from the India of the Raj. The story that unfolds throws new light on my ancestry with an atmosphere of romance, which is sadly missing from the saga of the Hutchisons of Dalgig.

Copies of letters passing between James Hutchison MA writing from the Calcutta Turf Club and his Mother, Mrs Mary Hutchison at Lochar House, Dumfries; then aged 83/84. The letters undated but from internal evidence, late 1906 and January 1907 respectively.

From James to his mother

I have often thought of writing and asking you to put down in black and white some of the history of your side of the house, which I think will be much more interesting, if not so orthodox as the Hutchison side. You really should leave us some, as much as possible, of your family reminiscences. The Virginian and West Indian Connections were always far more interesting to me than all the Patersons and Gillespies etc. decent folks and yet they are mere names. Your mother's relations and forebears I think of as specially elegant and romantic folk and even wee George Mc.Morrin who liked his peas young and esculent had an air about him that was quite impressive. Of course, I have heard that some parts of the history might not be quite highly respectable. Time hallows that and under the circumstances it would have more attraction for me than all the other family history put together. I have a hankering after these Old World or

New World Stories. It is queer that I never heard of them from other folks. They were above the ordinary run and the West Indian hauteur combined with a refined daintiness must have inspired respect. They may be all imaginary but it is my only impression and I never heard anyone hint at a discription more definite. Anyhow let's have all you know and have heard, it will give you something to do in the winter evenings.

From Mrs Mary Hutchison to James

My dear Jamie,

— In the meantime I must try to give some sort of reply to the questions that you wish to ask viz. who was Mama's father? The only name I can give is Sir Harry Burrard, an Army man I fancy in America. Mama was born in St. Augusta and that's all I can tell except in a big volume on the War I was reading I came across Sir H.B.'s name but can't remember anything about it. My grandmother died in the Bahamas where she must have lived many years. I suppose she must have had a queer life I cant tell, that's all I know. Cousin Louisa (Mrs Litt) and coz. Eliza knew her. The latter was called for her. I remember seeing her death in the newspaper once when I was at Satterness – as being 82 and highly *respected*. The latter made me think people have different opinions. There is nobody living that I have any knowledge of now who can recall more. I remember Mama going into mourning and not saying who for and I wondered, but little children should be seen and not heard.

There were two sons I fancy – a John Forbes who was in the Navy, a Lieut., and a George, Miss Pordmore's father. I think he was either killed or killed in a duel in W. Indies and now I expect I am the last of both W. Indians and decent old Hamiltons can think no more. —

Your affecte. Mater
M.L.J.H.

My grandmother was writing about a period when irregular unions were not considered to be particularly blameworthy among the upper classes: the emerging middle class, and the Presbyterian Church most positively, took a harder line. In the church registers any child born out of wedlock was labelled 'bastard'. She had gone so far as to admit the facts but was unwilling to go into detail. The church registers in St. Augustine, even if such existed, were not on view in New Abbey, yet the Rev. Hamilton must have known and was clearly a man of courage to go through with it.

So this was the skeleton that had been rattling its bones in the family cupboard all those years while two generations of Hutchisons grew up in the fear of God and the certainty of the punishment for sin in the hereafter. I like to think of the manse echoing to the sound of merriment and laughter as Harriet's relatives came over to stay and show off their fine attire and elegant manners on the long single street that is the entire village of New Abbey. A charming, delicately carved gravestone in the

Hamilton enclave records the death of George Mc.Neill of Charleston, South Carolina in 1834, aged 22 years. Sir Harry Burrard, father of Harriet Smith is well-documented in the biographies. Typical of the well-to-do officer class, he served two spells of duty in the American War of Independence, taking time off in between to be elected Member of Parliament for Lymington. He was with Cornwallis at the surrender of Yorktown and could have served his internment in St. Augustine or lived there as an officer on parole, where his daughter had recently been born.

The only clue I have to the identity of Harriet's mother – Eliza Smith – is the reference to Cousin Louisa (Mrs Litt) in my grandmother's letter, together with inscriptions on an imposing stone that stands on the left of the Hamilton Memorial. It records the death of Captain Murray aged 56 years, in 1843. A smaller tablet below records that 'here also were interred his sister Louisa, relict of John Grierson of Larbreck, in 1843 in the 69th year of her age, and her beloved grandchild Louisa, daughter of John Litt Esq. in 1842 aged 12 years'. All three had died at the Manse. From this we may infer that Louisa Grierson and James Murray were half-sister and half-brother respectively of Harriet, and that Louisa Grierson's daughter was my grandmother's 'Cousin Louisa Litt'. Also the dates fit:

Louisa Grierson	b. 1774 d. 1843
Captain Murray	b. 1778 d. 1834
Harriet Hamilton	b. 1781 d. 1849

The father of the first two was probably a local man of property for we learn that Captain Murray was brought up in the locality of New Abbey. He commanded the brig. *Oberon* in an engagement with the French privateer *Ratisia* in 1810. His victory was celebrated in style by the inhabitants of New Abbey on 11 January 1811, when they met for

> A public Testimony of high esteem and affectionate regard for Captain James Murray of His Majesty's Ship Oberon in the recent encounter – *many inhabitants among whome he had resided in his youth* – toasting of health to loud and cheerful Huzzahs – dancing to a late hour – partaking of Bread and Cheese and Brown Mulled Ale.

and a good time was had by all – Presbyterians and Seceders alike.

James Murray had the rank of Commander at this time and was promoted Post Captain in 1818. He had his portrait painted, a miniature by F. Stump RA in 1824 and was in the list of Sea

Officers as Captain in 1833, after service in the Mediterranean and Newfoundland. We have a portrait of Harriet Hamilton, of great charm, charcoal on paper heightened with white paint, by Daniel Marree, 1846, a sampler which she embroidered at the age of 8, signed Hariot Smith and an enamel watch-back ornamented with diamonds set in a gold frame as a brooch. It was probably a gift from Harry Burrard; the discarded watch part I remember seeing in a drawer, before the dispersal of the contents of our home in Edinburgh when my father died. But of Eliza I know no more than when I started. My grandmother must have known, but she wanted no part of it and was only too glad to see the end of the Virginian Connection.

When James Hutchison, my grandfather, offered his hand in marriage to the daughter of James Hamilton, Minister of New Abbey, he must have known or at least guessed the secret of the 'Virginian Connection'. That was to be the least of his worries in the years ahead. In her will his mother, widow of Thomas, last of our name to be born at Dalgig, forgave James a debt, because at Ingleston he had succeeded to a 'dear farm'. The great days at Tinwald, when they sat down twelve to dinner at a Georgian mahogany table and the men continued long into the night drinking hot whisky toddy mixed each to his taste in cut-glass goblets, were becoming little more than a memory when James left Ingleston in 1862. The death of my great-grandmother had coincided with the repeal of the Corn Laws in 1846. Great changes in the economics of farming resulted and not all farmers were able or willing to adapt. James went to Mouswald, where it seems that things were not going too badly for him and his young family of six sons and two daughters. In 1873 he was busy setting up James, an MA at Glasgow, and John the next oldest in a nearby farm, where James was to try out the advanced ideas he had learned at university. William, my father, was about to go to Glasgow to study engineering. Sometime after 1875 things went badly wrong and he had to retire from farming and sell out to meet his debts. James, our Uncle Jim, and our father both went out to India to Tea Gardens in Assam, where the culture of selected stock was creating a new growth industry.

My father went to a small garden called Dooria, which he managed with great success. He produced only the highest grades of tea specially for blending and remained connected with it all his life. He was able to indulge his love of all sporting pursuits and even had at one time a pack of hounds, of which a photograph survives. He was 44 years of age when he met Barbara

The Virginian Connection

Murray — Eliza Smith, died aged 82 in the Bahamas — Sir Harry Burrard, Captain later General with Cornwallis at Yorktown in 1781

Children of Murray and Eliza Smith:

- Louisa Grierson* of Larbreck, b.1774 d.1843
  - Mrs Litt, 'Cousin Louisa'
    - Louisa Litt*, b.1830 d.1842, 'Beloved'
- Captain James* Murray, b.1778 d.1834

Child of Eliza Smith and Sir Harry Burrard:

- Harriet Louisa* Smith, b.1781 d.1849, m. Rev. James Hamilton 1817
  - Mary Louisa*, b.1823 d.1909, m.1848 James Hutchison — **My grandparents**

'Coz. Eliza' and the two sons, 'John Forbes' grandchild' and 'George Pordmore' have not been identified.

*Buried in the Hamilton Enclave

The Hutchisons of Dalgig

William	'possessor of Dalgig' in 1619
Hugh	tenant in Dalgig 1685
John	in Dalgig 1694. Several brothers, one of whom Captain William Hutchison as Lieutenant was embodied at the original muster of the Cameronian Regiment on 14 May 1689.
William	in Fardenreoch, later in Dalgig. Married four times, had families by all except the first.
Hugh	left Dalgig 1765 for Fardenreoch then Blackfardin and finally in Kirkconnel.

William
b.1738
d.1819
m.Susan Logan

Thomas
b.1760 at Dalgig
d.1837 at Ingleston
m.1805 at Glentaggart
Jean Paterson who
d.1846 at Ingleston

4 daughters
all married

Hew
'Shot and
robbed in
Norfolk'.

Eliza Smith (see above)

William
d.1837
unmarried
2 Daughters

Rev. James Hamilton
M. of New Abbey
b.1782
d.1858

m.1817

Harriet Smith
b.1781 at St.
Augustine
d.1849 at New
Abbey

5 Daughters
3 married
d. young

Thomas
b. 10 Oct 1810 at
Mersehead
d. 13 Oct 1845
at Erie Lodge

James
b. Mar.1821
at Tinwald
d. 1890 at
Mouswald

m.1848

Mary L. Hamilton
b. 1823 at the
Manse New Abbey
d. 1908 at
Lochar House

Harriet
b.1849
d.1934

Thomas
b.1850
d.1882

Unmarried

James
b.1851

John
b.1853
m.1880
Mary Munn

William
b.1855
d.1932
m.1899
Barbara
M. McCormac
b.1880
d.1906

Archibald
b.1858
d.1944
m.1896
Annie
George

Douglas
b.1860
d.1932
m.

Jean
b.1860
d.1938
m.1890

No issue

John Hamilton

Mary Stuart

James
b.1904

Muriel
b.1906

Robert
b.1910

Archibald
Maxwell
b.1900

Patrick
Hamilton
b.1902

William
Kenneth
b.1903

Barbara
Hamilton
b.1905

Shelagh
Mary
b.1905

McCormack, then only 19, in Calcutta. They married without delay and our family of five followed. Tragedy struck when our mother died of appendicitis at the age of 26. It was before the age of antibiotics and the surgeon hastily summoned arrived three hours too late. Father was devastated and, before he left for home, he destroyed everything that could remind him of his all too short and so happy married life. At Lochar House we never spoke of it.

Breakfast at Lochar House

In the morning room at Lochar House we were taught reading, writing and the elements of simple arithmetic by a governess. The day began with breakfast round the schoolroom table under the watchful eye of Aunt Harriet at one end, and the governess at the other. It was a frugal meal but nourishing and adequate by the standard of those days. The main filler, porridge of course, was greeted with loud protests if it contained any lumps. No sugar: that was acceptable if the porridge had been made as it should be with well salted water; followed by one slice of bread with butter, and another with marmalade; never butter and marmalade on the same slice. Our grandmother never came down for breakfast and quite often stayed away from mid-day dinner in the dining-room. She was over eighty and preferred the peace and quiet of her bedroom until she knew we had all been safely consigned to bed. Sunday was special with a boiled egg for breakfast and a boiled suet pudding, preferably the one with layers of black treacle inside, for dinner; otherwise sago, rice or tapioca, literally, and how we hated the skin on milk puddings.

The year was 1906 and I could not have been more than three years old. I can recall quite clearly the scene at breakfast on the morning when the house-maid knocked and came in to place a telegram in front of my aunt. Telegrams in those days usually meant bad news and Aunt Harriet was forewarned. But she went on to open it and read out in a curious flat tone of voice – 'Barbara died today coming home with twins'. I knew that something dreadful had happened and that things would never be the same again. I had been little more than an infant in my Ayah's arms when our father and mother left the three of us in the care of Aunt Harriet and returned to the Dooria Tea Estate in Assam of which he was the Manager. Archie, the oldest of the three brothers was six years old when that fateful telegram arrived and probably explained it all to Pat and myself; confirming the feeling of loss and desolation that had already invaded my conscious memory.

Until that day we had never doubted that soon we would be re-united and live happily ever after with a mother and a father like the children of our neighbours and even those in the village.

Aunt Harriet knew better: experience warned that she had been allotted a task in life, bringing up a family of three boys and twin girls, after their father returned to India in order to earn the money that would be required to provide for us all. She was 55 years old and unmarried. She had been the oldest child in a family of eight and had been expected to help her mother as soon as she was able. So Harriet ended by becoming indispensable, even after the last of her family, our Aunt Jean, married and left the family home in 1890. Then my grandfather died and left his widow with almost no provision for their future. Father took charge and with his elder brother, our Uncle Jim, took a lease of Lochar House, as a home for them; it was also somewhere to spend the long leaves from India. Both were unmarried at the time and it was handy for the social life of Dumfries and the sporting facilities of the county. In between their several visits there was the quiet, genteel life of the middle class, with two maids and a gardener who doubled as coachman. There were long letters to be written to the four brothers overseas, two in India and two in Australia; large packing cases to be ordered and filled with all those delicacies impossible to obtain in India, such as local Dunlop cheese and home-made jams and marmalade in stoneware jars, secured by bladder skins tied firmly round the necks, and other luxuries for which the exiles craved; not forgetting patent medicines on which Uncle Jim asserted his very life depended. Dr Smith's Chlorodyne comes to mind as one of them.

Lochar House was in our time a building typical of its period. It was built of red sandstone and double-fronted with bay windows, isolated from any neighbours by walls and fields on both sides of its garden, a road in front and a railway embankment at the back. Hardly recognizable today, it is the centrepiece of a roadhouse or small hotel. Inside it seemed strangely familiar when I called in for a nostalgic drink in the bar where once was our dining-room. But the long vista across fields to the distant hills is totally obscured by a large shapeless structure seemingly left over from the last war. Most of the three miles to Dumfries is scheduled as a trading estate. That however was nothing new: the Arrol Johnstone Company had already built a large factory for motor cars before the First World War, on the half-way mark between us and Dumfries. The meadow beyond the railway where a friendly farmer allowed us to mark out a cricket pitch is covered by a housing estate. Houses are encroaching also on the quarter mile of open meadow by which Lochar House had distanced itself from its nearest neighbours. Locharbriggs was a small village housing the workers in the large sandstone quarries nearby. They have long been abandoned and the railway which served them and us has gone too.

The village had no church of its own. The nearest and officially our parish church was at Tinwald, nearly a mile away. Due to some doctrinal difference or personal preference we favoured Kirton church even further away in the other direction. All we had in the village was a red sandstone mission hall to which we were dispatched on Sunday afternoons to sit with the village boys in Christian amity on benches ranged round a teacher. We had come to be instructed in whatever it was that Sunday schools existed for and were rewarded at the end by a highly-coloured text to keep us in the paths of righteousness. Most of the village boys came barefoot in summer and a few reserved their boots for the coldest days of winter. Far from pitying them I envied their freedom to wriggle their toes in a friendly effort to make me laugh. There was little common ground in other encounters. Soon after we came on the scene Archie had sallied forth from Lochar House, with Pat as his faithful lieutenant, both unobserved, to demand the obedience and respect of these sons of coolies. It had always been freely accorded to the Sahib's eldest son at Dooria: this being denied they returned to the attack suitably armed and were repulsed by superior forces even better armed. After this unseemly fracas all further contact with the villagers was sternly forbidden. I thought this was rather a pity. I might have found among them a friend and soul-mate; the boy who wiggled his toes at me might have had some message to convey. I tended to be left out of the secret alliances which make up the life of a family, somewhat isolated between two elder brothers and the twins, inseparable as identicals always are; anyway who wants girls? So I settled for 'pig in the middle' as my ordained place in the scheme of things, until Archie went off to a prep school at Lee-on-Solent to prepare for Osborne and a career in the navy. Pat, then as ever the opportunist, demanded my unswerving obedience, until on the first day of the school holidays I was firmly relegated to where I belonged and as firmly restored to favour on the day that the holiday ended.

There was one thing in my favour which was worth all Archie's intermittent advantages. Pat and I shared a bedroom. From beds on opposite sides of the room we were deep into the longest serial of all time. We took it in turns each night as soon as the candle was out to begin where the previous instalment had left off. No one, not even Archie, was ever let into the secret of how our hero Bob was faring in his many battles against hordes of villains (who needless to say were Germans). Bob was handsome with fair hair (golden would be sissy) and blue eyes (our hair was mouse-to-darkish and our eyes in varying degree on the greenish side of blue). Bob was tall and strong. The retelling of his good looks and many virtues caused a stirring down below the bedclothes. We loved him dearly. The day when he was ready to blow up the entire German navy had to be postponed indefinitely. Our story, like a good soap opera, had no beginning and must never be allowed to end.

Archie was never in doubt as to his future career. The Royal Navy was the greatest fighting force the world had ever known, guarding the greatest empire. Like Lord Louis Mountbatten, his exact contemporary (they even shared the same birthday), he always felt destined for the navy. It was the fashion of the time to dress children in sailor suits for Sunday best. An early group photograph shows all three boys in seaman rig. In an even earlier one I appear for no good reason in what looks like an outsize Petty Officer's uniform. You had to settle early in those days for the navy. There had to be three years at least at a prep school specialising in the subject to prepare for an awesome interview before a Board of Admirals at the tender age of 13 and then Osborne for two years and Dartmouth for another two tough years, before the real hardening up process was completed in a gunroom afloat. By a cruel stroke of fate Archie caught measles shortly before the date set for the interview. Although pronounced fit he was in no condition to shine before the Admirals' interrogation. Nothing daunted he settled for the Conway, a Merchant Navy Training Establishment, afloat in the Menai Strait in the hull of an old four-master. They had the option of sending a limited number of cadets for selection and entry into the Royal Navy at the Dartmouth stage. He survived all that and achieved his ambition to be a Naval Officer.

I too felt committed to a future career since ever I can remember. I was going to be an engineer. That was quite natural: my father had been in his second year at Glasgow University in preparation for a career in engineering when the crash came and the family dispersed. Anything that could be taken apart I tried to dismantle and usually managed to put together again. (That was long before the days of our first Meccano set.) But Heaven was just round the corner in the shape of the first motor car to become resident in our village. It was my father's new single cylinder 'Adams' which was destined to go out with him to India at the end of his leave. If it refused to start in the morning, which usually happened when he was all kitted out for fishing or shooting or whatever, the whole body had to be yanked up to reveal all the lovely mechanical devices which contributed to the successful working of the massive cylinder. While Harkness puffed and panted at the starting handle to speed up the equally massive flywheel someone had to let go a string or actuate a lever precisely at the word 'Now'. It was my dearest wish to be that person but I doubt if I ever was. They were indestructible, those old cars, built like the Forth bridge to last, by real engineers. It was reported that our old Adams was seen twenty-five years later working a milk round in Calcutta.

There were others. Uncle Jim became an eager novice and I guess that the T-Model Ford that appeared a few years later was probably his. At the age of ten I felt that I knew enough to drive it on the road. I had mastered the principle of the epicyclic gears and the two pedal control, but theory was not enough. I was never allowed to try and had to make do with my favourite day-dream – 'Harkness had died at the wheel while taking the family out for a drive in the country. Quick as thought I crawled over into the driving seat, took charge and drove them all home in perfect safety.' But there had to be a happy ending and Harkness recovered to utter the final words of the drama: 'Well done, lad.' Then there was Father's Vulcan, very posh that. Much more to my taste was an early model of the same make with many additions by the previous owner. There were three ways of clearing the road ahead, an exceptionally large bulb horn, a loud but quite melodious whistle, actuated by a lever which placed a stopper over the end of the exhaust, and a bell for use in crowded places. It also had a windscreen wiper, a complete novelty then and though worked by hand most effective, while on the dashboard there was a device, borrowed from steam-engine practice, which showed the flow of drops of oil through glass tubes filled with water, to each of the four cylinders; never a dull moment. Uncle Will was the proud possessor of this handsome vehicle but I never heard of him driving it. He left that to Aunt Jean who went about it with the same dash and *brio* as she had shown when driving her four-wheeled dog-cart in the farming days at Gledenholm.

Aeroplanes were my next obsession. When I read about a rally to be staged at Ayr I guessed that Lochar House could be on the route to be followed by participants from the south. For some reason Colonel Cody in his Deperdussen became an instant hero. The family showed no interest, rather disbelief. When I raised the cry of 'There, I can hear it' someone said, 'Rubbish. It's only the farmer using his reaper in the hay field.' But I was right.

I doubt if I ever got any credit for my forecast; after all who wants to fly anyway and it had all been over in two or three minutes and there was nothing much to see when it was there. My secret ambition to see one on the ground and speak to the owner was so far outside the realms of possibility that I rather think I lost all interest in those flying machines. More to the point, our first Meccano set arrived as a present towards the end of our Lochar House days. It was probably no. 1, with a maximum capability of delivering a load to the first landing on a string stretched from the winding gear at ground level. But that was enough; the swivelling and luffing jib crane in no. 4 would have to wait until broad hints dropped before birthdays and Christmas had produced the wherewithal to buy the conversion sets required.

Pat had no declared ambitions except to improve his golf and when the time came win the Amateur Championship. He also wanted to learn to play cricket on a real wicket against real fast bowlers, to run faster than anyone of his age at the annual sports, to kill things with Father's 12-bore and catch salmon with his Greenheart rod; and if he had to earn a living to do all these things, well that was just too bad. But Pat had something in the performance of which he left us far behind: he had a huge capacity for making friends, hordes of them in all stations of life, and they never forgot him. Many years later, at one of those Old Boys' reunions people kept coming up to me and saying, 'Why of course, I thought I knew you, you were Pat's young brother.' Pat was far away in Canada and had spent most of his working life abroad. When the time came he could work as hard as anyone. It was just that his motivation was different.

The death of our grandmother passed almost unnoticed. One night there was a great commotion with servants hurrying up and down stairs with cans of hot water and everyone talking in hushed whispers. Next morning Aunt Jean drove over from Gledenholm and we were all carried off to stay at the farm, which was a great treat anyway. When we were delivered back some days later it was as if nothing had changed. We saw very little of 'Grannie' who, like Florence Nightingale, found refuge in her bed when the turmoil of our arrival became too much to bear. She was an intelligent well-read woman with the reputation of being a bit of a bluestocking. One of her childhood friends was a granddaughter of Burns and she had visited the poet's widow in her Dumfries home. Of diminutive stature and usually dressed from head to foot in black or darkest blue, she resembled Queen Victoria for whom she had a very deep respect. She had demanded to be interred in the Hamilton enclosure in New Abbey with her own people. There was nothing anywhere to so much as hint at the mystery of Eliza Smith and Sir Harry Burrard, her grandparents.

I cannot recall seeing our other grandmother, the Irish one, at Lochar House. Archie and Pat went off to spend a delirious holiday with her in Newcastle-upon-Tyne and returned with tales of great fun and good cheer and no nonsense about children being seen and not heard. When her twin sons, our Irish uncles, came on a flying visit to Lochar House, they seemed like beings from another world. They were clearly free from any feeling of guilt about things said or done and unaware of the promise of eternal damnation prominent in the teaching of our Protestant faith. Since Fred had been selected to play at stand-off in the Irish XV and Bertie was in the running for a place in the three-quarter line they were heroes in our eyes. Both joined up in the Enniskillen Fusiliers in the 1914-1918 War and Bertie was killed in action and Fred never returned to an Ireland torn apart by strife and bloodshed. In 1916 their younger sister, our Aunt Eileen, witnessed a cold-blooded revenge shooting of a man in a tramcar and she left never to return.

Our Irish grandmother had been widowed while still quite young with a family of five. She then married a scoundrel, presumably of great charm for she remained faithful and forgiving all the days of his life. His periodic disappearances were of a kind not to be mentioned above a whisper and not in front of the children, and my father if at home would hurry off south to sort things out. Mr Savage, such was his name, contrived to keep his head above water, and lived for quite a long time. My grandmother survived him by many years and never lost her irrepressible sense of humour.

Looking back now over the years I can see that we were growing up in a strangely impersonal environment. Our father was a friendly but rather indistinct figure appearing like a spirit from another world endowed with human attributes, at intervals of two to three years. We never queried his authority but equally we never ran to him for advice. He never forgot our birthdays but all communication was through the weekly letter to Aunt Harriet. She would produce the ritual gold sovereign on birthdays and at

Christmas; all of which were quickly recovered at the end of the day and put into our individual accounts at the savings bank in Dumfries. I think that after the death of our mother he had no love left to give to any other person. What he did give and gave freely was friendship and understanding. They can be as powerful as love and much less demanding. He never administered punishment of any sort. The nearest he came to doing so was once when Pat went into one of those tantrums in which he specialised. He would be about five at the time and Father could stand it no longer. He tucked the miscreant under his arm and made for the back kitchen and the cold water tap, an old folk remedy. Before he could get there Pat seized the opportunity to wriggle round and asked 'Please may I turn the tap on, Daddy'. Father dissolved into gales of laughter and they both rejoined the family the best of friends.

Aunt Harriet had complete authority over our upbringing during our father's long absences in India. How she managed it I cannot now imagine. Although as a family we were not by nature unruly we were very determined and she like Father never resorted to physical means to enforce her rule. She too had no love to give. She spoke occasionally of a younger brother Thomas who had some weakness and died young. In fact he was two years younger than Harriet and lived to be 35. He has his own gravestone in the Hamilton enclave in the churchyard of Sweetheart Abbey. I feel certain that his weakness was in the intellect and that Harriet had to devote a large part of her early life to caring for him. Just when she had settled down to a comfortable middle age at Lochar House with her aged mother we three boys came, and then the telegram arrived and she knew she had what amounted to a life sentence looking after all five of us. I believe that she found the solution to that problem was to have no favourites and to treat us all alike and with strict impartiality.

The boys were to start school at the Dumfries Academy and as was customary in those days the twins were to be taught by a governess at home. We were taken in a pony trap at first, under the charge of Harkness. On account of some real or fancied weakness in my constitution I was to return at lunchtime on the local railway. There was one nightmare episode when I could not, try as I might, open the carriage door at Locharbriggs. I relapsed in a flood of tears with a fearful vision of being carried on forever, even as far as England. But reason prevailed and before we reached Amisfield, the next station on the line, I had managed to lower the window and there attracted the attention of a porter who unlocked the door and let me out. My solitary walk back, two miles of it, was the longest of my life, until rescued by Harkness presumably alerted by some kindly Stationmaster.

Dumfries Academy occupied a handsome building of the local red sandstone on a dominating site on a high bank of the River Nith. It was co-educational and in the Junior School we were taught by mistresses who were kind and efficient and kept good order. A private tutor had to be engaged to give us a grounding in Latin, but otherwise we were at no disadvantage when being examined for entry to the Edinburgh Academy. The decision to move to Edinburgh had been taken early in 1914 and schools selected both for the boys and for the girls in the family. The actual move was delayed some months by the outbreak of war in August. Father who held a Commission as Captain in the Assam Valley Light Horse heard the call of duty and rode off on his bicycle to Dumfries to offer his services. To our relief his offer was rejected; not surprising as he was in his sixtieth year. He faced greater danger from enemy submarines in voyages to India than in any post he might have held here.

4
The Edinburgh Academy

Η ΠΑΙΔΕΙΑ ΣΟΦΙΑΣ ΚΑΙ ΤΗΣ ΑΡΕΤΗΣ ΜΗΤΗΡ
Motto of The Edinburgh Academy

Life in a terrace house in Edinburgh put an end to the intimate contact with the countryside which had been ours at Lochar House. True there were compensations – light, all of thirty candle-power at the flick of a switch. (Oh! the wonders of gas and electricity after coal, paraffin and candles.) Then the cable tramcars clanking mournfully along, ready always to take you great distances for one penny. Many new friends, including the boy next door, who introduced himself by pushing up the bathroom window and viewing myself hot and steaming fresh from the bath. Our visits to the local baths taught me more than just how to swim (could this be Adam's first sin?) As to the 'sinfulness of that estate' into which it seemed I had now fallen, it was a cause of some remorse and anxiety until a few other experiences and a great deal of idle talk in corners assured me that, if this were indeed so, then by a process of extrapolation the whole school and all in it were (and always had been) destined for eternal damnation, and since nobody was much bothered about it I felt quite reassured.

My brother Pat and I were ready to start school on the first day of the second term of the session of 1914/1915. The Edinburgh Academy began life as a day school and still is, although one quarter of the boys were boarders by the time we joined. It was founded in 1824 by Sir Walter Scott and a group of Edinburgh lawyers; they had all been pupils at the High School and were now convinced that the only cure for the low standard of teaching, the appalling sanitary conditions in the Old Town, where it was situated, and the savage and indiscriminate use of corporal punishment, was to make a completely fresh start elsewhere. The founders met strong opposition from the Town Council, who wanted no competition, but were unwilling to find the money for a new High School. There was criticism from some, who saw a threat to the old egalitarian traditions of Scottish education; the new school was to be situated a the far end of the New Town, into which the well-to-do were fast moving out of the stinking Wynds of the Old. Fortunately, the opposition became divided on some irrelevant issue and the Edinburgh Academy was opened by Sir Walter Scott on the first day of October 1824.

The main building exists today almost unchanged except for some internal rearrangement; fronted by a classical portico supported by six Doric columns, it had consisted at first of four large airy rooms, each capable of seating 110 boys and surrounding an oval asssembly hall, with the Rector's room for 160 at the north end. Class 1B, to which I had been consigned, and you can't go lower than that, occupied one of the four and was exactly as it had always been except for the desks, now for four instead of six, and the gas lighting, which dated from the middle of last century; Welsbach's invention of the incandescent mantle had passed unnoticed and the electric light had to wait until 1927. Numbers in the classes had been steadily reduced over the years and now averaged about 30. Suffix A or B represented level of ability and not subjects on the curriculum. I felt aggrieved at being in 1B, more so as my brother was in 2A, and worked hard enough to win the third prize in two terms. That is as low as you could go at the annual prizegiving, but it secured my transfer next session to what I felt to be my rightful place in 2A.

I am glad not to have missed the experience of being taught by one of the legendary figures of the past. Caleb Cash seemed enormous; he was in fact very tall and erect with a large square black beard. He had clearly established his authority over Class 1B by the time I arrived and if he kept the Tawse in his desk I never saw it used or heard his voice raised more than was needed to gain an instant and respectful hearing from some chattering group at the back. The legend of his timepiece being checked each day against the sound of the Castle gun is not quite correct. He confided in me as one worthy to be let into the secret that the sound of the gun was bound to be some seconds late and why. What he went out in the yard to do was to observe a large ball on the post on Calton Hill released by signal from Greenwich.

The Classical tradition was central to the Founders' plan for their new school and so remained for at least the first hundred years, and the title of Dux for the best scholar in the school could only be awarded to a member of the Classical 7th. or Rector's class, as it was originally. At the Inauguration, Dr Williams, the first Rector, hoped that by the time the youngest new boy had reached the top class they 'would no longer shrink from comparison with Eton in Latin versification – nor with the Charterhouse or Winchester in Greek'. To stiffen their resolve he composed the school motto, which I have used to head this part of the chapter and which is still clearly to be seen in uncompromising Greek letters carved on the portico.

In the organization of classes and its teaching methods, the Academy had followed the traditions of the High School. Each intake of pupils, Geits so-called, formed a Class which remained together for four years and became known by the name of the master who had charge of it until ready to be handed over to the Rector for the last two. Not that the master had to teach all subjects – there was still room for specialists in the system – but the boys could identify with a group which had come together on their first day under a man, whose every foible and prejudice they would soon get to know and respect or else! In my time we stayed together as a class, but there was a change in master every year, until at or about the fifth we split up to follow our own specializations. Increasing numbers of options for specialist studies at ever earlier ages will erode the benefits of the 'class' system in a large day school, but I suppose that is the price of progress.

My only conspicuous success outside the classroom was in a military role, when I rose to be a Sergeant in command of No. 3 Platoon in the OTC. Although the war was over, military training was still taken seriously and we paraded twice a week in the uniform of Seaforth Highlanders. Some of us studied seriously to gain Certificate A, the magic key, which in the event of another war would open the door to instant officer rank. And the week of camp at Barry was enjoyed by the day boys – the boarders just wanted to be back home. When the day of the annual platoon competition came round I could not rate our chances very highly. We were, to be frank, rather an undersized lot; some of those in the rear rank, included to make up our number, seemed little taller than the old Lee Enfields with which they were to demonstrate efficiency in the complicated excercises laid down in the drill manual. However, they made up in keenness what they may have lacked in stature and we survived to take part in the final round of tactical exercises in Inverleith Park. Here we would be able to show our true metal. The enemy was deployed at the far end of the park and we advanced in 'short rushes' over the open and made good use of cover where available. The kilt is not a satisfactory battle dress; at the end of every short rush and inevitably with a following wind, it finishes up around your shoulders and it was a cardinal offence in the eyes of drill sergeants to break cover by using a hand to smooth it back over that which it was there to conceal. (Our corps commanders were English schoolmasters and they used to deliver lectures on the desirability of wearing trews in the interests of decency. 'I'll not take a lot of half-naked young savages into the park for those young nursery-maids to see.' But trews were not an army issue and we did nothing about it). And so to the last stages of the attack, when one of my four sections became detached, I won't say lost, and surprised the enemy and possibly themselves by capturing the enemy headquarters. And that was how we won the platoon competition and had our name inscribed on the plinth of the Ceylon Cup.

At an early age, I declared my intention of becoming an engineer and was excused Greek. In spite of its classical tradition and the fact that there was no science taught until 1890, the Academy had produced a great crop of eminent scientists in the nineteenth century. Without a doubt the greatest was James Clerk Maxwell, 'Dafty' to his class-mates, whose portrait was reported to be one of only three in Einstein's study in Berlin. Then there was also his friend P.G. Tait, who beat him to first place as Senior Wrangler at Cambridge. They were in the class of 1841-1847; another burst of scientific genius occurred thirty years later, when some boys, who were determined to teach each other science if nobody else would, formed the Eureka Club. Four members became Fellows of the Royal Society. In my last year at school, I was designated for the daunting task of acting as demonstrator for a Christmas lecture to be given by one of the former members of the club, Professor Sir D'Arcy Wentworth Thompson FRS. He had a commanding figure and a beard even longer than the one which had secured for Caleb Cash the respectful attention of his class of Geits. It all went well; the soap films projected on the screen did what they were intended to do and proved what he foretold they would prove. I was rewarded with an invitation to lunch at the University Club and he remarked, as we were about to enter the doors of the club, that the achitecture of Prince's Street was in most respects inferior to that of the Mile End Road. I could not comment as at the time I had not set eyes on the latter and treasured up his dictum for possible use in the future.

From its first beginning the Academy had been staffed almost entirely by graduates of Oxford and Cambridge. The senior science master was a hirsute Scot from Peterhouse, Cambridge, M. McCallum Fairgrieve. His humorous mannerisms and side-splitting rendering of 'When Father Laid the Carpet on the Stairs' at the annual 'Free and Easy Concert' concealed an utter dedication to science, not just as something to be taught to reluctant schoolboys, but more important as something that was shaping the future of the world. At the end of the lecture on the kinetic theory of gases, he took me aside and said in a hoarse whisper, 'I am going to let you into a secret, but you must not tell the others: the atom is not hard and indivisible as I have been telling them. We are breaking it open all the time at Cambridge.' This slight lapse on the part of the atom did nothing to shake his conviction that physics is an exact science and should be taught before chemistry, which in a school laboratory it is demonstrably not. Those of us who cared enough could spend two extra hours in the laboratories on subjects of our own choice. I was encouraged by 'Fairy' to spend the whole of one term designing and assembling some equipment and using it to measure the conductivity of electrolytes in gels of varying concentration. I must report with regret that the results led to no significant conclusions and I was unable to emulate Clerk Maxwell, who had a paper read to the Royal Society of Edinburgh while still at the Academy. When I look back, it was a fairly hard working day, with those two extra hours at the end of six periods in the classroom and one hour of obligatory OTC drill and then, still in the uniform of a Seaforth Highlander, a three-mile journey home by tram or bicycle.

The signing of the Armistice and the end of the Kaiser's War happened just half way through my school life. It made little difference to our home life; food was still scarce and servants unobtainable and our aunt, now 70, was no longer able to take the same active part in the running of the household as she had in the past. At a later stage, there arrived on our scene two 'lady helps', whose mature attractions my brothers seemed instantly to recognize. I was too young or too shy to try to find out what it was all about or perhaps was discouraged from doing so and nobody told me; just one more step up the ladder of ignorance. My father was now permanently at home and settled down to a regular routine of golf in the morning, evening at the Conservative Club and home for supper at eight. Except of course on Sunday, when there was no golf and he could settle down to three hours steady writing to the manager of the tea estate, in the peace and quiet of our compulsory church parade. He was comfortably off by the standards of those days, but there was one flaw. All his investments were in tea and rubber, where 10 per cent was the very least to be expected and double that from a prosperous concern, and they were among the first to feel the impact of the post-war slump, beginning a decline from which they never recovered. The customary month at the sea in August at North Berwick or Anstruther in Fife was supplemented by long visits to friends in the Highlands; and there was always a hill sheep farm called Rivox, to which Aunt Jean and her husband had retired after the calamity of his investments in, of all things, Austrian Railways.

Here we led a simple life and worked quite hard at times, what with the lambing, the hay harvest and the mucking out of byres and pig-styes; helping the shepherd to collect and fold the sheep and persuade them not too gently to immerse in a tank of tar oil emulsion, with a careful search in the evening to be sure that no wandering tick had attached itself to the friendly shelter of some hairier part of one's person. In September the lambs had to be graded, faces washed and fleeces tinted a delicate shade of ochre with a bright vermillion patch at the back of the head, all in preparation for Lockerbie sales.

One year, my brother Pat and I were both at Rivox, and just about to return home for school, when the great April blizzard struck right in the middle of lambing. Despite all the efforts of the shepherds, two in number now for the lambing, about a third of the flock were trapped in drifts, where they had taken shelter on the lee side of the stone dykes, some with their lambs and some about to give birth. We went to work with all possible speed, as soon as conditions moderated, looking for tiny blow-holes in the snow and prodding with long poles. About half of the missing had been rescued alive and some even of the lambs by the end of the week, when the roads were open again and we had to return, late for the new term but with a good story to tell. Our reward for any contribution we might make to the prosperity of the farm had come already, when my uncle acquired the shooting rights; he had been engaged in a long series of disputes with the landlord and his gamekeepers over the burning of the heather and this was the price of peace. We were now free to roam at will over the moors in search of 'one for the pot' and locating the coveys of grouse for a future walk up when our own Uncle Jim came up from nearby Moffat.

The small house was frequently full to bursting with relatives and other guests. Nothing daunted, Aunt Jean would bake scones of several sorts for ten hungry mouths twice a week on a griddle suspended over an open fire of peat and coal, as well as preparing four meals a day, milking the two cows, making the butter (my special task when available), preparing food for the hens and for the one duck, which could by some miracle lay two eggs a day if satisfied with her rations, and for the two sheep dogs. The moment supper was over, she would announce 'That's all for today' and, when satisfied that everything was clean, dry and put away, would sit down at last to knit a stocking and read the paper, while keeping up a running commentary on the day's happenings and the state of the world, all at the same time. Sharp at ten, candles were lit and lamps extinguished and everyone went their several ways to bed, to be ready for next day's activity, beginning in her case at 6.30 am.

It was a remarkable performance for one who had married well and lived in some comfort until uprooted by the failure of her husband's investment strategy. She deserves a chapter to herself and I should be the one to write it as her favourite; partly out of compassion I suspect, at a time when I felt somewhat isolated between two elder brothers and two younger twin sisters. And I did not always have the robust good health of the others, psychosomatic symptoms no doubt or a cry for sympathy. Whatever the reason, I spent some happy periods at one or other of her husband's residences, Gledenholm first, then Kindar House in New Abbey (visit to the Hamilton grave), Bankside near Lockerbie (first sight of a gasworks – two hand-charged stop end retorts, which served the 'Big House', Castlemilk, residence of Sir Robert Buchanan-Jardine) and then Rivox as I have been telling. My aunt had an engaging habit of calling the farm animals after members of the family, so that I might return for another holiday and enquire after the health of my friend Kenneth, the pig, only to find that Kenneth was hanging up as hams and bacon in the farm kitchen. The bull remained anonymous, which when I watched what he was up to with the half wild Galloway cows of the paddock was just as well; I might have felt embarrassed if he had been, so to speak, my 'alter ego'. It was not so much what he succeeded in doing as the spectacular results of any failure to do so that caught my eye.

Meanwhile at school, my early ambition to become an engineer was quenched by the condition of the traditional engineering industries of Scotland at the end of the war; rumour had it that trained engineers were having to go out on the road selling whisky. My sixteenth birthday was a time for decision and Fairy was quick to take part in it. Science, and by this he meant physics, was what he wanted and he had set his heart on Cambridge as the only place where physics was taught, practised and researched to his satisfaction. This meant a scholarship, since it would be out of the question to expect my father to bear the whole cost. The Scottish system of education was still as good as anything in the world and there was no brake on anyone who felt the stirring of genius, as witness James Clerk Maxwell or in a lesser way myself with every confidence in an ability to excel. I already had all the five Higher Leaving Certificates, which would qualify for entry to any university in the Kingdom, even Oxford after 1920, and all without much effort on my part.

It was a very different matter, when only five clear terms remained before the date of the first group of scholarship examinations at Cambridge. The volume of papers from previous years left me in no doubt that it was all too short a time, in which to rise to the standard of mathematics expected of a scholar. As to the rest, I was fairly confident, when in December of 1921 I sat down in the hall at King's to find out what it was that the examiners had in store for me. It was as I thought it might be, only worse; with devilish ingenuity they had introduced abstruse mathematical problems into what I had considered to be straightforward physical phenomena. I romped through the chemistry, but guessed the game was up. At the 'practical' in the Cavendish, I was engaged in long conversation with no less a figure than the legendary J.J. Thompson, discover of the electron. I could only hope that the invigilator would give me some bonus marks for the half-hour that he held me spell bound or I would have to write it off to experience as time lost in a good cause. Then there was a General Knowledge paper; all the clever English schoolboys got to work at once churning out neat essays and finishing each with a flourish of the pen and a satisfied smirk. Or so it seemed to me as I sat paralysed, like a rabbit I had once seen facing a weazel, for although I felt that I knew enough about the subjects I had never been taught to write English. Opinion at school had inclined to the view that a good grounding in Latin would provide all that was required to master English grammar and, as to writing English, anyone could do that. But I had fallen deeply in love with the kind of place that Cambridge was, with the kind of life that people led there and in a nice kind of corporate way with all the other boys, especially those from the Public Schools, who were trying like me to get there. The ones I came to know in the short time we were together seemed so mature and well-mannered and friendly. It occurs to me now that they may have been intrigued to meet a boy from a Scottish public school, albeit a day school, setting foot on English soil for the very first time, for that was how it was.

In the interests of economy, I had travelled to Cambridge by a route which involved changing trains at Peterborough and Grantham and I had not yet set foot in the capital city, a defect which I decided must be remedied without further delay. After negotiating the exchange of my return half, I reckoned to have about five hours and something under two pounds in which and with which to 'do the town'. King's Cross as a leisure centre was not exactly a Piccadilly Circus, even if it offered, as I was informed later, grave pitfalls for the unwary young traveller including the possibility of a lapse into sin. But with a stern sense of purpose I dined respectably with a self-conscious half-bottle of wine on the table, followed that with a visit to a local and long defunct music hall and returned to Edinburgh as a seasoned and blasé traveller, there to await a telegram from the porter at King's. The message, when it came, was brief and to the point, 'Sorry no award at King's'; it came as no surprise and I scarcely felt it worth any crumb that might have fallen from the rich man's table by way of an award at a lesser college.

'Fairy' was disappointed but not disheartened and readily fell in with my suggestion that I should try for Oxford next time. He was prepared to concede that chemistry was being taught there and research carried out to standards as high as those of physics at his beloved Cambridge. So I settled for Oxford and made Corpus my first choice of the colleges. It was the smallest in the university, with a strong classical bias and there had been a steady stream of scholars from the Academy. This would be my last chance, as I would be nineteen in October, and less than three months remained in which to prepare myself for the ordeal; and I was not going to be caught out again. I bought several volumes of the collected 'Fourth Leaders' of *The Times* and soon learned how to say something about almost anything without too much commitment to any firm opinion about the subject; and at just about the right length to suggest to an examiner that I had in fact heard about it, but with no presumption that I was trying to impose my opinions on the examiner, whose wisdom and right to differ I would in no way question. There was no simple way out of my other problem, although I was Dux of the top class in mathematics and recipient of the Gloag Silver Medal in evidence thereof. A serious hiatus had developed in the teaching of mathematics to scholarship standard during the war years and the temporary master in charge was a nervous wreck by the time he had finished with us and we with him. My serious question as to what proof he had that parallel lines never meet drove him into a frenzy, because he knew that I knew that in hyperbolic and elliptical space quite different rules apply, which he was desperately anxious not to have to debate in front of a class, whose attention he was hard pressed to hold with far simpler concepts. With no help coming from that quarter, I had to make do with some intensive study in advanced textbooks at home and even in classes supposed to be for other matters, where the master was tolerant and understanding.

When I arrived at Oxford, it was to find that Corpus had no chemistry tutor of its own and relied on Hammick at Oriel. His translation of Perrin's *Les Atomes* had by chance come my way as a prize for science the year before and I had no difficulty in working in a reference to 'M. Perrin's outstanding contribution to our understanding of the behaviour of atoms' and was probably tempted to add 'now available in a masterly translation', but happily refrained, which knowing Hammick as I did later was just as well. The final interview was warm and friendly and I left Oxford with very little doubt as to the outcome, which was duly confirmed by telegram as a scholarship worth £80 p.a., and that was how I came to be in the train entering Oxford where my story began.

5
A View from the Gasworks

How soon hath Time the subtle thief of youth.
Stol'n on his wing my three and twentieth year!
John Milton 1631

As my taxi turned into Grosvenor Road, SW1 on a September morning in 1926 and delivered myself and my luggage at No. 94, I reflected that here with another journey ended, another new life was about to begin. This time there were no options and no dreaming spires – my final commitment to a life in the gas industry was symbolized by those four monstrous gas-holders which came into view as the night express slowed down for its final run into King's Cross. I surveyed the uninviting scene with the jaundiced eye of an overnight passenger in a third-class carriage. Down here on the Embankment it was all different and I soon cheered up.

My future landlord greeted me on the doorstep with dignity ('welcomed' would be going too far) and showed me to my room, contriving in the process to indicate all the work that had gone into converting the ground-floor-back into a bedroom for myself at very short notice. Mr Short was a tall upstanding West countryman, a pillar of the Church and a sidesman at the fashionable St. Michael's Chester Square. He himself was a retired policeman and having put our relationship on a proper footing I was ready to be introduced to his wife. Mrs Short was small, friendly and firmly Chapel, and an excellent cook as I soon discovered. John Brooks had found the rooms and shared them for a year with Robert Curwen, also Corpus, who, having completed his indoctrination into the Colonial Service, was about to leave to take over his allotted corner of our African empire. Arthur Gott was to have his room and when John heard that I had finally settled for the Gas Light and Coke Company he prevailed on Mr Short to make space for me. It was all very agreeable and vastly preferable to the alternative – a solitary life in a bed-sitter. Our large sitting-room occupied the whole of the first-floor frontage with a view of the river (just) and its myriad activities and, for myself, a first-class view of the Nine Elms Gasworks on the far bank.

'A Young Lady'

Arthur went back to his home in Lymington most week-ends and John was often away visiting friends or relations. It was all most convenient when the following year opportunities arose of meeting the 'young lady' mentioned briefly towards the end of Chapter 1. Her name was Dorothea Bluett, and she was the only daughter of Lt. Commander Bertie W. Bluett RN. In 1914, under the threat of war, he was appointed to be First Officer of *Monmouth*, a veteran armoured cruiser which was being commissioned in haste to join a Squadron of four equally old vessels under the command of Admiral Cradock, flying his flag on the cruiser *Good Hope*. Their objective was the defence of merchant shipping in the South Pacific, and, obeying as he understood them, the Admiralty's rather confused orders, Cradock went in pursuit of a crack squadron of German cruisers under the command of Admiral Graf von Spee, and when he found them at Coronel engaged him in battle. The result was a foregone conclusion; hopelessly outgunned, *Good Hope* and *Monmouth* were lost with all hands. It was no consolation to the relatives that the Navy's revenge came a few months later at the Battle of the Falkland Isles.

At the outbreak of war the Admiralty in its wisdom closed Dartmouth and sent all the cadets to sea. A group of ten fifteen-year-old cadets arrived on the *Monmouth* to the dismay of the First Officer;* Cadet Mandley wrote in his diary, 'I heard a marine say 'Here's some more poor little chaps being sent to be killed.' Fortunately for them when they reached St. Vincent they were transferred to HMS *Caernarvon*. Among their number was Cadet Patrick M.S. Blackett, who fifty-two years later, as President of the Royal Society, performed the solemn ceremony of admission by which I became a Fellow in 1966 and signed the Charter Book, first used by Charles II in 1664.

Mrs Bluett never re-married and lived mostly just outside the small town of Annan in Dumfriesshire where her parents had a commodious house, while Dorothea went to the Royal Naval School at St. Margaret's, just a short mile from where we came to live in Twickenham. She became Head Girl, although no scholar

* *Coronel and the Falklands*, by Geoffrey Barnet 1962.

as she is the first to admit, but fortunately for the success of our marriage plan, gained the trust and friendship of the Headmistress, Miss Chaplin. Meanwhile Mrs Bluett was trying to bring a little life and joy into the Scottish scene at the nearby village of Powfoot, on the Solway, where there was a golf course and hotel that my father favoured. She converted the village hall into a dancing place, all very respectable, I need hardly add, and there we met in the long vacation of my third year at Oxford. Dorothea was nineteen and had just left school; I was twenty-one and had still a year to go before I could even begin to earn a living, clearly a most unsuitable match. I run into difficulty in trying to explain our situation to readers of the present generation. The settled middle class, not only in Scotland but there particularly, encouraged flirtation but abhorred consummation, reasonably perhaps in view of the risks in the pre-pill era; marriage was the triumph of continence over desire with virginity a prize to be cherished. These crude mores were expressed in a code of polite behaviour which gave licence for a period of tactile investigation after which it was to be expected that intentions would be manfully expressed as towards the marriage bed, supported by a declaration of financial resources adequate to support the bride in the circumstances to which she had been accustomed, or at least some hope thereof, and I had neither. To declare our intentions was to invite unrelenting opposition, so we agreed to admit nothing until at least I had a firm promise of employment. Meanwhile Dorothea's mother was encouraged by the hope that our enforced separation in the following year would solve the problem of what she considered to be (and rightly, as I will cheerfully agree) a hopelessly improvident match.

These considerations were very much in mind as I set about looking for employment in the spring of 1926. It should not have been too difficult with an assured first and three papers published and more to come, yet the full implication of the 1929 recession was already casting its shadow before. We were having to learn the hard way that it is not enough to win a war; it is essential also to win the peace. Heavy industry had profited by the demand for munitions yet continued to produce with the pre-war tools of its trade. We failed to learn from Germany the lesson that the rapid assimilation of the results of research at the universities into industry was the secret of their success. Teams of experienced engineers, trained in the Technical High Schools, took over and the integration of all branches of science in further development behind the security of the factory walls completed the process.

There was one outstanding example of good management over here and that was the Brunner Mond Works at Northwich where they produced alkali by the ammonia-soda process. They recruited regularly from the Oxford School of Chemistry, and it would have been my first choice had there been a vacancy; only one place was offered and that was pre-empted by the Trinity scholar of the previous year. It came down to a choice between the Gas Light and Coke Company in London and ICI at Billingham. Harold Hartley had joined the Board of the Gas Company a few years before and was already exerting his influence to good effect by the establishment of a research department for gas manufacture with the promise of a new laboratory. He could be very persuasive if his mind was set on a matter and I undertook to attend an interview at the head office in Horseferry Road, Westminster, although I had reservations about the sort of salary being talked about, 'without commitment, of course'. The interview was friendly and the surroundings impressive.

I was offered the job and a salary which was remarkably like the one mentioned at Oxford and to that extent disappointing. I went away to think it over, and came to the reasonable conclusion that it was only fair to ICI to offer them the opportunity of assessing my worth. Several of us arrived together for the interviews and were hospitably received in a country club atmosphere at the guest house in Old Stockton. Dinner with our hosts was probably a part of the interviewing process. The appointment when it was offered was in the research department. The salary was half as much again as at Horseferry Road and I was now in quite a dilemma; I wanted the money and I wanted a wife, and a short walk round Stockton-on-Tees left me wondering whether there was much hope of pursuing my courtship to a satisfactory conclusion there.

I came back to Oxford torn by doubts and in great confusion of mind. Quite by chance next morning I came up with Harold Hartley pushing his bicycle along Long Wall. He was looking for a quiet spot at which to perform the near acrobatic feat of mounting over the back wheel from a projection called the back step (my father had always used that approach). He saw me and gave his mind over to my problem – counselled patience – thought all was not lost – mounted triumphantly and disappeared down the Broad at a good pace. A few days later another summons came to attend at Horseferry Road. I placed my difficulty fairly before the Gas Company: had always wanted to work in London, disliked the secrecy rules of ICI, presumed that in a public utility there would be freedom to publish and so on, touching delicately at the end on the matter of my salary. There was a long pause, both sides rather embarrassed (it was not the kind of subject normally discussed in that room with that person) and then came an improved offer and that was how I became a gas man and worked happily (well mostly happily) ever after.

Life on a gasworks

My introduction to the research department of the Chief Gas Chemist took place at an interim laboratory they occupied high up on the top floor at the back of the headquarters building. It revealed nothing of the Victorian splendour which surrounded my two earlier visits to Horseferry Road. Space had been found for it by extending the Chief Engineer's department, the acre of prime building land at the back of the head office being still occupied by two elderly gasholders. They at least provided a change of scene as they rose and fell in response to the changing demands for gas by the citizens of Westminster. Two of the occupants of the laboratory were Oxford chemists and they made me welcome, offering every facility except bench space, of which there was none to spare.

All difficulties were resolved when I was introduced to Stuart Pexton, leader of the group to which I had been assigned. He told me how he had migrated to a gasworks at Stratford (atte Bow, not upon Avon) where there was a laboratory large enough to share with the works staff. The works, though small by the standards of the Gas Light and Coke Company, offered a good variety of plant and equipment well adapted to the programme which he outlined over beer and sandwiches at the Albert Tavern. He would meet me there the following morning, assuming always that I was careful to follow the travel instructions which he gave me. A green open-top no. 24 bus to Victoria, a District Line underground to Bow Road and a tram to a stop convenient to Stratford Works saw me launched on my gas industry career. The thing that I best remember about the journey was the succession of appalling odours that appeared endemic to the part of the East End which begins at Bow Road. Since no one I spoke to ever mentioned them I let it pass. When finally I could restrain my curiosity no longer I was told that the less offensive was a tallow and soap factory and the worst offender was something to do with rabbit skins, and when you had worked long enough on a gasworks you would not be able to tell the difference.

L.A. Ravald, my senior by some years, was waiting to introduce me to the arcane system of units in general use in the gas industry. Grains per 100 cu. ft. was the measure of the ammonia present in the gas, ounce strength the measure of the ammonia in the 'gas liquor' produced by washing the gas with water (it was the number of ounces of sulphuric acid required to neutralize the ammonia in one gallon of the stuff), pressure of gas was in inches on the water gauge, and temperatures in Fahrenheit of course; a long way from the CGS units of the research laboratory and further still from the SI code, but a useful eccentricity because it was the language of the men who operated, and those who supervised, the processes. Years later I noticed that in a hydrogen plant designed by ICI for the Balloon Barrage all the instruments which gave readings in atmospheres and degrees centigrade had been covered by paper scales reading inches water gauge and degrees Fahrenheit.

Dr Pexton (the prefix fitted him so well that he was always thus addressed on the works – indeed his visits had something of the character of a family doctor visiting a sick patient and prescribing a cure) arrived at Stratford bursting as ever with enthusiasm and full of new ideas. There was plenty of room for new ideas in an industry which in many respects belonged to the second half of the nineteenth century. The complex mixture called coal gas which emerged from the retorts laden with every sort of impurity had to be brought under control without delay to prevent the deposition of pitch or naphthalene or ammonium chloride, any or all of them, during the process of cooling the gas to ambient temperature. Many and diverse were the opinions held and stoutly defended about how best to achieve these aims and about the equipment best suited to the purpose. It was mostly rule-of-thumb and if it worked, that was good enough for the man who ran the works, and who shall blame him for that? The scrubber yard was the name of the area which had so intrigued me on my first voyage of discovery and here ammonia was removed by washing with water and tar fog by a variety of ingenious devices, none of them very efficient; and so forward to the purifiers, where hydrogen sulphide was absorbed in layers of a special kind of iron oxide and the gas was given a final clean up in the process. I may say that this stage was so efficient that it became quite difficult later to think up anything in modern technology to take its place.

The economics of gas manufacture in London and the south east depended on Durham run-of-mine coal brought in by the cheap sea route. It had been thought unsuitable for the new continuous vertical retorts which were revolutionizing the gas industry in the rest of the country. Thomas Hardie, appointed Chief Engineer in

1922, would have none of this and the vertical retorts he introduced added to the problems of the purification of gas just about as fast as they could be solved. It was all in Pexton's character to tackle each or any of the problems which presented themselves, with cheerful confidence, attacking with almost uncanny accuracy at the point where the minimum of laboratory research could yield the maximum reward in terms of progress at the works. The problem when removing ammonia from crude gas by washing with water was how to finish up with the maximum strength of solution compatible with the minimum escape of ammonia in the washed gas. Our simple tests, they could hardly be called research, on the multi-stage rotary washers, which had replaced the huge pre-war tower scrubbers, had shown how their performance could first be assessed and then improved. It was some years before L. Silver at the new Fulham Laboratory could elucidate the mechanism of what turned out to be a very complex process.

All our experience pointed to the need for more efficient cooling of the gas, and led Pexton to a fresh examination of the design of the condensers, so called, used to cool the gas before it could be further purified. Early in 1927 he came down to Stratford highly delighted with a recently published treatise on Chemical Engineering by Walker, Lewis and McAdam. It opened my eyes to the value of the methods used in America to design for improvement in many industries having problems in common. We could now predict how new designs with higher gas and water flow rates could handle the gas from vertical retorts where heavy steaming to increase production of gas had mutiplied the heat load on the condensers by a factor of two or three times.

There was also a substantial increase in the amount of naphthalene in the gas which could affect the performance of the condensers even to the extent of complete blockage. Pexton appreciated the scientific approach of Dr Carpenter of the South Metropolitan Gas Company in his young pioneer days. He had shown how by reversing the flow of gas and water, deposits of naphthalene could be melted and and then washed out in a stream of hot tar; but his condensers were inefficient due to their low gas and water flow rates. The new condensers developed their own problems. Serious corrosion of the water tubes led to failure in some cases in a matter of weeks. This was brought under control by better choice of the tube material and attention to the method of fabrication. The condensers were later redesigned to eliminate the trapping of air bubbles on the inner surface of the tubes, a frequent source of corrosion, and we heard no more of the problem.

I will mention just one more project which came to a successful conclusion during the three years that I worked for Pexton. There was a growing market for benzole, the name given to the mixture of aromatic hydrocarbons, predominantly benzene, always present in coal gas. Benzole was in demand as an additive to improve the quality of motor spirit by increasing the anti-knock rating. Toluene, the second member of the family, had been in great demand during the war for the manufacture of the explosive TNT. Many gasworks co-operated to produce toluene by washing gas with oil or tar in simple improvised equipment. One obvious approach was to substitute efficient washers, such as those used for ammonia, and to increase the oil flow sufficiently to recover the benzene as well as the toluene. An alternative was to use activated carbon, a material similar to, but not identical with, that used in gas masks during the war. An early trial plant registered total failure – the carbon gummed up and became inactive. It looked as if the laboratory investigation would take a long time to come up with a solution and we decided that the best plan was to miniaturize the equipment but in all other respects run the process as it would be carried out on the full scale.

Eight replicas in miniature were required to identify and evaluate the variables. They were designed and built in the 'Stove and Meter Shop' on Stratford Works with the co-operation of the Superintendant and his skilled brass fitters, all in a remarkably short space of time. Once installed in a hut on the works we organized shifts for round-the-clock working for as many weeks or months as it would take to get the answers we wanted. We were able to pin-point the trouble as arising in the desorption stage where the carbon is first heated and then steamed to remove and recover the benzole. The recipe for success was to:

(1) Heat the carbon as quickly as possible.
(2) Introduce the steam early in the cycle.
(3) Steam countercurrent to the flow of gas.
(4) Avoid excessive temperatures.

All very simple, it would seem, and not very much to show for the time taken and the man-hours involved, but it worked. Before long a plant to treat 2 million cu. ft. per day was installed at Harrow and working satisfactorily; followed closely by one at Beckton for 80 million cu. ft. and said to be, like the works itself, the largest in the world. I regard those first three years as my apprenticeship to the real hard core of the gas industry – the places where gas was made. Meanwhile if progress might seem rather slow at times (and salary advances might seem even slower) I never regretted the long hours spent in the works.

The opportunity to get even closer to the heart of the business came when I was appointed to carry out, jointly with Eynon Davies, the Station Chemist at Fulham Works, an acceptance test on a new installation of vertical retorts. It was one of the first, and certainly the largest, retort house yet designed and guaranteed for use with sea-borne Durham coal as part of Thomas Hardie's new look for the old company. When the time came to carry out the test Durham coal was not available – an aftermath of the General Strike of 1926 and the long-drawn-out miners' strike which followed. Imported American coal had to be used and it was agreed to shorten the test period to 7 days. We thought it over and decided that we could cover the day in two twelve-hour shifts and I took over the night shift, leaving Davies free to carry out his other duties as Station Chemist.

There was much more to it than just those seven days. When you are planning to measure an input of 700 tons of coal a day and everything that comes out of the coal after it has been admitted to the top of each of the 120 vertical retorts that make up the settings in the retort house; brought up to bright-red heat during the first 20 feet of its passage through the retort, then cooled with steam on its way down to the iron lock hoppers; from here discharged as coke to be graded and stored in hoppers before being weighed out for sale to customers; some of it to be weighed and sampled and sent direct to furnaces where it was turned into the gas used to heat the retorts; as if that were not enough, the waste gases to be 'weighed' by the device of measuring the water used to produce the steam generated during their passage through waste heat boilers; finally everything to be accounted for and reconciled as mass and energy balances. None of this is possible in seven days unless, as in sea trials of a new ship, you put the vessel on a straight course and bearing and at steady speed before entering and after leaving the measured mile. In terms of our test that entailed about four weeks of close observation and testing of equipment; it did not require me to be on night duty until near the actual test.

There is something rather special about a gasworks at night. The captains and kings have departed to the comfort of their respective firesides, with high tea or dinner as may befit each one his station. Now the shift foreman reigns supreme. Fitters and other maintenance staff, so prominently in the way until desperately wanted, have disappeared. Coke lorries, and at most works a great variety of horse-drawn vehicles have finished their day's work and there is hardly ever a man to be seen outside. Even the machinery seems to settle down to a quieter rhythm and on a fine night the stars have a special brilliance when you emerge from the dim light inside for a breath of air and a chance to cool down.

Inside the retort houses work goes on as usual, periods of intense activity alternating with rest periods in the lobbies. Horizontal retort houses still represented three-quarters of the company's carbonizing capacity. Hand-stoking was a thing of the past but the machines that had taken over were of necessity large, complicated, yet surprisingly accurate in the hands of a skilled operator. It is a time of intense activity as the machine traverses the length of the retort house using a powerful ram to push the spent charge out of the retort, from whence the red-hot coke falls in clouds of steam on to a scraper conveyor and is quenched with water sprays. Coal is projected into the empty retorts from a fast-moving band and, by varying the speed, the skilled operator can lay a uniform layer the whole length of a 20 ft. retort, leaving just the right amount of space for the free passage of the gas to the iron collecting pipes at either end. My vertical retort house offered a more orderly regime to replace the smoke, steam, fire and fury that seemed to dominate the scene I have described. Here the coal slips quietly into the top of the retort and emerges from the iron lock hopper at the bottom, cool enough already to be conveyed away on a quiet rubber band. The only heavy manual labour involved appeared to be the 'poking' with long iron rods to ensure that the coal was passing smoothly through the 'plastic' zone. But it could be very hot indeed on top and wherever samples had to be taken and temperatures measured with an optical pyrometer. On one occasion with my hands full of samples, my face blackened by coal dust and a bright-red pencil in my mouth I was near to being whisked off to the ambulance room as a casualty in urgent need of attention. The several weeks required for the verification of all our results did indeed end in satisfactory material balances, the essential criterion of a valid test.

Pexton welcomed the results as an early contribution to a study of the principles and practice of the carbonizing process to which he was now committed and which was to occupy much of his time in the future. Carbonization was at the heart of the gas industry's business as it had been for a hundred years and would continue to be for better or worse for another twenty. Most of the improvement, and there had been considerable advances in design and performance as evidenced in the retort house at Fulham, had come though the efforts of the engineers and designers using methods that were essentially empirical; scientists where they came into the picture at all, were operating on the periphery, studying such matters as the behaviour of refractories. Pexton's incursion into the field (taking on where Dr Carpenter had left off nearly twenty years before) was to prove timely and effective in the gas industry's struggle for survival in the years that lay ahead.

Marriage

When John Brooks left us to go out to Australia, Kilmeny Simon, an Australian friend of his, who had been encouraging him in his pioneering venture, offered us one floor of her furnished maisonette at 43 Mecklenburgh Square, with a pleasant outlook over the gardens in front and the grounds of the old Foundling Hospital at the side. It suited us both very well: Arthur Gott because he was pursuing his career as an architect in the offices of Sir Giles Gilbert Scott in nearby Gray's Inn; myself because Dorothea could come up from Twickenham in time-off from her duties as Assistant Games Mistress at the Royal Naval School. It had been organized for her by Miss Chaplin, the Head Mistress, who was actively on our side, against my future mother-in-law's plan to keep us as far apart as possible until a more suitable match could be arranged for her only daughter. Added to the comforts of my foothold in Bloomsbury, we might be invited to tea on a Sunday in Miss Chaplin's sitting room at the RNS. We were left to the ministrations of Molly, the friendly Irish parlour-maid, while our hostess busied herself elsewhere. Although I saw nothing of it, I later heard how my arrival and departure on the drive leading up to the portico of the former Kilmorey Mansion was closely monitored by many pairs of eyes from windows offering a good view of the event. An occasional invitation to lunch at 'High Table' in the school hall was a more daunting experience; there could be no mistaking the centre of interest nor the degree of the interest aroused. I had acquired scarcity value.

The time came when, having made the decision to get married in the autumn of 1929, the search for a home anywhere within the range of my scanty resources seemed doomed to failure, until we thought of the area that both knew best. The estate agent for the St. Margaret's district of Twickenham opened his book at the entry – 'Top floor flat in converted mansion, offering spacious accommodation comprising 2 living rooms, 4 bedrooms and all usual offices. Rent £90 per annum plus Rates.' Unbelievable!

This, our first home, was situated in what was then known as Twickenham Park, a Victorian housing estate of large houses built in Italianate style, in the fields surrounding a Georgian mansion called Twickenham Park House. It was timed to take advantage of the improved communications of the new London to Windsor line and a bridge over the Thames. The authentic Twickenham Park, of which no trace remains and even the site is conjectural, has earned fame from the residence there of one of its earliest tenants, Francis Bacon who found 'the situation of that place much convenient for the trial of my philosophical conclusions'. Verb. sap.

I went to work with a will and spirited contests in shops in the King's Road ended in the purchase of several pleasant, partially reconstructed antique pieces of walnut furniture, still around to recall the days when times were hard. We descended on a City warehouse with a letter of introduction which ensured a substantial discount on the price of one double and one single bed. There could be no second-hand stuff in that sector of our economy. I hoped we could be married in the Grosvenor Chapel where I had been confirmed by Bishop Gore, not long after coming down from Oxford. That turned out not to be possible and we settled for St. Paul's Knightsbridge. Arthur Couratin, with the vicar, performed the ceremony and Miles Clauson was my best man, so Corpus was well represented to see me off into strange uncharted waters, on which we appear to have navigated with some skill in a marriage which lasted for 56 years. Our honeymoon in France in Le Morvan was a great success in more ways than one. Within the statutory year our daughter was born, not perhaps a good example of family planning but a great joy and pleasure and never regretted.

Three years later when it came time to buy our own house, the very one that we had been coveting, on the other side of the Park, came on the market and, scraping together all I could muster, I paid the deposit, negotiated a loan and bought it for £1300, and lived here ever since. We have adapted the interior at intervals to suit our changed circumstances and re-designed the garden as the mood takes us, recalling what Bacon said about a garden: 'It is the purest of human pleasures.' That I was able to buy for such a sum, a relatively new architect-built house with 5 bedrooms and 2/3 living rooms was a measure of the depth of the depression in 1932; that its present value is well over 100 times what it cost me then is but a measure of the new evil of inflation.

My father's death in 1932 at the age of 76 came suddenly, although not unexpected; the state of his heart had been a matter of concern for some years. The family home in Edinburgh would have to go and the disposal of the contents followed inevitably. Uncle Will died a week later, hopelessly insolvent at the end as I suspect he had been for several years. Testy old Uncle Jim, now over 80, was a tower of strength and took care of Aunt Jean and helped with the arrangements to keep my father's estate intact until his tea and rubber shares could be realized at more nearly their true value than at the derisory prices ruling in the depth of the depression. Aunt Harriet lingered on for another two years and her death in an Edinburgh nursing home severed the last of my close links with the past.

Fulham Laboratories

While I was away at Stratford a new laboratory was growing up on space once occupied by the stables at Fulham Gasworks. The displaced horses were moved into new quarters 200 yards away, where unlike less favoured animals they went upstairs to bed in stables of revolutionary design which in the fullness of time were converted into new laboratories.

Most of what happened in those days stemmed from the driving force of Sir David Milne-Watson, Governor of the Gas Light and Coke Company. The war had brought him into contact with many of the leaders of other industries, like Mond and MacGowan, and Lord Moulton whose Report on the German War Factories was published as a White Paper. Where better could a Balliol man go for what he wanted than to Balliol? And so Harold Hartley became a Director of the Company in 1922 while continuing as a Tutor and Fellow of his College.

He told me that it had been quite hard work to win over the opposition when it came to deciding the objectives of the future research department and its location. In the same year that he was made a director Thomas Hardie became Chief Engineer. Although his training had been on the traditional lines of a gas engineer, when he came from Newcastle-upon-Tyne to the 'Gaslight' he was clear about what the company would have to do to fulfil its ambition to expand and succeed. He was aware of the contribution that science could make and ready to listen to the advice of the scientists. Beckton Gasworks was by far the largest in the company, the largest in Britain, and claimed to be the largest in the world, but most of its gas-making plant was representative of late nineteenth-century practice. The Beckton engineers knew this and were convinced that any future research department should be located at Beckton where so much modernization was required.

Across a closely guarded boundary fence lay the Tar Works, out-of-bounds to the public and the staff of the gas works alike, zealously guarding the secrets of its processes and claiming to be, like the gas works, the largest in Britain. It was under the able direction of W. Gordon Adam, the Superintendent, another graduate of the Honours School of Chemistry at Oxford. He came there as Senior Research Chemist and took charge in 1914 in the absence of his titular chief on war service. As Superintendent after the war he was building up a research department, with the purpose of branching out into the production of chemicals for use in peace time. There would be no doubt as to the advice he would tender if asked, or even if not.

In the end the Hartley view prevailed and the Court agreed to the proposal to establish a new research department as part of the Head Office establishment with a laboratory to be built on a site yet to be settled. As a first step they decided to appoint a Chief Gas Chemist and to find space for a small laboratory within the precincts of the Chief Engineer's Department. Harold Hollings from the South Metropolitan received the appointment in April 1924. He was a graduate of Leeds University with a Master's degree in Gas Engineering. When he arrived at his office in Horseferry Road he found a few files and documents of doubtful relevance, his responsibilities but loosely defined, with no indication of what might be considered an acceptable programme of work. All that had been decided was that he would take over from Gordon Adam responsibility for co-ordinating the work of the twelve station chemists. I feel sure that this situation did not cause him any permanent disquiet: he was now in a position to indicate to others what it was that they should be asking the Chief Gas Chemist to do for them. The new laboratory was authorized, the architect appointed, and the site chosen by the Governor himself, in the best tradition of authoritarian management.

The architect let himself go on the library; when three oak planks arrived, each twenty feet long, two feet wide and some three inches thick, it was a seven days' wonder until they were unveiled, pegged together, as the top of a refectory table of truly monumental proportions. I happened to be around at the time because, with the two senior chemists away on some assignment, I had been deputed to supervise the finishing stages of building the laboratory and installing the fittings and services. Here was something that I should have enjoyed – a young man's golden opportunity to acquire and exert administrative authority! – first faltering steps on the ladder of promotion! – I hated every minute of it and could hardly wait to get back to where there was real work to be done in the laboratory and on the gasworks. Before handing over I took care to stake a claim for eventual occupation of the desirable end bay of the No. 1 Laboratory, my headquarters for the next ten years.

Recruitment of staff proceeded at a steady pace for several years. Oxford was well represented among the newcomers and our number soon rose to eleven. When the company prudently abandoned its sortie into the chemical industry, some half-dozen chemists from the research group at the Beckton Tar Works joined the department. Recruitment from other universities brought our strength up to about forty graduates, at which level it remained, more or less, until the outbreak of war.

Our total effort owed much to the contribution made by a band of Chemical Assistants. These boys, mostly straight from school, worked very long hours. It was before the days of sandwich courses and day release, but the Company was generous by the standards of the time in such matters as tuition fees and expenses. The regular day was 9 until 5 with a half-day on Saturday, and then on to night classes from 6 to 9, at a Technical College, Chelsea or Battersea, or Birkbeck College of London University. Most of them received some reward by way of qualifications of one kind or another; several went on to the award of internal or external degrees from the university. Ian Dryden who was my first assistant achieved a second-class honours degree in physics at his first attempt. Dissatisfied with that, he went on to win a first in chemistry and, to crown it all, passed the stiff examination for Membership of the Institution of Chemical Engineers.

Gerard Daroux who qualified as a chemical engineer left to join a firm of chemical manufacturers and developed for Esso a process, for which he designed and and built a prototype in America during the war, to make acetic acid by the thermal decomposition of acetone. The attentive reader will recall how this reaction figured prominently in my Part 2 research with Hinshelwood at Oxford. We did not know at the time of the presence of an intermediate product, ketene, in the decomposition. Daroux planned to capture the ketene, on the wing so to speak, by heating the acetone and cooling the products as rapidly as possible to maximize the recovery. He then pursued his strictly commercial objective by hydrolysing the ketene to acetic acid. We could only claim to have been obedient to the precept of von Helmholtz quoted at the beginning of Chapter 2, having sought no practical utility while in the pursuit of science.

As I look back it seems that the important development was the evolution of an attitude to research in a laboratory not as an end in itself, but as directly related at every stage to the full-scale development of ideas in terms of their application to industrial practice. This led inevitably to the acceptance of chemical engineering as a branch of science in its own right, just as it had been accepted, taught and practised in America for two decades. The younger generation were quick to advance on this route and several who began as chemical assistants survived the hard slog of evening classes at Battersea and the gruelling test of the 'Home Paper' to qualify as chemical engineers.

As a senior chemist and group leader I was free to plan my own path within the broad outlines of a research programme never formally promulgated but well understood by all concerned. I continued to work in close co-operation with Pexton so that there was never any misunderstanding along those boundaries where our respective interests touched. They were being brightly illuminated by the researches of the one-time Station Chemist, L. Silver, discovered by Hollings at Kensal Green and brought to Fulham. Here he worked, at first alone or with one assistant and with the simplest of equipment, to determine the chemical engineering principles involved in the gas-washing process. Because he preferred to express his results in arcane units peculiar to the gas industry his first two papers in 1934 may not have received the recognition that was their due.

On my own

My brightest hopes – and greatest disappointment – came in our search for a better way of removing the one-per-cent of hydrogen sulphide in the crude gas. Some of the earliest legislation, continuing in force to this day, states that the gas shall be free from hydrogen sulphide. As any learned judge would propound, and the ordinary chap on the Clapham omnibus would respectfully agree, that could only mean that there must not be any! The Victorians, with pragmatic appreciation of the absurdity of the Absolute decided that 'none' meant that you could not see it. The Gas Referees obliged by ruling that if six strips of absorbent paper previously soaked in a solution of lead acetate and exposed to the gas for three minutes were not each of them perceptibly stained, there was no hydrogen sulphide in the gas. There were various guesses as to what that meant in actual figures and some degree of unanimity that it was in the region of one part per million by volume. I decided that we should try to settle this matter first of all; details of the method are of no current interest, but allowing for the fallibility of human reactions as to what is perceptible we were able to settle for 1.5 ppm. We had to have a method of measuring the hydrogen sulphide in gas down to a concentration of one hundredth of that figure. The answer was to pass the gas through a disc of porous paper impregnated with lead acetate and then to measure the optical density of the stain against a calibrated wedge. The method was simple to use; fulfilling a long-felt need in our industry and finding applications elsewhere.

Several 'wet' processes were examined, and rejected when they failed to satisfy the Referees' Test. One that did, and showed sufficient promise to encourage us to build a small pilot plant, was rejected in the end as not showing any real advantage over 'dry' purification by iron oxide. This last was a process which three-quarters of a century of practical experience had perfected, was universally used in the industry and satisfied the requirements of the gas engineers. A skilful operator could sleep soundly at night secure in the knowledge that the gas leaving his purifiers would be well within the limit set by the referees; he could dispose of the spent material without any public outcry; he could even sell it at a figure not far below the price of pure sulphur – unit for unit – to the makers of sulphuric acid. It had its drawbacks, or else the gas industry would not have been searching so long for a substitute.

The purifiers were large containers of cast iron or occasionally reinforced concrete, up to 50 ft. square with removable lids and inside them the bog-ore was spread out on wooden grids in layers up to 4 ft. deep. Four such 'boxes' constituted a stream, and they were interconnected by an ingenious system of valves and gas-mains to permit the operation of 'swinging' the boxes so as to change the order in which they were presented to the crude gas stream. Alternate sulphiding and regeneration of the oxide over a period that might be as long as two years served to build the sulphur level up to the 50% that the market demanded.

Any system that takes up to two years to complete a cycle of events is not one to lend itself to analysis on traditional chemical engineering lines. Instead we took just one box in a stream and tested it in all four positions over the whole period from the day it started life newly charged until it was ready to be discharged months later. We noted how the operator shortened the interval between swings from five days at the start down to one day when it was due to be discharged. What I was trying to do now was to quantify the rule-of-thumb judgements of the charge-hand whose skill I was in no position to criticize and could not hope to better. Here then are the results as they were published in 1935 in a joint paper with Hollings entitled 'Gas Purification':

H_2S in Gas

	grs. per 100 cu. ft.	*ppm*	*% removed*
Entering first box	550 (c.1%)		
Leaving first box	25		95
Leaving second box	0.5	8	98
Leaving third box	0.01	0.17	98
Leaving fourth box	0.001	0.017	90

The principal objections to this ancient, but reliable and quite sophisticated, process were the high capital cost, the waste of valuable ground space, and its labour-intensive nature. With few moving parts a set of purifiers might well last for forty years. The ground occupied had been halved by new three-level installations with oxide floors above and below the boxes, using mechanical handling wherever possible. But there was still a great deal of hard manual labour involved in the emptying and filling of the boxes and the mixing and preparation of the charges. There was to be in the end an engineering solution, not ours, in which trays filled with iron oxide were stacked in tall steel towers and most of the handling was by cranes and other machines purpose-built, thus eliminating the arduous manual labour of purification as I knew it, and with a great saving of space. In its new form our ancient process was to survive until with the rest of the traditional gas industry it was swept away in the oil-based and natural gas revolutions of the sixties. Efficient it might be, but it did nothing to solve the problem of the existence of another group of sulphur compounds, commonly called 'organic sulphur' present in purified gas to the equivalent of 25 grs of sulphur per 100 cu. ft. with carbon disulphide accounting for 80 per cent of the total, and thiophen for most of the rest.

'Sulphur must go'

There was growing awareness of the bad effect of sulphur acids on a new generation of more sophisticated appliances and the cry went up that sulphur must go or more realistically be very much reduced. Dr Carpenter of the South Metropolitan was first off the mark with a catalytic process designed to remove carbon disulphide by hydrogenation over a nickel-based catalyst. Plants were installed at several of his company's gasworks between the wars. They suffered from several quite serious drawbacks: the gas industry was not yet equipped to solve the problems he set it and there was no further development in that direction.

We knew that the active carbon benzole plants at Beckton and Harrow were recovering as much as 80 per cent of the organic sulphur and that the market for benzole was assured by an official policy of incentives through a subsidy on home-produced motor spirit. There was some uncertainity about using active carbon for the gas from vertical retorts and the company had decided not to be over-committed to this one method. There might also be a problem of supply of active carbon in time of war, and it had seemed prudent to settle for oil washing plants at most of the up-river stations. As normally designed they removed less than 40% of the 'organic' sulphur in the gas. I decided to see what could be done about it. The three seniors in my group had all qualified as chemical engineers: Hopton, product of the Dyson Perrins at Oxford with first-class honours in chemistry and five published papers to his name; Spivey, a graduate of Leeds, and Dryden who came up the hard way at evening classes; and a group of assistants varying in composition but generally about five in number, equally at home at the bench and on the works. I tried to leave nothing to chance and we began by re-examining published data on the sulphur compounds in gas. New analytical methods were developed after we established the presence, for the first time I think, of traces of carbon oxy-sulphide, a gas at normal temperature and unlikely therefore to be amenable to removal by active carbon or oil washing processes. We were relieved to find that the rate of circulation of oil required for carbon disulphide removal was only three times that for benzene, not the four times that had been predicted.

I visited most of the benzole plants at the company's works and found them unsatisfactory in most respects. Some of the shortcomings stemmed from the sludging of the wash oil, making it impracticable to use high-velocity multi-tubular heat exchangers to conserve heat. The steam stripping stills used to regenerate the oil and recover the benzole were poorly designed with insufficient spacing between the plates. I tested one and it had a plate efficiency less than 25%. It was not all the contractors' fault; there had been strong competitive bidding against specifications that were not tightly enough drawn. There was nothing to be gained by trying to adapt them; we must make a clean sweep and start afresh. In the laboratory we established that the sludging was due to the high temperature used in the stripping stills. By operating the still under partial vacuum at a temperature of 80°C sludge formation would be negligible.

Now everything began to fall into place. High-performance steam turbines of the de Laval type would be used to provide power for pumping the oil and the cooling water. The exhaust steam at atmospheric temperature would supply the still at its operating vacuum equivalent to a pressure of 12 inches of mercury Abs. and there would be enough left for the final heating of the oil to 80°C. Heat would be conserved by the use of multi-tubular, high-velocity oil to oil heat exchangers followed by an oil-to-vapour heat exchanger at the outlet of the still. This in brief outline is the plant we set out to design in detail sufficient to convince the drawing office and the engineers of our credibility. It took a year to convert this outline into a reality in which all the parts would fit together like any product on an assembly bench. Every part and element of the final conception was examined and tested in one way or another; while much new data was being developed in the laboratory.

Falconer Birks was an experienced engineer of forthright character and came by way of Beckton to occupy the post of Chief Mechanical Engineer at Head Office; it was not in his book that a research chemist was a fit person to select a steam turbine or even discuss the matter with those who by experience and training were. I had read quite deeply in the subject and knew that the only way I could have the efficiency needed to balance the steam and power of our concept was to use de Laval turbines with a single rotor at 20,000 rpm geared down to 2,000 rpm to suit the pumps. He thought not – I tried to blind him with science – it did not work – I played my last card – there was a small stand-by generating plant at a works I knew – might I turn it into a test bench? – permission granted. When I took the results to his office a few weeks later he hardly even glanced at them; he had probably been refreshing his mind in some textbook and in any case would guess that I would not have been there if they did not fit my case. He became a very good friend and adviser, and supporter of my plan to proceed direct to a full-scale plant, not wasting time and money on a pilot plant; finally quoting Admiral Jackie Fisher on battleships as the last word on the subject.

A second year progressing our preliminary outlines through the drawing office turned day-dreams into hardware to match the site and the duty selected for this first of its kind. It was to be built at Kensal Green, a medium-sized works of fairly ancient vintage. The Court approved and we were in business – a benzole plant to treat 7 million cubic feet of coal gas per day, to recover 3.5 gallons of benzole per ton of coal and to reduce the sulphur in the gas to below 10 grains per 100 cu. ft. (I had prudently left some room for carbon oxysulphide of which not much was known yet.)

It was going to look unlike anything seen on a gasworks before: its main feature two tower scrubbers 60 ft. high and 6 ft. diameter. 'But I thought you said tower scrubbers were obsolete!' 'And so they are, for ammonia.' 'So now you want us to design for a 10 to 1 aspect ratio!' 'It should have been 20 to 1. I cut them in two to make it easy.' And so the debate went on until we each understood the other's point of view, and the engineer designer appointed to the project was soon passing our project drawings through the drawing office at surprising speed and on out to tender. Meanwhile the site had been cleared and the foundations were well advanced. Birks had appointed a young engineer, A.G. Grant, a Whitworth Scholar and newly recruited to the company, to supervise construction. The third year saw the orderly arrival of equipment ready to be erected on the prepared foundations and construction went on apace, until in the last months we were able to move in and carry out test runs on the several parts of the plant. The station engineer, another Carpenter, but no relation of the redoubtable Doctor at the South Met., was of the old school and deeply suspicious of this new breed of experimental chemists. He always chose a time when I was not there to visit the site and make discreet enquiries as to the purpose of everything he saw, and especially as to the safety of his works, when as inevitably the whole thing blew up. We carried out the pre-commissioning tests discreetly and nothing blew up, or out, or at least so that he might notice, and I was able to announce that the plant would go to work at 11 am on a Sunday in February 1937. By the time that Chips got back from church and came on the scene there was a gentle hum of well-oiled machinery and pure white benzole was issuing from the separator. We drew some off in a beaker; he sniffed it and approved and left for lunch with the satisfied air of one who knew all along that everything would be all right. I can remember him with respect and affection as a man of few words and none of them unpleasant.

I took a report to the autumn meeting of the Institution of Gas Engineers and it was well received. Our plant had been working without interruption for six months and was fulfilling our design expectations. It was to continue working for twenty-five years until it and the works were all demolished in the first of the industry's two revolutions. It was the first of many such installations, some very much larger, some smaller and some for benzole only where the sulphur feature was not required. The only weak feature was the water-cooling tower of a type widely used in industry which failed by several degrees to meet its specified duty.

This was serious. A difference of 5°F in the temperature of the oil represented 10 per cent in the design paramaters, and the performance of the plant would be seriously affected if on full load on a warm day in summer. We cured it by fitting fans to turn our chimney-draught cooler into one of the forced-draught type. We tested some at other works under rigorous conditions, so far as the vagaries of our climate allowed, and they were no better. There emerged a set of empirical rules which enabled all concerned to buy against performance and not on the cheapest tender. Meanwhile I was having a good look at the current designs and decided that everything about them offended against good chemical engineering principles – and the forced draught ones were mechanically inefficient as well.

Spivey took over the investigations and we built a test rig, only 4 ft. square, in which all essential factors could be controlled and monitored, except the weather which we had to take as it came. The results were so consistent and encouraging that I decided to apply them to the water cooler for the first of the new large benzole/sulphur plants which was to be at Fulham, and it fulfilled all expectations. We were satisfied that the dark mysteries sometimes concealed under the name of 'best engineering practice' can be expressed more usefully in relationships between non-dimensional groups of units of measurement; so bringing together such disparate applications of chemical engineering as gas washing for recovery of ammonia, benzole and carbon disulphide, gas cooling in water tube condensers and now water cooling in forced draught and natural draught coolers. I offered our paper to the Institution of Chemical Engineers. It was read on 10 February 1942, and I set off next morning by flying boat from Poole bound for Cairo and Calcutta by way of Lisbon, the Congo, Abadan and Bombay, on Air Ministry duties. When I returned I heard we had been awarded the Moulton Medal with which I was well satisfied.

My last two years at Fulham were marred by a serious break-down of the health of my old friend and mentor, Stuart

Pexton. Our informal debates on the state of the world – the future of the gas industry, the economics of benzole recovery as misrepresented by the Company's accounting system, ways towards a more realistic statement of profitability, all had to end; and he was not fully recovered by 1940, when I left Research and did not return. In those first fifteen years Pexton made seminal contributions to the theory and practice of coal carbonization – a process which was to remain for a further twenty years the mainspring of the industry's activities. He was among the first to appreciate that the successful operation of continuous vertical retorts carbonizing Durham coal required correct alignment of the outward taper of the retort towards the base to accommodate the swelling which takes place during the coking process. He was critical of the practice of heavy steaming, prevalent among engineers anxious to be at the top of the carbonizing league table for which the sole criterion was therms per ton of coal. Some steam had to be introduced to keep the ironwork cool, and in passing up through the charge would produce some water gas. Beyond that the increased yield of gas from extra steam was being obtained at the expense of increased fuel consumption and reduced throughput. He showed how, in a redesigned heating system in which combustion air circulated through flues near the base of the retorts, the amount of steam required to cool the ironwork could be greatly reduced. It was then possible to produce gas at a calorific value high enough to compensate for the loss of calorific value due to benzole recovery. These considerations were decisive when it came to getting the company's approval for my Kensal Green plant. He saw that the first purpose of carbonization was to convert the volatile content of coal into a gas of high calorific value, in practical terms mainly methane and ethane: hydrogen and carbon monoxide were diluents which could often be made more economically in plant designed for the purpose. These thoughts led to the concept of the Hydrocarbon Enrichment Value. Starting from the calorific value and the volume of the inert free gas, the HEV was defined as the heat value in therms of the gas from a ton of coal, in excess of the calorific value of hydrogen or carbon monoxide (they are nearly identical). This deceptively simple concept was soon being used as a criterion of efficiency of carbonization.

On my way to being a chemical engineer

The Institution meeting, where I presented the paper on the

Kensal Green plant, included a preview by Griffith of a new process avoiding the pitfalls which led the Carpenter-Evans process to oblivion. There was a successful demonstration on the works scale the following year, and we now knew that a combination of an efficient benzole plant with the new catalytic process could reduce the sulphur in the purified gas by 90 to 95 per cent; but, the war intervening, there was to be no further development and the industry seemed content with what it already had.

New installations were to be designed and built to our design at four of the largest of the company's works. Each presented its own fascinating problems, none of them remotely related to the laboratory bench at Fulham where it had all started. A delegation from the South Metropolitan Gas Company visited Kensal Green with a view to installing a plant at their East Greenwich Works. It was the first time in twelve years that I had ever met anyone in that organization doing my sort of work. It would have been the largest yet, until with the threat of war they decided to limit their commitment to a plant designed to maximize the benzole recovery and to leave the sulphur to a later date. The vacuum distillation section could then be duplicated and the oil circulation trebled. I saw no more of the emissaries from across the water; until twenty years later in the South Eastern Gas Board, I came to know them both very well.

The one remaining of the company's larger works was Bromley-by-Bow, and it was nominated for the active carbon process. Falconer Birks, now Deputy Chief Engineer, had to be satisfied that a proposal of mine for a new method of heating and cooling the carbon bed would eliminate the corrosion of the coils that had plagued the Beckton plant. Quite simply, all it amounted to was to use superheated water at high pressure in a closed circuit to heat the carbon and another closed circuit of cooled water to cool it. Then with a simple ingenious device, to store the hot and the cold water in the same tank still under pressure, we overcame all objections about loss of thermal efficiency. The hot water from an absorber that had completed its regeneration stage passed into the upper half of the tank, displacing the cold water already there; which then passed out into the absorber to start the cooling operation essential to the success of the absorption part of the complete cycle. Meanwhile the next absorber in line for regeneration could draw on the hot water in the tank replacing it with the cold water from its coils. It was all so simple that everyone wondered why they had not thought of it before and some even thought that they had.

When I joined the Gas Light and Coke Company in 1926, it never crossed my mind to think about what the future might have in store for me. There was no shortage of work waiting to be done, without concerning myself about wider issues. The approval given for the construction of a plant to my design at Kensal Green was an opportunity not to be missed on any account. As self-appointed project manager doubling with Grant on site, I became totally committed to the realization, in terms of engineering hardware, of what had been at one time no more than a sheaf of specifications tied together by line diagrams. Now the dream had become a reality. Each section, each moving part, was fitted into place under Grant's watchful eye, and coupled up ready for test. In principle it had been a logical extension of those mental attitudes acquired in the laboratory at Oxford except that now the stakes were high indeed. Failure could not be written off to experience, or used to devise a new and better experiment; it could only result in my being discredited in my chosen role of embryo engineer.

The success of that venture was not marked by any startling improvement in my position, my salary or my prospects. A Senior Chemist I was, and that was what I looked like being to the end of my days in the company. There was no convenient niche in the Chief Engineer's department to which I might aspire and where I might combine what I believed to be a talent for innovation with an opportunity to design and construct a new generation of gasworks plant and equipment; anything in the nature of an advisory appointment had no attractions after I had been so close to the action at Kensal Green. There was always an alternative – to look elsewhere. The prospects were not encouraging. Except for a few government departments, where the status and salary of posts advertised seemed, if anything, inferior to what I already had, the great world of industry outside appeared to have no immediate need of my services. There seemed to be nothing for it except register for war service as a scientist.

One step towards being accepted as an engineer, without having to go back to 'school', was to apply for membership of the Institution of Chemical Engineers, on the strength of the successful design, construction and operation of the Kensal Green plant and others, and I was admitted without further formality. I had to convince the President, Hugh Griffith, who happened to be managing director of the firm that was to build the Bromley plant, that superheated water would heat the active carbon if not quite as fast as steam at least fast enough to avoid fouling the carbon. In this I succeeded by developing a step-wise approximation to the Fourier type series that a strict treatment demanded. More important it also satisfied the team of German design engineers, and we worked amicably together on the details. My conversion to chemical engineering was a final break with the Oxford tradition, inherited from the Brunner Mond connection. Oxford, alone among the leading universities, has no honours school of chemical engineering, with appropriate degrees.

6
Intermission

Pause, cessation, period of inactivity
Oxford English Dictionary

I cannot now recall what we and those around us thought about the prospects of peace or war in the years leading up to 1939. That already distant past no longer presents itself with the clarity of scenes imprinted on the adolescent memory and revived from time to time by the process of involuntary recall (the madeleine in the cup of tea at Proust's Combray). The stress of war offered few opportunities for 'sessions of sweet silent thought' and 'remembrance of things past': recall from the level of conscious memory at the desk or the word processor is a poor substitute, but it is all I have and must serve.

A speech by Winston Churchill, who was then in the political wilderness, came over the wireless with vigour and conviction and opened our eyes to the real danger that faced Britain in 1933. The occasion was a banquet on St. George's Day. As befitted the time and place, he began in lighter vein, but then came the message loud and clear. We must be ready to fight to preserve our country and all we held dear: it was not yet too late to start rearming but it soon would be: above all we must see to it that we had an air defence able to withstand any onslaught that an enemy might unleash on our cities.

A few months before, on 10 November 1932, Stanley Baldwin, who held high office in Ramsay MacDonald's coalition, had been addressing the House of Commons, with a message for the young men of Britain on the theme that 'the bomber will always get through' and concluded by warning them:

> When the next war comes and European civilization is wiped out, then do not let them lay the blame on the old men. Let them remember that they principally and they alone are responsible for the terrors that have fallen on the earth.
>
> Loud and prolonged cheers. (*Hansard*)

The young men of Oxford were ready to follow the lead and advice thus clearly presented, and a motion was put down for debate at the Union:

> That this House refuses under any circumstances to fight for King and Country.

It was debated in February 1933 and carried by 275 votes to 153. A harmless piece of folly, I thought: Churchill disagreed. 'A disquieting and disgusting symptom,' he called it, and the message went round the world, stopping off at Berlin to comfort the Führer, that England was finished and would never fight again. The speech on St. George's Day was Churchill's answer to Baldwin and to Oxford:

> Nothing can save England if she will not save herself. If we lose faith in ourselves, in our capacity to guide and govern, if we lose our will to live, then indeed our story is told. If we remain paralysed by our own theoretical doctrines or plunged into the stupor of after-war exhaustion, then indeed all that the croakers predict will come true and our ruin will be swift and final ...

Overnight I became a Churchill man. Meanwhile Hitler's inexorable path to world power continued unchecked, and it seemed to me that war was inevitable, much as we all hoped it might somehow be averted. March 1938 and the annexation of Austria passed into history and there was nothing that anyone could do about it, except wait for his next move. It came soon enough, at the end of August, while we were on holiday at Milton-on-Sea. Demands for the dismemberment of Czecho-Slovakia were a very different matter and the threat of war came much closer. The improbable figure of Neville Chamberlain, Prime Minister since 1937, and a gift to the cartoonists with his bowler hat and umbrella, soon became familiar as he was flown back and forth to Germany for his confrontations with Hitler, at Berchtesgarten, at Godesberg, and finally at Munich: whence he returned to a reception by cheering crowds all the way to Downing Street: and to them delivered words of comfort saying to the multitude that he had brought back from Germany peace with honour and, waving a sheet of paper, announced, 'I believe it is peace in our time.'

I returned to London alone to size up the situation and find out if anything might be required of me in the line of duty, to be met with the much-described scene of trenches being dug in unlikely places, shelters being hastily constructed for undisclosed purposes and great numbers of sandbags being filled and placed where some person in real or assumed authority had directed. The threat of war receded, the family returned from Milton and everything went back to normal. It has been a matter for debate whether anything was gained by the eleven months purchased at Munich at the expense of Czecho-Slovakia. As to our defences, that must remain a matter for the experts: as a member of the public I can only affirm that when war did break out we were much better informed about our duties and responsibilities, and prepared for whatever might befall us. In 1938 there might have been serious confusion, even panic, which could have been disastrous for the morale of the civilian population. The same people were to survive so triumphantly the test when it came, during the six years of war.

We stayed on in London while Ann, our only daughter, remained the only pupil at Miss Lee's pre-preparatory school. All the other families had evacuated to the country. Dorothea's mother had returned from Canada where she had been staying with her sister on a ranch in Alberta, feeling perhaps that her duty lay with her daughter and grand-daughter in these perilous times. Our house was amply large enough to accommodate all four, if need be on the ground floor, and we decided to stay put. With the help of our local builder I created a reasonable shelter out of a larder/wine cellar that the architect in 1922 had thoughtfully designed to be partly below ground level: it was also underneath a solid concrete-tiled staircase which was one of the features that finally decided us to buy the house at a price I could barely afford, because, you see, 'it saved us the cost of a stair carpet'. Small though the resulting space might be, we fortified ourselves with the thought that it was as large as the cabin of any yacht that we were likely ever to be able to afford. After enduring the discomfort of three long nights, and having observed what happened to houses of similar size following a direct hit from quite a small bomb, and there being no prescription for absolute security, we came to the reasonable conclusion that it would be as well to sleep in the comfort of our own beds; descending only when the noise of gunfire, aeroplane engines and sundry pieces of ironmongery falling out of the sky made further sleep impossible. Dorothea rationalized our decision by ruling that if your name was on a bomb it would get you wherever you might be.

At 11.15 am on Sunday 3 September 1939 Neville Chamberlain broadcast to the nation that Britain was at war with Germany. A few minutes later the sirens sounded the first of the many hundred warnings to be heard over the next five years; this time of course it was a false alert. Churchill, who was at his London flat, went on to the roof to see what was going on and was impressed to see 'thirty or forty barrage balloons in the clear cool September light'. Then, armed with a bottle of brandy and other appropriate medical comforts, he and his wife went into the basement shelter down the street, where 'everyone was cheerful and jocular, as is the English manner when about to encounter the unknown'.

I was on duty in a deep shelter which was the bomb-proof Control Room to which I had been seconded. It was in the wall of one of the Horseferry Road gasholders. Both had been demolished together with the early Victorian Chief Office where I was introduced to the gas industry all those years ago. The intention was to build a handsome new Chief Office on the large area thus vacated, but Whitehall got in first with a bomb-proof building and having got a toehold grabbed the lot. The Governor, the Court and a somewhat attenuated Chief Office had already moved to the Kensington District Office.

The thing I best remember was the eerie silence that followed the last wail of the sirens. Cars had stopped either to listen to the wireless if they had such a thing, or else just to listen; a cement-mixer stopped mixing; a crane stopped lifting. 'Gawd,' came the inevitable voice of our local wag, 'they must all be dead.' Then anti-climax: what sounded like a bomb exploding and everyone stiffened into tense expectation of the next, but it was only the heavy iron-clad door of the shelter being closed with unnecessary violence, the noise magnified by its echoes in the circular holder tank; and everyone anxious to be the first to laugh and say, 'Goodness me, I thought for a moment it was real.' And then the telephone bells started to ring as soon as the all-clear sounded. They had strange experiences to report from the works and the holder-stations all round the district.

In those days the traditonal Sunday dinner gave rise to much the highest hourly demand for gas in the whole week, summer and winter. Beginning at eleven o'clock and for about two hours, every gasholder, prudently filled to its limit overnight, came into service: every piece of spare plant was activated: gas boosters used to supply were running flat out: often enough the automatic governors controlling the pressure of the gas in the district mains had to be by-passed: and not until the engineer on duty saw the holders start to rise again did he feel free to go home for his lunch. It was just so on Sunday 3 September 1939, but with a difference. When the warning sirens sounded every housewife turned out the gas on her hotplate and in the oven and went to shelter as instructed. Meanwhile the attendants at the works and holder stations – those who had not themselves retired to shelter – were having to wrestle with a situation quite beyond anything they had ever experienced. As the readings on the pressure gauges rose inexorably they were shutting down everything they could as fast as they knew how. (Have you ever counted the turns of a large wheel required to shut off one 24 inch valve?) No sooner was everything under control again than the all-clear sounded. Families emerged from shelter and, seeing all was well, demanded restorative cups of tea. Gas rings were lit to boil the kettles and ovens lit again to complete the cooking of the Sunday joint. Demand raced up again to its Sunday level and now the unfortunate attendants were hard pressed to keep up any sort of pressure in the mains. At least it was all good practice for the real thing when it finally came in the Blitz.

The uneasy tranquillity of the next eight months was shattered in May when the German armies broke through – by-passed the famous Maginot Line, received the surrender of the Belgian king, overwhelmed the Dutch who were not even at war, rolled the French armies back to Paris and beyond and to a shameful surrender, and drove the British army into the sea at Dunkirk. When it was all over, with Churchill installed at last as Prime Minister, our armies reorganized and in the process of re-arming (Winston could offer nothing but 'blood, toil, tears and sweat'), we were ready to face whatever might come our way. The Battle of Britain, if we had lost, would have been the end of our struggle. The Blitz which followed was no better and no worse than predicted; the people in the great cities were well informed and well prepared. The several gasworks which I visited had survived remarkably well; responding well to the demands made on them as the damage to the district supply system was repaired, having to make do without several of the larger gasholders which had been destroyed by direct hits or had gone up in flames: none exploded.

We experienced only one concentrated raid. This was on 25 November 1940 and was aimed at Richmond with a substantial overspill across the river into Twickenham. It was just possible that the Luftwaffe arrived under the mistaken belief that there was a secret underground installation in Richmond Park.

One casualty of the raid, on our side of the river, was the Royal Naval School, onetime mansion of the Earl Kilmorey, the handsome classical frontage of which lent so much character to the river scene as we had known and enjoyed it for the past fifteen years. It was fortunate that the school had been evacuated to Surrey a few days before, and there were no casualties. The destruction of the RNS put paid to our plan for Ann's education as a day-girl at Dorothea's old school; however, she was accepted as a boarder and went down, in termtime at least, to the comparative safety of Fernhurst and Haslemere.

And then, quite out of the blue, came the kind of opportunity that I had been hoping for. It began with a visit by Hollings and myself to a newly established Directorate of Hydrogen Production, ostensibly for the purpose of discussing some technical and logistic aspects of the supply of hydrogen to the Balloon Barrage. I came away with no illusions about the real purpose of the visit. The Director, Viscount Ridley, whom we met, wearing the uniform and badges of a Major in the Northumberland Hussars, had just recently been seconded from his regiment. He had briefly studied chemistry as a pupil of Harold Hartley at Balliol, thought better of it and returned to his first love of racing cars in which he raced with some success at Brooklands, and became also a successful designer of racing engines with other applications of the internal combustion engine. There was a warmth of manner and an underlying sense of humour which belied the authority of his white hair (he was in fact some months older than me), and the serious nature of the supply problem which he outlined and which his new department had been set up to resolve. Two weeks later came a summons to see Sir David at the Governor's office now in its new location at Kensington. He had known and held in high regard Lord Ridley's father, the Second Viscount Ridley, at Balliol, need I say, and would I go to join his son's directorate as soon as might be convenient (it could not be too soon for me!) – the office would see to all the details, and he trusted that my wife and family were keeping well through these difficult times. With the war years intervening, it was to be my last meeting with the man who had represented all power and authority during my fourteen years of service in the Gas Light and Coke Company.

So that was how I found myself, on the second day of January 1941, ploughing my way, as it seemed, through layers of broken glass to spend my first day at the Directorate of Hydrogen Production in Kingsway. I had a feeling that this was to be a final break with the past, and so it was: to my great relief, for I had nothing more to offer by way of a solution from the chemical laboratory to the serious problems that the gas industry would have to resolve if it were to survive and prosper in the years ahead.

7
The Air Ministry

My arrival at Princes House, Kingsway had one thing in common with my arrival at the Corpus Annexe all those years before: now it was Mercer in place of Banci, whose smile of welcome was to give way to an expression of concern. It was this – the newcomer had neither rank nor title, nor even was his salary on record, for I was on secondment from the Gas Light and Coke Company. How then was I to be measured up for an office, for a desk (one pedestal or two?), a chair (swivel, padded or just hard?) and a carpet, if any? While pondering these weighty problems Mercer showed me round the offices.

The Director's office was unoccupied. Lord Ridley was away on leave at Blagdon, ten miles north of Newcastle where he lived and owned ten thousand acres. Fifteen miles to the south west of Newcastle was the great Consett complex, centre of his family interests in coal, iron and steel. There was a massive two-pedestal desk and armchair to match with a conference table and Axminster of impressive size, and two telephones. Next door was a suitably smaller office, smaller desk, smaller carpet and chair to match. It was also unoccupied but used, when he was there, by the (part-time) Assistant Director, George Evetts, known to me only by name; next a similar office occupied, this time very completely, by David Evans, the Chief Engineer, who had come over from the Works Department. Not a man to share an office with, I decided, and felt that the same thought was passing through his mind as we chatted. So to the General Office with linoleum on the floor and a minimal carpet for the Chief Executive Officer's feet. Here Mercer presided over the office staff of two secretaries, whose desks with a filing cabinet or two was all there was, as I can recall, but all in accordance with the rule book, beyond any doubt.

Evetts, contacted by telephone, had no objection to sharing his office with me. Mercer could now relax and turn to procedural matters on which he was an expert and I was only too glad to be instructed. The niceties of inter-departmental minuting, the complications attendant on communication between Ministries (best use the telephone and make a note on the file), the functions of the civilian departments of Contracts, Finance and Works and the service directorates of Equipment and Organization: these were all spelt out in detail, even the names of those to whom it would be seemly to address one's enquiries first. At Balloon Command I would find that anything to do with hydrogen could best be channelled through the Hydrogen Officer, an efficient and most obliging Squadron Leader. It paid to follow Mercer's advice and everything soon fell into place, with nothing to be gained by trying to circumvent the system.

The sequence of events which led up to the establishment of the Directorate of Hydrogen Production within the Air Ministry and not, as might have been expected, in the Ministry of Aircraft Production, was as follows. A balloon barrage for the protection of London was set up under Fighter Command in 1937 and was first flown over the Capital at the time of the Munich crisis. An independent command was established in November 1938 and in 1939 had reached a flying strength of 600 balloons. By the end of 1940 this had reached 2,400, and balloon barrages were flying over the cities and other centres of population and certain vital targets, the length and breadth of the land.

The decision to establish a Directorate of Hydrogen Production followed on the heavy losses of balloons during the air attacks in the summer of 1940. Balloons might be replaced from stock but the hydrogen was quite another matter and while the balloon might be recovered and repaired, its contents representing thirty days of normal consumption had gone forever. The Blitz revealed the deficiencies of a supply system which depended on long hauls of cylinders over the already congested railway lines from Billingham in the north to London and other centres of population in the midlands and south. Added to that there was the clear risk that Billingham and the alternatives of Runcorn or Widnes were all important chemical works and prime targets for enemy attack, although as yet not affected. The extensive re-organization which followed the appointment of Lord Beaverbrook as Minister of Aircraft Production left hydrogen production stranded between the Air Ministry and MAP, despite the fact that MAP had taken on the production of balloons. However, Beaverbrook made it perfectly clear on 3 September, in his most emphatic way, that he wanted no part of the hydrogen business and there was no one ready to argue with him about that. And when they tried again a few weeks later there was a curt reply which finished up in characteristic style, 'You must not speak of transfer.'

Sir Christopher Courtney, the Air Member for Supply and Organization, lost no time, and after taking the usual soundings he was able to write to Sir Archibald Sinclair, the Secretary of State, on 28 September 1940 with the recommendation that there should be set up a Directorate of Hydrogen Production within the Air Ministry, and putting forward the name of Lord Ridley as Director he concluded: 'You will see that the proposal will have to be put to him in pretty strong terms.' This was because Ridley had already made it clear that he would not accept any post that required him to relinquish his regimental duties as a Major in the Northumberland Hussars. Sir Harold Hartley had warned that after being released for work on the Committee for Alternative Fuels, he had insisted on rejoining his regiment when he saw an immediate threat of war. Sir Jasper Ridley wrote describing him as 'something of an engineering genius' and warned: 'He will decline an invitation that means leaving his regiment'. So a compromise was reached and he joined the Air Ministry, on secondment from his regiment, on 25 October 1940.

In the 1914–1918 war both contestants had persevered with airship design; the Germans with their Zeppelins and here the Navy with a fleet of dirigibles on anti-submarine patrol over coastal waters, to service which they built a chain of hydrogen plants. Several were based on a simple chemical process – the reaction of ferro-silicon powder with a hot solution of caustic soda. Mobile versions existed and crews of airmen were being trained to operate them. The alternative was the Lane steam-iron process of which the only survivor was a plant at the airship base at Cardington. This involved two distinct operations: in the first 'Blue Water Gas' was made by a process familiar to every gas engineer, by which graded coke was 'blown' with air to heat it to redness and then in the 'run' subjected to the action of steam to produce a gas consisting of carbon monoxide and hydrogen. The blue water gas (so called because it burned with a blue flame – it was in fact colourless, odourless and extremely lethal) was purified and passed through metal tubes containing graded iron ore in a heated furnace. The ferric oxide in the ore was thus reduced to the ferrous state, and at the right moment the supply of water gas was shut off and replaced by steam, producing hydrogen which after cooling and purification would be over 98 per cent pure. As in the manufacture of the water gas the two stages of the process were alternated at regular intervals.

This was the plant used to fill the R101, a giant dirigible of 'rigid' design on which the hopes of an Empire Air Service centred, with a refuelling point at Ismailia and a terminal with hangar and hydrogen plant at Karachi, ready for the inaugural flight. It ended in disaster when the airship plunged into the summit of a small hill in northern France with the deaths of all but four of those aboard, including the Air Minister and his several guests, bringing to an end any further development. A crew member, one of the survivors, became a compressor attendant at Cardington, and told me how, being in the forward gondola, he simply stepped out on the grass at the moment of impact, and turned round expecting to see the others follow, when in a few seconds the whole airship was engulfed in flames.

When the decision was taken to establish a balloon barrage, the old Lane Plant was rebuilt to an up-dated design by ICI and an identical plant was installed at Weston-super-Mare Gasworks. This was nothing like enough, and the Air Ministry was glad to accept an offer by the Power Gas Corporation to build three plants of greatly improved performance, incorporating the Bamag principle of internal heating of the iron ore, the first of which came on stream just as Lord Ridley was taking over. Meanwhile the rival firm of Humphreys and Glasgow was ready with a much improved version of the German Messerschmidt design, which had been developed by staff at the Warrington works of Crosfields. We were now assured of good competition and ample productive capacity.

The new Director must have put in a tremendous amount of work in the two months between his appointment and the time when I joined his directorate, as I realized when I looked through the files filled with outline plans and supporting papers. He was no stranger to the gas industry and as a director of the Newcastle Gas Company had been connected with one of the best-conducted of the provincial undertakings. His basic plan, still only a draft, was to build small to medium-sized hydrogen plants at a number of local gasworks, preferably those of medium size, since if too small they might lack the necessary expertise (he visualized the plants as operated and managed by the gasworks staff); if too large they would be more attractive targets for enemy bombers. Ridley was satisfied that sites could be found for all the installations required to meet the foreseeable future demands of the Balloon Barrage. He knew also that it was out of the question to obtain any more of the special high-pressure cylinders used for storing and transporting hydrogen. All available production of the high tensile alloy steel used in their manufacture was pre-empted for other purposes. His first priority then in siting the new factories was to minimize the turn-round time from factory to balloon site, so ensuring that the best possible use was made of Balloon Command's stock of cylinders.

I do not want to suggest that in just two months he had been able to evolve a complete working model of the future supply system. In all the time that I was working closely with Matt Ridley – it was in fact only fifteen months – I never failed to be impressed by his capacity to visualize a complicated structure of several interrelated variables in the simplest possible terms. Having committed that to paper and worked out perhaps a few examples, he was ready to turn the whole affair over to the staff. If their detailed calculations led to conclusions at variance with his own he would go through their figures in some detail, not hesitating to plead ignorance if only to extract an accurate statement of cause or consequence and then, if satisfied, accept the implied correction cheerfully and get on with the next business. But mostly we found he had got it right the first time.

He insisted from the very beginning that his appointment as Director of Hydrogen Production was not to be the first step towards the creation of yet another large new government department. We were to make use, wherever possible, of other departments in the Air Ministry, and to make sure that all contracts included the supply of detailed working drawings and designs. For most of the first year there were only four of us in the small office suite at Princes House, Kingsway: George Evetts, later Sir George, the (part-time) Assistant Director, a retired consultant engineer who had specialized in gas industry matters, D.A. Evans from the Air Ministry Works Department, as Chief Engineer, and myself as expert in the technology of hydrogen manufacture: plus that essential ingredient of any government office, a Senior Clerical Officer in the person of Mercer in charge of administration: with secretaries and typists and other essentials I think not more than ten in all.

DHP: the first twelve months

It simplified matters a lot when I was appointed Assistant Director, sharing the title, the duties and an office with George Evetts. We worked most amicably for several years and I learned a lot; including how not to get overheated about the stupidity and obstinancy of all those people who could not or would not agree with my every suggestion. George would always counsel patience, as being more likely to succeed in the end. My main concern was to ensure that the Master Plan was carried out with the minimum of delay, not easy in those days without any special priority. This entailed close co-operation with the Chief Engineer, David Evans. He showed no sign of resenting my appointment and I was careful to treat him with the respect due to his age and experience and his status as an old Air Ministry hand.

The three new hydrogen plants ordered by the Air Ministry, situated at Poole, Long Eaton and Kilmarnock, came on stream between November 1940 and March 1941. They were well located to give much-needed relief to an overstressed supply system and after the usual teething troubles were soon producing well up to specification. It had also been planned to build two large shadow factories on greenfield sites. Work on these was suspended pending approval of the new plan. Work on the plant items continued unchecked and eventually they were all diverted to new sites.

It was clear that the raids were developing on a widespread scale and that barrages might have to be deployed in many towns and cities in the United Kingdom and Northern Ireland. The large sources of hydrogen in the north which had supported the barrages so far should be covered by alternative supplies. Approval was given for a plan to construct up to twenty new plants and to invite the further co-operation of the gas industry in installing and operating them. They were to be smaller than their predecessors, and therefore easier to accommodate in gasworks of medium size, so providing a greater degree of dispersal than hitherto. They could be located near actual and projected barrages with useful savings on distribution and consequential better utilization of our limited stock of cylinders.

The first step was to enquire what facilities could be made available in the way of water gas or steam or gasworks plant at gas undertakings in parts of the country well placed in relation to actual or projected barrages. This limited the field of our enquiries, but the response was on the whole favourable: about half the quantity of steam and water gas required was offered together with some gasholders, buildings and sites. The new programme was to comprise six plants similar to those already built and commissioned, but on the smaller scale of 1 million cu. ft. per week and nine plants of the Crosfield design. Bulk orders for these together with their auxiliaries had been placed with the respective contractors and certain items of gasworks plant had been purchased on bulk orders.

The next step was to make preliminary surveys of possible sites and to start negotiations for the installation of the plant, for its operation in due course, for such supplies as had been offered and for the hire of gasworks plant where appropriate.

The task of fitting the plants into the sites available was not easy and there was the further complication that the new plant had to match whatever had been placed at our disposal from the gasworks. It would have been simpler to build an entirely new works, but we thought that in view of acute shortages of manufacturing capacity we should make use of whatever was to hand. A summary of the results of these transactions shows that out of a total 19 plants installed:

Water gas and steam were available at 10 plants,
Water gas only at 4,
Steam only at 1.
At 4 plants all services had yet to be installed.

One of the most valuable contributions that a gas undertaking could make was an offer to lease a large (by our standards) gasholder, to meet peak loads and level out demand and so contribute to maximum efficiency of production.

Adhering firmly to his declared policy that hydrogen production was not to become a reason for the creation of another large government department, Ridley planned to delegate the management of the plants to the parent undertakings. They had no difficulty in agreeing to provide management and technical supervision, but not surprisingly there was some difficulty about the matter of reimbursement. The main stumbling block was the unpredictable nature of the demand, dependent as it was on enemy action and the occasional thunderstorm. This ruled out the settlement of an all-in price, however geared to material and labour costs; further, some plants might have to be placed on stand-by from time to time. A compromise was reached whereby we agreed to reimburse the operator for all charges incurred for materials and labour up to chargehand, and thereafter a fee by way of remuneration and profit. The fee was in two parts, a fixed element to cover overheads arising whether the plant was used or not, and a variable related to the actual activity. Clauses had to be negotiated for steam and water gas supplied from the gasworks and for hire of plant and buildings. It sounds complicated and it was, with each plant a special case. We were fortunate in having the services of C44, a contracts branch which became expert in the language and practices of the gas industry; even if its stern sense of justice did require some tempering of mercy from ourselves on occasions when the undertaking found the going too hard to endure. Technical and cost returns were to be rendered monthly and drawn up so that variations in cost could be related to technical efficiency at each stage of the process, which was about all we needed to know.

Overseas assignment

Word had got about in the overseas commands that the Air Ministry had a new directorate ready and willing to solve all and any of their problems of hydrogen supply. Hydrogen was required for the Met. Office weather balloons – a few cylinders at a time; for balloons large enough to lift several men on a platform to a height from which they could learn or practise parachute drill – a large demand but intermittent; and for regular servicing of balloon barrages already flying or projected, in defence of ports and installations, notably the Suez Canal.

The balloons in question were much smaller than those used for the home barrages, flying at 2,000 ft. instead of 4,000 ft., but serving the same purpose by keeping enemy bombers up at a height where the AA could get at them. They were flown on a piano wire, incapable by itself of inflicting much damage. Instead they were armed with an explosive charge fixed to the wire near ground level and anchored by an inertia link which released the wire on impact with a plane. The drag of the balloon then quickly brought the charge up into contact with the enemy. It sounds complicated but was certainly effective although there were few opportunities to demonstrate this. Such was the respect that airmen felt for this deterrent that few, if any, would fly near a balloon; being in no position to stop and ask whether it was armed or not.

A Balloon Group had been established with headquarters at Ismailia and was flying a barrage for protection of the Suez Canal and shipping on it. Their source of hydrogen was from portable generators operating the ferro-silicon – caustic soda process. The fall of Norway had brought on a crisis in the supply of ferro-silicon, and most or all of what could be obtained from Canada was being directed to the producers of special steels. As information came in about the size and disposition of balloon barrages, existing, planned or contemplated, not only in the Middle East but at Aden and Abadan; Bombay and Calcutta were mentioned, and even Trincomalee in Ceylon; we decided that on the balance of evidence there was at least a case for a steam-iron plant somewhere in the Middle East. Logistics suggested the middle of the delta and there we found the name of a town called Zagazig, which gave us the code name 'Z'. I will hasten to add that, while the code name survived, the town was eliminated from the list of suitable sites within twenty minutes of my arrival to view it as a possible.

Middle East Command were pressing for action, and the decision was that I should go to review the situation and make recommendations. There was the option of becoming a temporary officer distinguished by the VR sign, with whatever rank was adjudged appropriate for an Assistant Director. There was not much time to spare so I decided against. It created no problem in the area of Middle East Command; outside that I carried a letter signed by some very senior person requesting that I be treated in the manner appropriate to a Group Captain, which worked marvels, even in India where a special sort of status system governed the allocation of places on the trains.

January and February of 1942 were months of misery on the home front. The news was uniformly bad from all those areas where we were engaging the enemy, and after the striking victories against the Italians in the Middle East and East Africa the full force of German Armour was being launched against us in the desert war. The debacle of Greece and Crete was behind us but Egypt was threatened, and Singapore had surrendered to the Japs. Winter added to our misery at a time when both fuel and food were in short supply. However, the Blitz was over for the time being at least and I never heard anyone suggest other than that it would be all right in the end, somehow – means unspecified. As a loyal gas-man I had equipped the house with a number of pieces of gas-burning equipment and as no one could devise a method of rationing gas we were well placed to deal with the worst that the winter could throw at us. Hens were installed at the end of the garden and by exchanging our egg ration for an issue of meal and conserving all scraps coupled with the foraging of the birds in the land at their disposal, we seemed to do quite well; but in all the time that we kept them I could never bring myself to the ultimate sacrifice of killing and eating one. I do not recall ever having any such scruples on the farm, but there the birds were strictly anonymous and here they all had names and even their pecking order had been noted as a matter of scientific interest.

All matters affecting my departure seemed to come under the category of secret information, including the route by which I should arrive finally at Cairo, Aden, Abadan and India. The RAF were taking no chances and inspected me medically with the greatest thoroughness before pronouncing me fit in all respects for training as a pilot. And to make doubly sure required me to sign a 'blood chit' absolving the service from any blame or liability for anything that might befall me while under their care. Even the date and place of my departure was a well-kept secret; I was to be ready to leave at a few hours' notice. When it came, on 11 March, I recognized Poole harbour, where our Sunderland flying-boat lay at a buoy. There is nothing I know quite like the thrill of taking off on a large flying-boat, as the water surges up past the windows (we were not pressurised) at ever increasing speed and then recedes as the lift increases, finally to disappear under the hull at take-off.

Looking round we seemed to be a rather motley crew of country parsons and schoolmasters, described on their passports as government officials. With some there lingered a certain air of authority, at variance with the baggy flannels and worn sports jackets. Meanwhile we were coming down on the Shannon and being taken to Limerick for an overnight stay.

*

Seven days later – still at Limerick, awaiting a call to resume our several journeys, each with highest priority to Cairo, Ceylon, Burma or wherever. It leaked out that the flying-boat intended for the use of Sir Stafford Cripps on his mission to convert Gandhi to our cause had gone U/S and ours had been called back to rescue him. Frustration soon gave way to a reasonable determination to make the best of a bad job. The weather helped – it was spring and it was Limerick race week. After rationing in England the food was out of this world: poached (it could well be in both senses of the word) salmon and large roasts of lamb or beef seemed to appear at every evening meal and any feelings of guilt about the loved ones left behind, making do on spam and Woolton pie, soon gave way to the consoling thought that this was the daily ration, Irish-style; ours not to reason why.

After seven days of this, the call came to be on our way. There was a large handsome Boeing flying-boat at a mooring on the Shannon, and off we went without delay – next stop the Tagus in Portugal. Then the longest hop, mostly at night, to Bathurst in the Gambia, in great comfort with separate sleeping berths for all, like those one used to see in the American trains. Next morning was the moment of truth when curtains parted revealing several spotless tropical white uniforms and yards of gold braid; it was like the transformation scene in a pantomime as parsons and schoolmasters were turned into admirals and generals and all the civilians could do was to keep a stiff upper lip. We were flying at about 9,000 ft. and I could see in the first morning light the tips of the high peaks of the Canary Islands pointing through the clouds. Then as we passed Dakar at a safe distance to port there was a welcome from puffs of anti-aircraft shells as a token reminder that this was still Vichy France. Bathurst had little to offer by way of entertainment, but it was my first African scene, with scores of girls operating old treddle Singer sewing machines on the water front making goodness knows what, but including perhaps the khaki shorts I bought as a first instalment of my tropical outfit, the traditional heaps of tropical fruits and vegetables and scrawny chickens tied in bundles of six to an old man's thumb, and what was said to be the only place where a drink could be found other than the white men's club. It was a small and cheerful bar presided over by a beautiful young black girl; she had discovered how to speed up service, with three glasses in one hand and two bottles in the other from which she extracted and replaced the corks with skill and precision.

The next day to Lagos where we separated and some transferred to that old work-horse of the African jungle, the three-engined Fokker with its corrugated wings, belonging to the Belgian airline, Sabena. From now on we flew at recognition height, below 1,000 ft. and, all navigational aids being suppressed for security reasons, we navigated by dead reckoning using what looked much like conventional road maps, with the many rivers the main method of confirming our position. Flying at that speed and height there were many opportunities to view the wild life when the herds took off at the sound of our propellors. With overnight stops in Douala and Bangui in Free French Equatorial Africa, we arrived refreshed and hopeful at Juba in the Sudan ready for the last lap.

Two hours out from Juba and Cairo seemed further away than ever, and even Khartoum doubtful, when the centre engine of our three gave up with a sigh and spread a coating of black oil over the nose of the plane, reducing visibility to nil. I was sitting up forward reading the map for my own satisfaction; the pilot seemed unconcerned and assured the passengers that he would make Khartoum on two engines – no problem. After clearing up the mess and securing a view ahead he was as good as his word, and next morning a relief plane came to take us to Cairo; it had been fifteen days door to door – 'time to spare, go by air', and rather more than it took my father to complete the first leg of his passage to India by steamer during all his life as a tea-planter.

Shepherds Hotel was full of rumours, mostly true unfortunately. Two battleships were indeed resting on the mud in Alexandria harbour, after a daring attack by Italians in one-man submarines, and a third was moving slowly through the canal on its way south for repair following an encounter with enemy aircraft in the Mediterranean, Rommel was promising to take Egypt in a month or two, and who could trust King Farouk with his court of sycophantic Italians? I reported next day to Air Vice-Marshal Pirie, the AOA at RAF HQ, down by the Nile. A desk in an office was at my disposal and any assistance I might require. Next morning I set out in the company of a young Egyptian surveyor from the Land Registry to look for a possible site for a hydrogen plant in the delta. He was helpful but not hopeful. It was all a matter of contours and he demonstrated how the water level in the thousands of irrigation channels was controlled by a sophisticated system of weirs which had to be adjusted continously to ensure that each of the millions of peasant cultivators had access to his fair share of the Nile's bounty. From then on it was a matter of how much man- or animal-power could be found to raise the water the next few feet to the level of the growing crops. Above a certain contour the answer was negative and these were the empty sandy spaces where we might look for a site. There were several, but all had been pre-empted by the cultivators for the burial of their dead and I was not prepared to start with the kind of conflict that might ensue if we tried to move in there. And at Zagazig, where we stopped for refreshment, my guide was careful to keep the car in view, explaining that there were people around who could have all four wheels off in about five minutes flat and another lot, on seeing your plight, who would offer to replace your wheels from stock they held at a price to be negotiated. After two days of this I decided to look elsewhere.

One obvious choice was the sandy area between the eastern side of the cultivated delta and the Suez canal, with its southern boundary, the freshwater canal between Tel-el-Keber (of Imperial fame) and Ismailia. The whole of the area was one vast military base under canvas, but I hoped to find a corner somewhere, and decided to make a start at the headquarters of the Balloon Group guarding the canal and its ports.

The Group Captain had his Command headquarters in the town, which had been pleasantly laid out and landscaped by the French. He was glad to hear that something was being done to replace the threatened supply of ferro-silicon and took me on a tour of the canal barrage. There were several of the standard 'portable silicol plants', about which I knew something, working into 'nurse balloons' which were new to me. They were in fact large cylindrical balloons with a valved connection at each end and an internal diaphragm shaped exactly like half a balloon. One end could be connected to the silicol plant or to the balloon to be inflated and the other end to a portable air blower. The secret was to maintain pressure on both sides to keep the balloon rigid; it could even be walked by a squad of airmen on a milkround to top up several balloons. I thought, 'Goodness, who thought of that?'

Another of the group's responsibilities was to supply balloons to ships leaving Port Said for the eastern Mediterranean, and Suez for the Red Sea and Aden, and presumably Alexandria as well. Possible sites for a steam-iron hydrogen plant were reviewed with the staff at the army engineers' office. An area near the village of Qassasin which I had spotted through an arch under the railway seemed to have a lot going for it, with good road and rail access and a plentiful water supply from the freshwater canal. They observed that the purpose of my archway was not for traffic but to release the water which would collect in the event of a flash flood, not that anyone could recall ever seeing one. I left them with an outline sketch of a hydrogen plant and they promised to give it further consideration, pending my return.

Back at Cairo I found arrangements well advanced for a flight to Aden in the company of Wing Commander Usher, an agreeable and resourceful companion for such journeys under wartime conditions. It was all of 1,500 miles, but at Khartoum with only 500 to go, we ran out of aeroplanes. The Wing Commander was not one to waste time arguing with authority and seeing an unmarked plane on the ground being refuelled and finding it manned by three Americans on some secret mission, he begged a lift, which was readily granted. With five minutes to spare (they had to be in Aden before dark) we were aboard with all our possessions and on our way.

Aden was a pleasant experience. Everyone was helpful and my business did not take long. Our quarters in the RAF station were comfortable and the nights cool even if the days were fairly unbearably hot, and I had been able to tropicalize my wardrobe in Cairo. The town was efficient and clean with scenes of traditional Arab life, and huge camel trains coming in past the RAF station in the last hours of darkness to reach Aden at dawn, the drivers asleep in the saddle. Even the camels seemed cleaner and better-tempered than those in and around Cairo. I best remember two events, one a sumptuous dinner with the captain of the port at his home in the 'crater': there was iced melon followed by grilled 'Karachi salmon' and sand grouse shot by our host the day before. Details of the wines escape me but I well remember their quality. The other was a race in the Bay as a member of the crew of one of the two RAF racing dhows, stripped out and re-rigged Bermuda-style. The lateen, though more efficient, is too slow about for racing purposes. It was a boisterous sail in the freshening onshore breeze which gets up every afternoon in the bay, with all the crew sitting out and the water just lapping the gunwhale; while the local wag was telling about what the barracudas do to unwary swimmers. I was encouraged by the sight of a very small boy in a tiny home-made craft, no bigger than an orange crate, going purposefully across the bay to leeward of us, with a small scrap of cloth as a sail, to visit, so they told me, his grandmother as was his custom every holiday. It was with great sorrow that I read, years later, accounts of the last days of British rule in Aden.

It was time to go and we had secured two seats in the bomb-bay of a Blenheim being delivered to Asmara in Eritrea, first stop Kamaran, a small island and one-time British possession off the coast of Yemen. We were met by the only white inhabitant, the British Resident, who with a few policemen, Indian I think, kept the King's peace in that tiny scrap of our far-flung empire. I was pleased to observe as we sped along the only highway a prominent notice saying 'Danger Crossroads' with the standard AA sign, and duly crossed what appeared to be no more than a camel track. 'Reminds me of home,' said the Resident, and took us into the Residency for tea and a welcome rest from the cramped quarters and hard corners of the bomb-bay. The second leg of the flight found the Blenheim climbing abruptly from stifling heat above Massawa to the bitter cold at 7,000 ft. to give us a clear path into Asmara. What with that and the low oxygen level I was literally frozen stiff when they opened the bomb-bay to unload its strange cargo. Yet when I read how Winston Churchill, at the age of 67, travelled from England to Cairo in two hops in the unheated tail of a Liberator, a few months later, I think I should keep quiet about my own slight discomfort. When I reached Cairo I heard that most of the objections to the siting of the hydrogen plant had been overcome, subject to confirmation when our detailed plans were delivered.

The way was now clear for my passage to India; in comfort by flying-boat to Karachi with one overnight stop at Basra. It was all right as far as our first stop on the Dead Sea. After that, flying at recognition height over the hot air currents of the desert produced a very bumpy ride, and several passengers looked happy again for the first time when we touched down on Lake Habbaniya. This was the last stop before we came to rest on the Shatt-el-Arab. Next day it was all fair-weather flying down the Persian Gulf via Bahrein and out over the Arabian Sea to Karachi, where I was delivered into the safekeeping and the comfortable quarters of the RAF at the old airship terminus. Here I found everything much as it must have been left on the day after the R101 disaster brought to an end all ambition for an Imperial airship service. The two Indian attendants who met me and conducted me round had been with the plant from the very beginning and took real delight in showing how even the largest of the gas valves could be spun round with one finger and every piece of working machinery was greased and oiled and ready to work; they had been doing just that for the last twelve years. The only thing missing was the crown of the gasholder, for they had not been told to empty out the water and dry it out and condensation and corrosion had done the rest. I made light of the matter and consoled them by saying it would be no great difficulty to replace the crown sheeting if, and I stressed if, we decided to commission the plant again. The Air Ministry had warned me against committing us to anything at this late stage of a war of words between London and India as to the responsibility for maintaining their white elephant which included a hangar as large as that at Cardington.

I went on by train to Delhi, sharing a compartment with a handsome young Indian Army Major who was on leave and on his way up country complete with a fine pair of 12-bores and a rifle with telescopic sights to enjoy the shooting on the family estates. I was slightly shocked, and hope I did not show it, at his complete lack of interest in the war and any outcome of it. But he was good company with a fund of stories about the reaction of the British recruits on their first exposure to the climate of India and the countryside, not to mention the inhabitants. The sergeant of his company when asked what he thought of it all, replied, 'Well, Sir, I reckon its just miles and miles of shit-coloured f*** all.' So true, I thought, looking out towards the last of the evening sun, but with one difference – there always seemed to be one solitary figure out there, walking slowly from nowhere to nowhere. I was too young when I left India to recall anything of it, and it was a very different India where we lived in Assam, but quite illogically I had the feeling that I was coming home again.

At Delhi on the following day, when I returned to my hotel after a round of calls at the government offices, it was to find two Indian servants packing all my possessions into my suitcases and seemingly intent on making off with them. When my fury subsided enough for them to get in a word, it came out that I was commanded to stay with Sir Gilbert Laithwaite, Private Secretary to the Viceroy. I had known Gilbert in London through Miles Clauson when they were both in the India Office, and Miles had presumably kept him in touch with my movements. I was most certainly happy to fall in with the plans that had been made for me. But, not for the first time, my arrival at some new destination was to witness the welcome at the threshold give way to a certain anxiety, as if something was missing, for I had no bearer. Still pondering this weighty matter, the Goanese major domo led me to the drawing-room where a large tumbler of *nimbu pani* (fresh lime juice and iced water) awaited me, most welcome on that day of great heat; while he set about resolving the problem of the missing bearer. Quite soon he was able to produce a young man (who was I believe the curry cook's second son, or it might be that he was the second curry cook's only son) and from then on I could not so much as light a cigarette unaided. He unpacked and took away suits to be pressed and shirts to be laundered, he prepared a bath and attended me to it, and waited at the door with clean shirt and freshly pressed trousers, into which I was assisted with near-reverential care; and that being the night of one of the Secretary's dinner parties, he was able to produce a passable version of the dinner jacket out of my darkest grey suit, a freshly laundered white shirt and a black bow tie conjured up from nowhere.

The guests, mostly official, were quite well aware of the great danger which threatened India when the Japanese had seized Burma and were making their first thrusts into Assam. The Cripps Mission had failed and the mass of Indians, while in no way favouring the Japanese, were at best non-co-operative if not actively hostile. The British judged rightly that any falling away from their high standards would be seen as the first sign of defeat, to be followed by a second Singapore. So dinner jackets were worn and there was to be a great race meeting next day. There was a sharp reminder of the realities outside when a senior officer just in from Assam, travel-weary and wearing shorts and bush-jacket was shown into the room by the butler and, after a drink, and waiving the formality of introductions, retired with Gilbert to his study for the best part of an hour. We finished the evening out on the lawn drinking coffee by the light reflected from the flood-lit eucalyptus trees which surrounded us, and listening to the music of Bach and Beethoven from a source tactfully concealed among the trees. I had to be up at first light next morning for a tour conducted by one of the guests with his car to view all the first six cities and be back in time for breakfast and further meetings with government officials. That and an evening visit to the fort was all the sight-seeing that time permitted.

At the end of a second day of discussion I had come to the conclusion that under the conditions prevailing in India there was no place for a Director of Hydrogen Production even if the demand were ever to justify one. It would be better to leave hydrogen to the appropriate supply department of the Government of India, with the help of an advisory service of one or more technical experts from London. They were all most helpful and I left with a list of possible suppliers: these were, in the main, electrolytic plants producing chlorine for bleach and for water purification, with hydrogen as a by-product, and fat hardening plants using the familiar steam-iron process for hydrogen to make 'ghee' from a variety of vegetable oils. So it was on to Calcutta and Bombay where the demand for barrages was thought most likely to arise and where such plants were known to exist. As to Karachi and Ceylon where the naval base at Trincomalee was a distinct possibility, I thought that the commissioning of a steam-iron plant in Egypt would release enough ferro-silicon to meet all foreseeable demands for a year or two ahead.

I left Delhi and the hospitality of the Viceroy's Secretary with many regrets, and boarded the night train for Calcutta on which I was to share a commodious six-berth saloon with five army officers. They were expert in the art of securing the maximum of comfort on long train journeys and adept at securing a fresh supply of ice at every stop. Our saloon not being air-conditioned, a block of ice some 100 lbs in weight was placed on a grid in the centre with a fan at each end placed so as to direct a current of air over it. It seemed slightly ridiculous that there we were sitting round a block of ice cooling our hands and ourselves, for all the world like boy scouts round their camp fire at some jamboree.

All I can remember about Calcutta was the heat – the monsoon had failed to arrive on time but announced its intention with 100 per cent humidity and a temperature of near 90°F at night. I would like to have seen the racecourse where Uncle Jim had ridden his horse to victory in the equivalent of our Grand National (there was no possibility of going up to Assam and Dooria where I was born); on the other hand there was every good reason to get out and on my way as soon as possible, and that I did, riding the famous night express to Bombay in air-conditioned comfort, and booking in at the famous Taj Mahal in all its colonial splendour. There was hydrogen to spare at the first plant I visited and a willingness to double the output if required. Enough to be going on with, so I cast about for the quickest way to get out and on my way to Abadan. It was a plane of uncertain vintage, its body and wings all covered with canvas, and a notice 'Do not step off the gangway', but it got me to Karachi in time to join the Sunderland on its scheduled flight up the Gulf to Basra.

The Anglo-Iranian Oil Company's refinery at Abadan had one thing in common with my own company's Beckton Gasworks – each was said to be the largest of its kind in the world. It had been built in the first instance to supply the navy with fuel oil when the change from coal firing was decided before the First World War. Petrol was then a by-product to be disposed of however possible, until market forces led to some diversification. Now, somewhere down the line, hydrogen was being produced as an ingredient in the synthesis of high octane petrol for the RAF.

A fast motor launch collected me at Basra and delivered me direct to the refinery jetty: which perhaps was just as well: being a civilian, my RAF Middle East pass might have failed the scrutiny of some Persian official, whose country was still technically at peace, and I had not thought to get a Persian visa. The scale of the refinery plant and equipment was an eye-opener, dwarfing in its scale anything you might see in Britain at that time, or indeed even now. The man at the head of it all was J.M. Pattinson: he made me welcome, put me in charge of one of his process managers and offered the hospitality of the guest house at Khorramshah with an air-conditioned bedroom, which I was very glad to accept. He was later to be Managing Director and Deputy Chairman of BP, and when next we met, fifteen years later, it was to negotiate an agreement for the South Eastern Gas Board to build a new works at the Isle of Grain using as its raw material oil products from the adjacent BP refinery. It was the forerunner of a change which brought new growth and prosperity to the gas industry, until in the fulness of time oil was replaced by natural gas.

That was all in the future: the immediate purpose of my visit was soon accomplished, and I undertook to have the manifolds, hoses and the other equipment of a filling station sent out from the UK, and any compressors that might be needed when future requirements had been properly evaluated. Among the more bizarre of these was an order from very high up to supply balloons and several trailers each with its pack of thirty cylinders charged with hydrogen, to be put on rail to Tehran for the Russians. I never heard what happened to them and to my knowledge, they never returned to be refilled.

It was time now to concentrate on getting home again. Any problem (there probably never was one) about my return was settled when Air Marshal Tedder, the AOC-in-C Middle East Command, sent for me. He had been well briefed by AOA and wanted me to get on with the job of securing supplies of hydrogen for the Middle East. To that end a seat was reserved for me on the flight leaving next day. So it was good-bye to the pyramids which I planned to visit that very day, and back to the African pub-crawl, only in reverse and with no mishaps and with only one day's delay at Limerick due to German bombers being decoyed to Brownsea Island in Poole harbour instead of Southampton.

Major the Viscount Ridley CBE, TD 1902–1964

When I returned from my travels overseas on 26 May 1942, Ridley was already doubling with the post of Director of Alternative Fuels at the Ministry of Transport and under pressure to go there full time. His master plan for hydrogen was going well and would soon be in full operation. We tidied up any loose ends. and on 1 July 1942 he left me in charge as Director and shortly after returned to his beloved north as a civilian in the appointment of Regional Controller. I had known before leaving England that he had been suffering a great deal of pain from an old injury to his leg and would have known that any hope of active soldiering was gone. It was the long-term consequence of a very serious accident in 1931 on the track at Brooklands and further complications were to lead ultimately to his death in 1964 at the early age of 62.

He was by inclination, training and experience a mechanical engineer and the brilliant designer of some very advanced internal combustion engines, prompted thereto by his love of fast cars and motor racing. MG and Austin, with all their resources, were fighting it out at Brooklands, to win and hold the record for the 750 cc class, when Ridley surprised them both, coming out from his small workshop with a completely new engine featuring wet liners and a bronze cylinder head. He had the record in his pocket, with a capability of 112 mph and a good lead over the rivals when he went out on the track on the last day of the 1931 season. Then disaster struck and car and owner were both badly smashed up.*

It was possible that a too flexible chassis had allowed the undershield to come in contact with an uneven part of the track. The engine was recovered undamaged, and, detuned, was to be the basis of a new fast sports car when the war put an end to all such activities. They all finished up in the billiard room at Blagdon, converted into a workshop where Matt might adjourn after dinner to discuss design and the prospects of further improvements.

I find it hard to realize that my active association with Matt Ridley extended only to a bare fifteen months. We were under intense pressure throughout; he would read, work and write at immense speed, never failing to grasp the significance of a proposition in rather less time than it took to describe it. I believe this was because he had the gift of immersing himself completely in any subject that was engaging his attention, and his mental processes were sharp enough and fast enough to encompass what some might consider to be unnecessary detail. Impatient as he might be at the intricacies of Civil Service procedure, he would always treat the most junior of those who might cross his path with the utmost courtesy, insisting that not only the department, but that he himself, should follow the laid-down procedures.

High up on the list of things he detested was pomposity, soon to be detected by unerring instinct. Milder cases could be cured by a gentle process of deflation, but if it involved vulgar pretentiousness as well there was a more vigorous reaction which left the victim wondering what he had done to offend. What he found utterly intolerable was any attempt to secure personal advantage out of work done as part of the war effort. A Member of Parliament had sought to enlist his interest in a possible new method of making hydrogen which a leading industrialist (now dead) was prepared to put at the disposal of the Air Ministry. I was present at the meeting in the Director's office where it was suggested, ever so delicately, that the new idea could be applied and used to inflate a barrage balloon over the House of Commons with the fitting sequel of a title or even some lesser honour for the leading industrialist. Matt listened in agonized silence only long enough to be sure he had heard right, and when he was convinced that it was so an icy chill came over his features. He let out a kind of guffaw, got up and, reaching for his Sam Browne and cap, was at the door before anyone could utter. 'Good bye, I must be off now,' he said

* Based on an article by John Bolster in *Autosport*, 18 April 1952. He knew Lord Ridley and admired 'his astonishing technical achievements'.

and was gone. I was left to pick up the pieces and needless to say nothing more was said about what had been proposed. However, their process, which I judged to have some merit, was given a full and fair trial, but proved unsatisfactory.

Every so often there would be occasion to visit the establishments. Much had already been done in the short time before I joined for the purpose of singling out possible sites and discussing outline agreements for hydrogen production with gas engineers (several of whom privately told me of their astonishment at the depth of insight into such matters displayed by a Lord in khaki), and we made some notable tours together. At Torquay, arriving on a presumably peaceful Sunday morning with Matt at the wheel of his khaki-coloured Lancia, we were greeted by a furious bombardment of bags of flour from a fiercely armed Home Guard detachment at the gasworks gate. We had taken an involuntary part in some exercise which, knowing of the spirit of the Devon men, we reckoned we were fortunate to survive. After explanations all round we adjourned with the Captain of the Home Guard, who had turned out to be the engineer and manager of the Torquay gas company, to a charming meadow in a valley, where we sat on the grass and decided the layout of a future hydrogen plant.

In Wales we made a start at Pontypool. The gasworks had nothing to offer but we were taken to see a site with a large empty retort house down the middle of which there flowed a stream of sparkling clear water. Why it existed, and what happened to it when we built our Cwmbran hydrogen plant there I never learned. Other prospects producing nothing of use to us, we left in the dusk to find the way up and over the valleys and hills to the home of the Hon. Oscar Guest, a cousin of Matt's where invitations had been sent to stay the night. It was not easy – there was an invasion scare and all signposts had been obliterated and the natives were, to put it mildly, unfriendly; fortunately there was a compass on the dashboard. As always when travelling with Matt there was a warm welcome, and our host claimed that it was purely by chance that he had come across the two bottles of old genuine Montrachet in the cellar and produced them for dinner, knowing well that next to very old vintage champagne it was his favourite wine.

We flew to Belfast where I confirmed that everything we might require in the way of site and services would be made available. Then to a splendid lunch with the Lord Mayor and for the night to Mount Stewart as guests of Lady Londonderry. Here we dined off silver plate, our hostess explaining that this had come about because, after the butler and all the male staff had left for war service, the youths who took their place were breaking the china faster than it could be replaced; the worst they could do to the silver was to dent it. Everywhere we went people were so pleased to see Matt that they would go to endless trouble to make his visit as agreeable as possible in those days of ration cards and scarcity. He was just the same as host, and on the occasions of my visits to Blagdon would bring up from the cellar a bottle of his oldest champagne, dating from the turn of the century, quite dark in colour and with most of the gas gone but delicious even to my untrained palate.

Forty years have passed since the events recorded here occurred. It has helped that fifteen years ago I was asked to write a note for the family about Lord Ridley at the Air Ministry. While searching my conscious memory for what it could produce, an incident occurred that had all the force of the madeleine in Proust's cup of lime tea. The occasion was a dull meeting I was attending, when someone produced a packet of the old original Gold Flake cigarettes; recalling vividly a day during the cigarette shortage in 1941 when Matt arrived at the office in a state of great elation to report that the lady at the tobacco kiosk had saved for him a packet of genuine Gold Flake when all else was as dust and ashes. And so to the end of a day of tiresome discussion and fruitless conference. 'What have we done today? Nothing – absolutely nothing', and the files would sail across the desk into the nearest tray. In, Out or Pending, it did not matter. 'Let's go and have a drink', and he never failed to marvel at what he considered to be my eccentricity in the matter of drinking ginger ale instead of soda water with my whisky. And if by chance there was some minor triumph to be celebrated and there was an R in the month there could be fried oysters at Rule's. When I think back over a friendship which gave me so much pleasure, I know too that it was a unique experience to be able to watch and learn about the handling of men and affairs. The Guermantes Way had much to offer to one who had only known the more prosaic path that was the Méséglise Way when the Prousts chose it for their Sunday walk.

*

It is appropriate here to recall how the family adapted itself to a war of which as yet we could see no certain end. With Ann away at boarding school and her grandmother living with us and able to keep house during the holidays, Dorothea felt that the time had come to take part. Her first contribution was to join the WVS. It was nearly at the end the Blitz. She was serving coffee and refreshments to the rescue workers at bomb sites somewhere near the Royal Hospital, Chelsea, but that was not enough, for soon there were no bombs and nothing much of what she looked on as real war work to do. So she transferred to another organization, also voluntary, called the Women's Legion. What appealed to her was the fact that they had the right to wear uniform. This was a left-over from the First World War, but the attractions of the uniform did not compensate for the humdrum nature of the duties they were called on to perform, such as serving coffee to the dockers. At last she found something to do that was really worthwhile, entitled her to wear a uniform and gave her a six-wheel 2½ ton GMC truck to drive, as part of the American Army Transport Service assigned to duties in Dockland. She claims with justice to have been the only one of the sixteen or so women in the transport unit who had never so much as brushed the wing of her truck against an obstacle nor allowed anyone close enough to cause any damage. It was hard work and she enjoyed it, leaving the house at 6.30 every morning to catch the underground to the docks where they were based. On one occasion, she was called out to an urgent assignment to carry a load of 'caskets' to an undisclosed destination, which turned out to be in Weymouth. There she had to deliver coffins following the disastrous exercise in Torbay when a tragic misunderstanding led to confusion and the needless loss of many lives among American servicemen.

8
Director of Compressed Gases

Hydrogen and other compressed gases

Halfway through 1941 we had moved into new offices in Holborn. In June 1942 I succeeded Lord Ridley as Director of Hydrogen Production and in January 1944 with increased responsibility I became Director of Compressed Gases. The first few of the new plants were being commissioned towards the end of 1941 and in the relative calm that prevailed then and through 1942 our programme was almost complete by August of that year. This provided for a total of 26 production centres of which 19 were steam-iron plants at gasworks, one to be reconstructed at Cardington and one electrolytic plant, a left-over of the Air Ministry programme, at Keith in the north of Scotland, making 21 in all for which DHP had direct responsibility, however delegated. The remaining five were independent suppliers who sold the hydrogen under contracts at negotiated prices.

Production policy was controlled from Headquarters and output planned in line with Balloon Command's forward estimates, which might vary, sometimes at quite short notice, with changes in the deployment of the barrages. Under normal conditions a group of balloon units was allocated to a single hydrogen plant in the knowledge that their average demand (topping up and the occasional replacement) was about right to keep the plant operating at an efficient level with some margin for minor eventualities. But after a period of heavy casualities due to weather or enemy action or consequent upon changes in the deployment of barrages we might have to take over control and divert supplies from one area to another. Our first objective was always to saturate the capacity of the nearer plants before going further afield and so maximize the use of the cylinders. In some cases the withdrawal of a barrage meant that a plant had to be shut down and placed on standby, possibly indefinitely.

Four regional production engineers were appointed. Their duties included regular visits to each plant for routine checks on the records and to advise on any matters arising from the functioning of the plants. They attended regular meetings at headquarters for exchange of information and evaluation of the efficiency of plants in their respective groups. These summaries were not circulated outside: something in my past experience warned that such comparisons would be misleading without full allowance being made for all the circumstances and might lead to angry remonstrance and tedious explanations. As it was, regular increases overall in production efficiency were recorded from 1941 right through until 1944 when Balloon Command was stood down and hydrogen production came to an end in September of that year. One thing that impressed me was the enthusiasm, and eventually skill, of the mainly young technical assistants, to whom was delegated at many gasworks the immediate control and management of the hydrogen plants. They were soon thinking intelligently not only about improving technical performance but also how to compromise with the unpredictable demands of their customer, the RAF concerned only to have the cylinders filled without delay.

My first eighteen months as Director were fairly free from enemy action and offered me an opportunity to start some experimental work on the hydrogen generators. One discovery of interest was that the reduction of the iron ore by 'blue gas', a mixture of carbon monoxide and hydrogen, proceeds in two distinct stages, first to ferrous oxide and then on to metallic iron. We learned how to turn this observation to our advantage by control of the operating schedules, leading to very substantial improvements in efficiency. I need not go into any further detail here – the results were published in a paper which I presented to the Institution of Gas Engineers in 1946.

In my travels abroad I had been impressed by the need for portable equipment in a rapidly changing war situation. There being no foreseeable improvement in the supply of the traditional ferro-silicon, I decided to put to some good use my experience of the kinetics of gas reactions, a subject which had occupied the whole of my last year at Oxford, and went to consult Hinshelwood, now Dr Lee's Professor, in his new laboratory in the Parks. Of several options the best starting point appeared to be methanol, also known as methyl alcohol or wood spirit, which was being produced on an industrial scale from blue gas of modified composition, by ICI at Billingham. In the usual chemical terms:

$$2H_2 + CO = CH_3OH$$

Treated with steam under the right conditions in the presence of a suitable catalyst the product would be hydrogen, which was what we wanted, and carbon dioxide which would have to be removed:

$$CH_3OH + H_2O = CO_2 + 3H_2$$

ICI produced a catalyst and laboratory tests were favourable, so we ordered equipment from Foster Wheeler designed with a view to mounting on a heavy-duty chassis, and with the ICI catalyst all went according to plan. An improvement in the carbon dioxide removal stage was under consideration about the time when the US Army Air Force moved into Britain. Under the exchange of information agreements we learned that they had been working on exactly the same lines and with more resources had reached the stage of production of a standard mobile hydrogen generator. So with more than a little regret I decided to call off further work. But all was not lost: twenty years later when most of the gas industry's production was oil-based, with the light fractions reformed catalytically to hydrogen, it was found that methanol, added to the reactants, gave a powerful boost to output at times of peak load due to weather or other factors. And if ever the need were to arise again, I should think hard before passing over the methanol route to hydrogen for use in almost any circumstances, in fixed or in mobile plants.

My recommendation for the Quassasin site for the Middle East hydrogen plant was approved and one of our younger production engineers was enterprising enough to take on the task of building and then running it, reappearing as Squadron Leader A.H. Pinder RAFVR before departing for Egypt. We decided on a plant to the Power Gas Design with priority over the tail end of the home programme. I had confirmed that coke of suitable quality could be brought in from India or South Africa and caustic soda, the only chemical used in any quantity, would present no difficulty. James Cross, an assistant engineer from the Gas Light and Coke Company, who had been seconded to Cardington to help them out of difficulties before we came on the scene, took up the offer of a posting to the Supply Ministry of the Government of India, to look after all hydrogen matters there. Anthony Bacon, a Parsons-trained engineer, came over from Balloon Command for the high-pressure end of our business, which included something approaching 100 compressors for up to 3,600 lbs per sq. in. and all the filling gear involved at the trailer bays. With a retired chief accountant from the Gas Light and Coke Company to supervise the costings, and a retired chief gas chemist from Beckton to keep an eye on all technical matters, we went into 1943 well-equipped to meet all problems that might come our way, while still maintaining the Headquarters establishment within the figure of twenty persons which had been our aim throughout.

Twice in that year came opportunities to observe, at last, our system's response to a sudden emergency. During one brief period of four days in April, a total of 1,320 balloons was destroyed with 942 casualties on the last day alone. Output of hydrogen was more than doubled as plants came quickly up to their full capacity and others on standby came on stream: there was never any failure to meet demand with something in hand. In five days the barrages were at full strength again after the balloon crews had recovered 4,000 feet of cable and the remains of balloons from the rooftops of neighbouring houses. The main features of this incident are recorded graphically on p. 128. Towards the end of 1943 we received calls of increasing urgency from one of the directors of equipment, first to advise and then to assist in the matter of the supply of high-flying oxygen for bombers and fighters both British and American, and this was soon to occupy most of my time up to VE Day and beyond. It will be better to leave that part of my story until later and continue with the history of hydrogen production up to the day when the balloons were hauled down for the last time in September 1944.

The first of the two important events in 1944 was the supply of hydrogen for 'Overlord', the plan which was to come into effect on 6 June with the launching of what Churchill called 'the greatest amphibious operation in history'. Balloon barrages were to be deployed in defence of the ports of embarkation: there was nothing new about that, although on a much larger scale than ever before. In addition large numbers of the smaller Mark VI type were to be inflated at other embarkation points and each vessel sailing was to be provided with one; and if the operation were to be aborted, they were all to be deflated and kept ready for a postponed start. Bournemouth and Torquay were best placed for the operation and bore the brunt of the load on the day. On the principle of belt-and-braces we put together a reserve or stand-by made up of a mobile Silicol plant with a nurse balloon and a skid-mounted compressor and mobile generator on the freshwater side of the creek at Keyhaven, first left as you enter the Solent from sea-ward. And it gave me the opportunity of inspecting my first sea-going

Figure 1. Two weeks in the life of Balloon Command

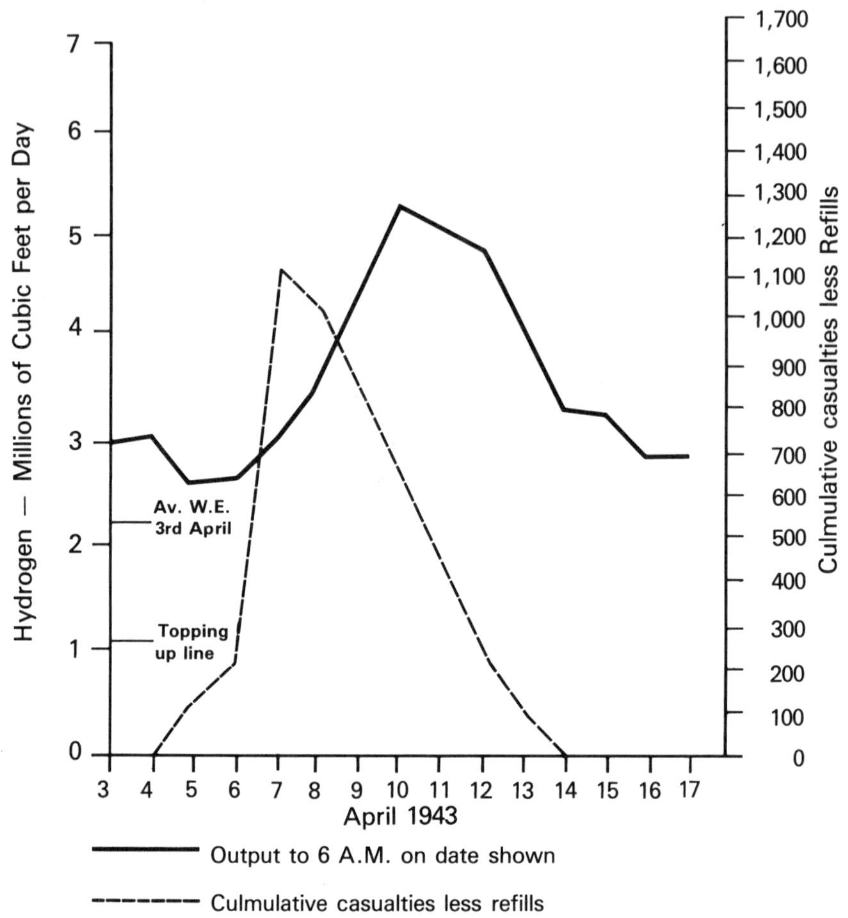

Daily casualties

4th April	100
5th April	191
6th April	89
7th April	942
8th April	30
9th April	15
10th April	15
11th April	10
12th April	13

vessel, the centreboard sloop Loreen, hauled out over the sea wall in the main Keyhaven Channel, and there for the duration.

I had soon realized that servicing a wartime operation on the scale of Overlord was no task for a civilian supply department up at the Air Ministry, and found a keen young engineer who had been managing our Long Eaton plant before it went on stand-by. Equipped with all necessary passes and driving his own fast car, he was able to get around all over the area, and if there were problems, as I am sure there were, they never got as far as my desk. Lord Ashburton, then a Group Captain in Balloon Command, in charge of the operation, has written, 'The one shortage that never hit us was lack of hydrogen.'

Seven days after D-Day the flying-bomb, or V1, assault on London began and lasted for eighty days. It was a most unpleasant, but not necessarily frightening, experience, though frustrating in the knowledge that there was no German airman up there who could be killed in retaliation. After a few false starts the final disposition of our defences was:

A fighter belt at sea 10,000 ft. out from the coast line.
Anti-aircraft guns ranging from the shore to 10,000 ft. out.
An inland fighter zone from the shore to the balloon boundary.
A barrage of 2,000 balloons to the south and south-east of London.

With speeds up to 400 mph the small V1 was a difficult target for the guns and just about at the limit for interception by our fastest fighters, who had eventually to fly continuous patrols. At its flying height of 2,000 ft. the V1 was essentially a target for the balloon cables, and they were effective, but there was a limit to what they could do: the statistical chance of contact with a cable of the 2,000 balloons flying a barrage the length of London was only 20 per cent. I have estimated that the barrage accounted for 16 per cent of the V1s that survived the AA guns and the fighters.

While it was interesting to speculate on the effect of flying four more barrages, if space could be found in the pleasant countryside of the home counties, my pressing problem was to find the hydrogen for the one we had. It was an area which for reasons of safety had not been chosen for siting hydrogen plants, and the concentration of most of the balloons in the country into this small space put a severe strain on the transports and distribution resources of Balloon Command. Although we had plenty of hydrogen to supply the barrage it became essential that the plants best sited should take a large part of the load. They were the eight which had fed the London barrage, with another two not far away.

The response was gratifying: all ten of them sustained for nearly ten weeks close on 100% overload, bringing all their spare and stand-by plant on stream; doubtless cutting a few corners here and there. We did our best to help them and, with the aid of RAF transport and despatch riders, set up a service of urgently needed spares. From Chelmsford it was reported that an additional hydrogen compressor they had asked for arrived from Belfast within twenty-four hours – a day or two in advance of the notice of despatch. When it was all over we found that in the ten weeks the barrage was deployed it had consumed 179 million cubic feet of hydrogen and destroyed 279 V1s which would otherwise almost certainly have reached London. But in spite of the courage of the fighter pilots, and the skill and endurance of the gunners and the passive resistance of the balloon cables, some 40 per cent of the flying bombs were getting through to London.

Victory, when it came total and complete, had to await the arrival of consignments of radio proximity fuses from America, the very existence of which was about the best-kept secret of the war. Even their name was secret as revealing too much, and replaced by the non-committal VT, variable time, as being meaningless. Credit for the name is given in a recent book, *The Deadly Fuze* by Ralph B. Baldwin, to my brother, Commander Hutchison RN, who led a delegation to Washington entrusted with the task of taking this essentially British invention for development in the United States and seeing it through development in the United States to the production stage. The secrecy which surrounded every aspect of the development and production of the fuse extended into our family circle and it never occurred to me to ask what he was doing over in the States; so that when he came to stay with us for a week his day-long disappearances to some undisclosed destination passed without comment. I never thought to connect them with an unusual request received some few weeks before for deliveries of hydrogen to a site on the east coast for flying trials of an outsize balloon. It was in fact for balloons from which the targets were suspended in the first definitive test over here of the radio proximity fuse, which my brother had come to witness.

Churchill in his war memoirs mentions early attempts to develop a proximity fuse capable of exploding a shell within certain distances of the target, thereby increasing the accuracy of fire of anti-aircraft guns by whole orders of magnitude; earlier tests of photo-electric devices failed here and in America. The radio proximity fuse was first conceived at the Radar Experimental

Station at Malvern, as consisting essentially of a radio pulse-emitter sensitive to reflection from the target. The decision to entrust its development to the Americans was logical in the circumstances of 1942, and they were quick to appreciate its potential, putting ample resources into the problems of miniaturization and shock-proofing involved. My brother stayed with it throughout and was awarded the OBE for his services, and from the Americans he received the award of the Legion of Merit, Degree of Officer, in 1946. He returned to rejoin the Ordnance Service, and was promoted Captain in 1949; and in 1958, a year after retirement, he became manager of a shadow factory making radio proximity fuses, until 1966. So that from start to finish he had spent twenty-six years with a secret weapon which for a time was to change the face of warfare, at sea and on land.

There was undoubtedly reluctance on the part of the Americans to release the VTs prematurely or without specific undertakings about how they were to be used. It was vital to the interests of the Allies that in no conceivable circumstances should the device fall into German (or Japanese) hands as it could so easily be copied, but firing out to sea satisfied security criteria. With three pieces of American-produced equipment, the proximity fuse, the SCR-584 radar and the M9 gun director, the V1 was defeated, and the record of the anti-aircraft rose in four weeks from 24 per cent to 79 per cent success in the last week of the attack. On 28 August when 94 bombs approached our coast all but four were destroyed: fighters took 23, the guns 65 leaving the balloons to pick off two of the six that reached them. In Churchill's own words, 'The V1 had been mastered.' The balloons were hauled down and put away – they could offer no defence against the V2 rocket attack that followed – and hydrogen production ceased except at Cardington by mid-September. There remained however some activity in the wake of the German retreat. Barrages for the protection of shipping on the Scheldt and in Antwerp, using balloons of the smaller type, made no great demands on our supply system, although the cylinder trailers were using up valuable shipping capacity. So I decided to go across to survey possible local sources, and spent an interesting few days seeing what a newly liberated country looks like. Regrettably our best option, a fat-hardening factory, had been wiped out in error by American bombers in a high-altitude daylight sortie. It was a fascinating experience to go down to the bank of the Scheldt and look across at where the enemy was still in occupation; and an uneasy moment as I watched a V2 rocket take off a few miles away and head for

London, wondering where it might land when it arrived there. So then back to the flesh-pots of Brussels where the RAF had acquired part of the Residence Palace, a luxury block of flats, recently the headquarters of the German Army. They had blown up the telephone exchange before leaving but left behind their wine cellar as compensation, which some thought to be fair exchange. I returned as I had arrived by way of Ostend and a fast ferry boat used by service personnel.

By the last months of 1944 we were already making plans for the disposal of the hydrogen plants and the return of the hired plant to its rightful owners, while Balloon Command was being run down in preparation for the final act by which it was stood down in February. Air Commodore Lincoln, the Deputy AOC, came to Bournemouth and paid a generous tribute to the work of the gas industry, saying that the operations of the barrages had never been affected by lack of hydrogen: 'It might be truthfully said they were only possible because of the ready availability of the gas.'

Oxygen and other compressed gases

A call from Group Captain Butt, a Deputy Director of Equipment, alerted me to a serious deficiency that had developed in the supply of oxygen of the quality required for use in high-flying aircraft (HFO). It was during the second half of 1943, probably about October, but I cannot be more precise than that. The short-fall had become acute after the arrival of the American Eighth Air Force to occupy airfields prepared for them or vacated in their favour. The point was this: among the preliminary arrangements agreed before their arrival there had been an undertaking by AMSO to supply them with HFO. It turned out that the Americans were using much greater quantities of oxygen than had been specified in their list of requirements – several times what our crews used for comparable sorties. I was asked to advise, quite informally at this stage, on steps that might be taken to alleviate the immediate shortage and to consider what longer-term plans could be made for a substantial increase in the near future. It was a matter of great urgency because plans were already agreed for operations on a greatly increased scale.

I readily agreed to see what we in DHP could do to help. Our hydrogen situation was now well under control and for the next month or two I was able to devote most of my time to oxygen. I found that once again it was a case of shortage of supply, aggravated by a limit on the number of high-pressure cylinders available to transport the oxygen to where it was required and to act as reserve storage at the point of use. There was a further complication: while the RAF had opted for a pressure of 1,800 psi in the aircraft system, the Americans used a lower pressure of 800 psi in their aircraft: so that while we had to have transport cylinders designed for 3,600 psi, made of scarce high-tensile steel, all this was wasted on the supply to the American airfields. I will tell later how we were able to turn this to our advantage.

There was no shortage of oxygen. Produced at several works of the British Oxygen Company, conveniently located for their industrial customers, it was transported efficiently and swiftly in liquid form in spherical copper containers suspended from chains in containers packed with a thermal insulating powder. At local distribution depots it was regasified and compressed to the normal pressure of 1,800 psi. A few depots had been equipped with special compressors for the RAF with a terminal pressure of 3,600 psi and driers to reduce the dew point to the specified safe figure for HFO. Any laxity here might cost the life of a pilot of a Hurricane if the control valve were to ice up at 10,000 ft. and sub-zero temperature. The bottleneck was in the supply of the compressors; for oxygen they must be lubricated with water since compressed oxygen in the presence of grease is a sure recipe for disaster. They were all made at one factory by or for BOC and the factory was already at full stretch.

A visit to the US Office of Supply confirmed my fear that their present rate of consumption was the correct figure to use in any plan. The officer I met agreed that the current figure was several times greater than the estimate which had been forwarded to the Air Ministry and he could not account for the discrepancy. I could only think that it was something to do with those 'damned dots', or there might have been some confusion in the units used: mutual recriminations could generate great heat but would produce no oxygen, and all I had to suggest was that they try to economize in the use of oxygen for the next month or two while we sorted things out. (Someone told me later that US Airforce crews had got in the habit of turning on the oxygen at take-off – what had begun as a remedy for the occasional hang-over had become an addiction. From such small causes do great muddles arise.)

According to records produced for my englightenment, production of oxygen was running at the rate of about 7,800 cylinders a week. BOC were filling 5,300 of these at their 12 depots and the RAF at maintenance units and forward filling stations, five in all, were responsible for the remaining 2,500. It was estimated that, on the projected scale of operations, consumption would rise to double the current level within six months at the very latest. The only way that I could see of tackling this situation with any hope of success was to do what had been done in 1940 for hydrogen, and delegate responsibility for the entire operation to one department, in the Air Ministry preferably, not the MAP. I was spared the embarrassment of suggesting my own, when I was asked if I was willing to take it on. Air Marshal Sir John Bradley who had come to the Air Ministry in 1942 as Deputy AMSO gave the proposed change his full and unqualified support and continued to keep a close watch on all that happened in the next critical six months, and so on 1 January 1944 we became the Directorate of Compressed Gases. I undertook to alert the Director of Flying Operations if at any time during the critical build-up there was ever any doubt as to our ability to meet the combined demands of both air forces. That situation arose only once and followed two 'thousand bomber' raids on consecutive nights; but a third which was planned for the next night was cancelled on account of fog. In this way we were spared the painful necessity of halting the war effort then or indeed on any future occasion.

Time spent on reconnaissance is never time wasted, as they say in the army, and I entered on my duty as Director of Compressed Gases with a more than adequate appreciation of the problems ahead of me. The first thing was to cut through the tangle of red tape, book-keeping and store records that surrounds, and frequently impedes, the simplest of transactions in any sector of public accountability. My considered advice was to write off the contents of every cylinder of oxygen at the time it left the BOC factory or depot or any one of the RAF's own filling stations. The cylinder was much more valuable than its contents and should thereafter constitute the only accountable unit except for the brief period at the filling station. Here its contents formed a basis of charge from BOC to the RAF, before being written off to the cost of making war. I justified any breach of the sacred rules of accountancy by the argument that no one but a saboteur had anything to gain by blowing off the contents and I knew of no black market for oxygen without its cylinder or even with it.

That left me free to make a virtue out of necessity and use the difference between the working pressures of the oxygen systems in the aircraft of the RAF and the USAAF to our advantage. Freshly charged cylinders would go first to the RAF where, in the process of charging the aircraft system, the cylinder pressure would fall from 3,600 psi to 1,800 psi. At this pressure or somewhat higher they should be passed on to an American airfield and used there to recharge the oxygen systems of the aircraft to their working pressures of 800 psi before returning to the depot to be refilled. By maximizing the usage of cylinders we achieved two purposes; first to maintain a good stock of oxygen at the airfields ready to meet the heavy demand which must follow a large raid; equally important to maintain a stock of 'empties' at the depots so that the compressors could operate continuously.

These measures and a general tightening up all round gave immediate relief: they only touched the fringe of the problem – how to increase our compressor capacity. I looked over the hydrogen supply system to see whether any help might come from that quarter. BOC were using the equivalent of one whole depot, 600 cylinders a week, to supply purified compressed air. This duty was taken over in March by the hydrogen compressors at Worksop, requiring only the addition of a few pieces of equipment to clean up the air and dry it. Our electrolytic plant at Keith in the north of Scotland had no problem in changing over from hydrogen to oxygen and went on stream in February.

A real breakthrough came when BOC suggested a 'warm evaporator' to augment the output of compressor stations. This simple device consisted of a large pressure vessel of high-tensile steel in which was suspended a copper pot. The pot was filled with liquid oxygen through a hose from a road tanker and the cover refastened. In a few hours the oxygen evaporated and we had a large reservoir of gaseous oxygen at a pressure of 1,800 psi which could be used to give a preliminary charge to the cylinders. (Regardless of where they came from they had all been blown down to zero as a precaution against accumulation of impurities, especially water.) The cylinders then passed to the compressors at pressures between 500 and 1,500 psi depending on the state of the evaporator as between fillings. On average one might expect an increase of 40 per cent in the output of the filling station. At the end of March deliveries reached a high of 127,000 cylinders a week, still just ahead of demand. In the week ending 10 June we reached a figure of 157,000, exactly double that of January, beating my target by three weeks.

Sir John Bradley, never a man to waste words, wrote a minute:

Air Ministry, Bush House, 3rd July

DCG. I wish again to congratulate you and your staff upon the excellent increases in oxygen production which you have achieved.

J.B. D/AMSO.

It may have been his influence that secured top priority for oxygen at the Ministry of Production with the improbable code name 'Furcoat'. Delivery of new compressors began to improve: they were of the standard BOC design. Our contribution was to rebuild some of our much more powerful hydrogen compressors, with water-lubricated cylinders and pistons, on the existing crank-cases. Cardington started compressing oxygen on 1 May 1944, and one of the 'shadow' hydrogen factories, at Morley, went to work as an oxygen filling station in August. Together they were soon filling cylinders at a rate equivalent to nearly one quarter of the output of the entire system. Apart from these, all the new development took place at RAF Maintenance Units and forward filling stations. This was in continuation of a trend that was already in evidence when I took over. There was never any shortage of liquid oxygen which could be delivered by BOC in their insulated tankers to any specified destination. The MUs were geared up to supply replacements and spares: they had a skilled labour force available at all hours of the day or night; they were generally conveniently placed with respect to the airfields, all this making for a quick turn-round of cylinders; these continued to be at the forefront of our thinking.

The following table of representative figures, for the weekly rates of deliveries of full cylinders at three monthly intervals from January 1944 to March 1945, illustrates this point:

Weekly deliveries of HP oxygen cylinders

W/e	5/1/44	1/4/44	21/6/44	16/9/44	16/12/44	14/3/45
BOC	5347	7061	6722	4403	3488	4431
AM/RAF	2506	5279	10688	10888	11088	15188
Total	7853	12340	17410	15291	14576	19619

These figures do not tell the whole story: as time went on and we were able to build up some excess of production capacity over demand it was no longer essential to maintain a stock of empties at the filling stations in order to keep the compressors continually at work. Instead we were able to maintain a stock of full cylinders at the operational airfields where they were really needed.

From 1 January 1944 I became responsible also for the supply of nitrogen to the RAF. It was a relatively small matter then of some 500 cylinders of the gas, purified to the standard of HFO and compressed like oxygen to 3,600 psi each week. Now as every schoolboy knows the air we breathe consists of 79 per cent nitrogen and 21 per cent oxygen, and one might have concluded that there would have been no problem in obtaining all we could ever need from the air separation plants which were supplying our oxygen. But it does not work like that and the nitrogen they discharge in the process of making pure oxygen will always contain some oxygen as an impurity. The RAF was obtaining all the nitrogen it required from Billingham where ICI had adopted a policy of purging all pressure vessels with nitrogen before opening them to the air and had installed a piped supply to all parts of the works, from, I presume, an air-separation plant designed for the purpose. This, however, was our only supply and clearly vulnerable and I looked around for another. Recalling that the Fisons Fertilizer Plant at Flixborough had a nitrogen plant, I sought their help. They readily agreed to install compressors and a purification train to our specification and the RAF took on the responsibility for handling and filling the cylinders.

Meanwhile demand continued to rise, following, as might be foreseen, the level of activity of Bomber Command and the US Air Force, until by November it was running at 1,500 cylinders a week. This was about the comfortable limit of what the cylinder traffic could bear. I thought again of the hydrogen plants, looking to see where there might be capacity to spare. I planned to use a piece of equipment which had been coming into general use in the gas industry for the safe purging of large vessels and the crowns of gasholders. It was quite a simple device in which gas was burned in air in the correct proportions and cooled to give a mixture of carbon dioxide and nitrogen. If we were to burn hydrogen in such a machine we should finish up with nitrogen, and we had the compressors to fill the cylinders, after drying the gas and eliminating any oil fog. It turned out to be not quite as simple as that but the difficulties were soon overcome, and Wellingborough went to work at the beginning of December 1944 and Cambridge by February 1945, both in time to assist in the great peak of activity in March of that year, when deliveries reached 3,900 cylinders of nitrogen a week.

This was much more than had been planned for originally. The RAF had come to appreciate the risk inherent in a nearly empty tank at very low temperatures when the petrol/air mixture might breach the explosive limits: a simple remedy was to provide an atmosphere of nitrogen. We had also acquired another customer. The army was using nitrogen as a propellant for the flame throwers, and had used most of the supply they had in testing and exercises before D-Day, only to find that it would take several months to refill them from the source of very pure nitrogen that had been specified. We offered them what we had and they were happy.

The success of the Normandy landings which carried the Allied armies right up to the Rhine, and finally deep into Germany brought a few new problems in the supply of oxygen. The Tactical Air Force was operating on captured airfields with squadrons of fighters and fighter bombers and I suspected that, whatever estimates had been made of the consumption of oxygen, the planners might have overlooked the delays inherent in any supply system which involved the refilling of spent cylinders. The RAF had anticipated such a situation in pre-war days with the design and construction of a few small mobile air-separation plants, mounted on a vehicle and powered by an offtake from the main engine. This is always a doubtful expedient: motor vehicle engines are not designed for round-the-clock operation for days, even weeks on end, which is what it takes to run an efficient air-separation plant capable of supplying oxygen on demand. However, they were operating with some success and there was no immediate crisis, but I understood that the equipment branch concerned would like to be reassured about future supplies.

We had come up with a simpler concept for emergency use at home, where three transportable units had been operating successfully from July 1944 onwards. They were not strictly mobile or self-contained, depending on the supply of liquid oxygen from BOC in their standard tankers, but each unit had a capacity to fill 500 cylinders a week, many times that of the RAF's mobile units. I satisfied myself that the LO tankers, slightly modified, could safely cross the Channel, and we had hopes that alternative sources of supply of LO would be found in liberated France and Belgium.

A stage had been reached when all logistical problems could best be left to Maintenance Command and the appropriate equipment branch at the Air Ministry. I observed that No. 1 Transportable was withdrawn from service in February 1945 and the last of the three left in April of that year and assumed they were to go to northern Europe to supplement the RAF mobile units: we had no further obligations to the USAAF. I had reached a stage when, unless somebody asked a question or raised a difficulty, it was far better to ensure they had the tools and leave them to finish the job. I was determined not to become yet another small cog in a huge administrative machine: that stage was over and it was time to go, but D/AMSO was still reluctant, and sure enough there was an informal request from E44, the equipment branch concerned, for information about the supply of oxygen in the NW Europe theatre of operations. It was January and bitterly cold when I left Northolt in a small plane and reached Belgium in what appeared to be near fog, out of which a church steeple suddenly appeared in direct line with our starboard wing. A sharp banked turn to port seemed to this interested observer just enough to clear the weather-cock, as we came back on course for a small airfield near Brussels. What passed for a runway in a sea of mud was a half-submerged metal grid off which we duly skidded to end up axle deep in the stuff. It gave me time to re-arrange my thoughts about the safety and convenience of air travel while a tracked vehicle ventured out across the morass to rescue us. A day was usefully spent checking up on potential suppliers of liquid oxygen and other sources of oxygen from which the gas might be drawn to be compressed and purified to the RAF standards of HFO.

In the shops and in the restaurants and in a hostelry we visited later in search of entertainment, I seemed to detect a certain reserve, a sense of wariness, after the euphoria of recent liberation which had been so much part of the scene on my first visit to Brussels. In the interval Rundstedt's thrust through the Ardennes on 16 December with ten Panzer and fourteen infantry divisions had come near to reaching its first objective of the River Meuse, from whence they intended to recapture Antwerp and sever our main supply route to the British armies. It was not until 16 January that the gap had been sealed off and the good citizens of Brussels could breathe again. The thought of old scores which might have had to be paid off if it had gone otherwise and Germans had been back in Brussels on 27 December was deeply sobering.

The mobile oxygen unit that I was to visit was located somewhere up beyond Eindhoven and it was a fine frosty morning when I set out in a jeep with an RAF officer as guide and driver; if there was any map-reading to be done, I was there to do it. As we went on further north the roads began to show the scars of recent battles, relics possibly of the ill-fated attempt to force a crossing of the Rhine at Arnhem. We found our quarry well-camouflaged and comfortably established in a small valley with a stream running through it. The sergeant in charge was clearly 'a man of infinite-resource-and-sagacity': instead of beefing on about the shortage of distilled water for lubricating his oxygen compressor, he had set up a neat little distillation plant with a jerrycan for a boiler and a copper coil cooled by water drawn from the stream, as a condenser. It occurred to me that in a place where one English shilling would buy a gallon of wine there might be other uses for a still, but good manners forbade any such suggestion, although my ancestors, Scottish and Irish alike, would have had no hesitation in the application of their skill. A routine check of the test equipment proved that the oxygen they were producing satisfied the RAF standards for HFO, and we were soon on our way in the gathering dusk. It was only ninety miles or so, but the night was all blackness with no stars to guide and precious little to guide us in the way of road signs; and when I pointed out, on our right and distant only some half a mile, a large house or small chateau on fire and burning fiercely, the same thought occurred to both: there being no fixed front line in that sort of war, had we perhaps strayed too far to the east? And would perhaps our first question about the way to Brussels, addressed to some shadowy figure in the dark be answered in guttural German? For the first and only time I did indeed regret my failure to take the commission that was available to me: the rules of war make no provision for the treatment of persons suspected of spying for some alien power.

My main preoccupation back in the office was to secure my release, if not immediately, then at least in good time to begin overtures for return to the Gas Light and Coke Company. I had written to Sir John Bradley in December but he was slow to reply and I soon found out why: victory in the west was no longer a matter of whether, it was only a question of when. The heavy bombers had just about finished their task of pulverizing the German war effort and much else besides. The forward planners were looking to means of deploying them in support of a combined operation against mainland Japan, and Churchill relates how glad he was when General Marshall came forward with a positive plan for our co-operation in this last phase of the war. It included the Island of Okinawa as a base but no supplies were available from American resources and our base must be self-contained as to 'airfields, installations, ports, roads and pipes', and that for me meant oxygen and any other compressed gases. It took three months 'of the largest and most prolonged amphibious operation of the Pacific war' to capture Okinawa and this was not accomplished until 22 June. Meanwhile we were well-advanced in the procurement and assembly of an oxygen plant to be erected on the island in time for the first instalment of two squadrons in October and ten early in 1946, with twenty squadrons comprising four hundred heavy bombers as the ultimate objective.

After consideration of the various options open to us, I decided in favour of a fixed type of oxygen plant from a standard production line, for which we could provide the oxygen compressors out of equipment now surplus to requirements in the UK. We found what we wanted in the United States, and had it modified to form a 'break-down' unit, ready to be assembled on site out of transportable components. Flight Lieutenant Skinner, the second-in-command in what had come to be the Balloon and Oxygen Centre, Middle East, came home to take command. He had successfully erected and commissioned the plant, having trained RAF personnel to operate it, when an event occurred which made this and many other activities of no further consequence. Churchill again, now at Potsdam, on 17 July was handed a message, 'Babies satisfactorily born' – the experiment in the New Mexican desert had come off – the atom bomb was a reality. Faced with the alternative of the loss of a million American lives and half that number of British and Dominion troops in an all-out assault on the mainland, the decision was unanimous; after a fortnight of warnings and a call to surrender, the first of two atomic bombs fell on Hiroshima on 9 August, followed by the second on Nagasaki, and Japan capitulated immediately. It was in my last month of duty at the Air Ministry and when I read the news on posters at Holborn underground station my first thought was that no one could possibly want me any longer; and then my mind went back to the day when Fairgrieve, my science master at school, had drawn me aside to confide in me the news that the atom was not really indivisible as he had been teaching us in class. 'They are breaking it open all the time at Cambridge but don't tell the others.' Well, now at least they all know, I said to myself as I went down to the train.

9
A Fresh Start

My hasting days fly on with full career,
But my late spring no bud or blossom shew'th.
John Milton 1631

There was a chill in the air when I paid my first visit to the Gas Light and Coke Company's Products Sales Office in Queen Street, EC2. I had never met the Products Salesman and my friends had been free with advice to the effect that a cordial welcome was unlikely to be included in any plan to entertain me. J.H. Olliver had been the Products Salesman for about as long as anyone could remember. He was a highly respected member of a small group of buyers, traders and salesmen who together managed most of the tar trade in London with its continental ramifications and a lot of wheeling and dealing. He had always considered himself as responsible only to Sir David Milne-Watson, the Governor, in person. Together they hatched schemes for rescuing the by-products of gas manufacture from imminent disaster when first one and then another of the refined products leaving the Tar and Ammonia Products Works at Beckton lurched out of control from boom to slump. Now Sir David was gone and my arrival that morning was a herald of CHANGE; even if it had been explained that mine was no more than an exploratory mission. My presence was symptomatic of all those changes that were rocking the very foundations of an ancient structure. Who, he asked himself, could tell where it would all end? – as he offered me the use of a small dark office and a table and chair, and that was about all. It was too much for him and he soon opted for retirement, which was in any case several years overdue.

A.E. Sylvester, Governor 1945-1946

The changes that upset Mr Olliver had their origin in 1941 when Robert Foot, the General Manager, in the opinion of many the heir apparent, was seconded to the BBC. (He it was who had granted the salary concession which finally determined my decision to join the company in 1926.) He later left to head up the Mining Association and did not return. That left the way clear for A.E. Sylvester to be appointed Managing Director. He had come in before the war to overhaul the company's financial and accounting procedures and much else besides. He was ready to assume the mantle of power which Sir David, under the stress of war and increasing ill health, was ready to shed. Sir Harold Hartley, who had introduced me to the company while I was still at Oxford was appointed a Second Deputy Governor in the expectation that he would become Governor when the time came. But it did not turn out that way. In April 1945 when Sir David announced that he would not seek re-election the court elected Sylvester Governor. At the end of the year Harold left to join the board of British Overseas Airways.

Michael Milne-Watson, the younger son of Sir David, gave up his appointment as Commercial Manager to join the navy as an Ordinary Seaman, qualified as a Navigating Officer and saw service in a corvette off the coast of West Africa. Before he left and while I was still at the Air Ministry he invited me to dine at his club and meet Edgar Sylvester. It was a cheerful evening, and Sylvester showed some interest in what I was doing to involve the gas industry in the war effort. So in early February 1945, when my hopes were rising of securing my release from the Air Ministry. I asked for an interview to find out what if anything he might have in mind for me. He was in the throes of reorganizing the management structure and was not ready to come up with any positive offer. At least I reckoned he had accepted my determination to be done with research.

Even so it came as a shock when my old chief, Harold Hollings, sent for me and seemed confident that it was not a matter of whether, but only of when, I might be free to rejoin his organization and how best I might fit into the post-war scene. I listened, said little and left in what I believe can best be described as high dudgeon. H.H. left me in no doubt about the seriousness of his purpose: he had informed the Managing Director of his intention before sending for me. Well, if that's the way they want to play it, I grumbled, I'll show them, and applied for the only suitable alternative job on offer. To my surprise I was short-listed for the final interview and I made no secret of it. I was genuinely relieved when it went to a man whom I knew, and knew to be much better qualified than I could ever claim to have been. I had made my gesture and felt all the better for it. There was plenty remaining to be done at the Air Ministry in preparation for the construction of an entire new oxygen supply complex on Okinawa in time for the final assault on mainland Japan. All of that and much else became irrelevant when the first atomic bomb fell on Hiroshima. Free to go at the end of August, I took my overdue leave and went with the family to Barton-on-Sea, handy for the beach and for our centre-board sloop, Loreen, hauled out in 1939 over the sea wall of Keyhaven Creek. After two weeks of hard work, scraping, painting and varnishing, we were ready to launch. Then a few days more waiting for the planking to take up and the hull to be watertight again and I was ready to go to sea. My destination was Moody's Yard on the Hamble, to be our home base as it had been before the war.

It was also a time for decision about Ann's future. She had been a clever enough member of her class, especially in history. Miss Hussey, the teacher who taught history there must have been brilliant. She was well-liked and, of her twelve pupils taking School Certificate in 1945, all but one got distinctions in her subject. However, the other subjects, such as science and mathematics, were not taught to a standard which would have given any hope of entrance, much less of a scholarship to Oxford. Miss Chaplin, the Headmistress of the Royal Naval School who had been so kind to Dorothea and me in our 'courting days', had been on the staff of the Cheltenham Ladies College. Our combined efforts, including a call by Dorothea driving a six-wheel truck in battle-dress, succeeded in getting an entrance. In the autumn term of 1945 Ann left the RNS to go there, in St. Helen's House with a very distinguished house mistress (as at Eton, they did not teach). It certainly broadened her mind because the house mistress was an ex-missionary, with four Siamese, two Indians and two Abyssinians out of a total of sixty in the house. Miss Popham, the famous Headmistress at Cheltenham, was pressing for Ann to stay on an extra year and try for a scholarship. After a short tussle in which we all took part it was agreed she should go up at the first opportunity. Based on my own experience, I suggested that instead of taking a Higher Certificate, she should take the Oxford Prelims in Natural Science, which several of those who had places at Oxford also did. Ann reports that with all that behind her she spent the summer term at CLC organizing the lighting for *The Tempest*.

Meanwhile nothing further had come out of Kensington and I was less than confident about my hopes for a future career in gas when I reported for duty at the end of August. I had blotted my copybook by applying and being short-listed for a job outside; forgetful of the legendary curse attributed to a former Secretary and said to have been invoked on those who escaped: 'We never thought much of him while he was with us', this followed by a heavy sigh. Worse still I was accused by Sylvester of ingratitude. He would not have known what prompted my reckless action and I did not think it was up to me to tell.

While I had been at the Air Ministry he had been putting the finishing touches to his plan for reorganizing the management structure. At the top were to be the Governor and two Managing Directors. These appointments had been made and, with Falconer Birks and Michael Milne-Watson in office, I felt that at least I had friends in high places. There must have been some smoothing of ruffled feathers by the time appointed for my interview with the Governor. He was at his most genial and friendly when assigning me to the task at the City Office. It was to evaluate the economics of the processing of the by-products dealt with at the Company's Tar and Ammonia Works, past, present and future. Thankfully I knew next to nothing about the subject and was able to accept my brief with the cheerful confidence that only total ignorance sustains. In the eyes of our small world I was on to a good thing with the chance of promotion to follow. I was not so sure and felt that I was still on probation.

With his two Managing Directors in office, Sylvester addressed himself to the next line of command. There were to be nine Chief Officers, three of whom retained the traditional titles of Chief Engineer, Chief Accountant and Commercial Manager, and six Controllers, each with responsibility for some branch of the company's operations. The decision to bring Coke alongside Tar and Ammonia was what interested me. Controller of by-products was what I hoped to be and before long became.

Controller of by-products

I was appointed Controller of by-products in December 1945. The first item on my agenda was to find myself an office. It was not easy. What had started life as the Kensington District Office and Showroom was taken over in 1938 as temporary accommodation for the Governor, the Court of Directors, the Managing Director and the Comptroller; with their supporting staff under the Secretary they filled the place to overflowing.

My appointment was with Mr W.E. Gooch, the Staff Controller who was in charge of such matters at that time. I stated my modest requirements, an office and a secretary with the possibility of a PA later. He was polite but firm. There was no vacant office, no way he could partition one and no hope whatever of building one. He could however warmly recommend the office recently vacated by the Products Salesman. I was ready for that one – Roberts, about to be promoted, had moved in already. Fortunately I had got to know Bill Gooch when he was still Manager of the Brentford District and I was a frequent visitor to the works, trying to sort out problems as they arose in the siting and construction of the last of my new style benzole plants; part of it had to be accommodated on a narrow strip of land at the extreme far end of the works and the rest on the other side of the busy Brentford High Street. We met quite by chance in the office of the Station Engineer where I was explaining to Mr Perry the urgency of some impossible request and Bill had dropped in for a chat and a neighbourly drink. In that hospitable atmosphere all problems were speedily resolved, as I reminded him. Surely, I continued, now well into my stride, if Perry could accommodate a large benzole plant on a narrow strip of land between the road and the river, could the all-powerful Staff Controller not find the few square feet required to house an old friend? He took me off to inspect what were positively the last square feet left anywhere. It was a junk room filled to the roof with stores of all kinds. I said OK and how soon can I move in? Not to be outdone he said three weeks and that would include another window, a carpet, a desk and a filing cabinet, also a space for a secretary in the general office; and yes, he had someone in mind who might well suit, and he was as good as his word. So that was how I became a Head Office Man with a toehold on a ladder which might take me who could say where? Or to what heights? Or depths? Perish the thought!

Meanwhile there was work to be done. My time at the City Office had not been wasted. Roberts, the Assistant Salesman, was helpful and answered all my queries, while his Chief remained incommunicado to the very end. I spent a useful two months learning about the tar business from the records of sales for a period going back more than twenty years. I hoped that this might provide an indicator of what to expect when the present controls were swept away and filled many pages and graphs in my Filofax notebook which had served me well at the Air Ministry; and came to the conclusion that in business nothing is so certain as the uncertainty of forecasts based on prices in the market place. However, I used my time there to learn the language of the trade and met several of the leading figures who appeared to be operating on a good percentage basis at the periphery of the tar industry. I had also found a friend in the person of W. Gordon Adam, one time Scholar of Christ Church, Oxford and, since well before I joined the company, the Superintendant of the Beckton Tar and Ammonia Products Works.

An Aberdonian by origin, he had been attracted by what, before the First World War appeared to be limitless opportunities in new markets for chemicals derived from coal tar. When his Chief, Colonel Wilton, left for war service Adam found himself in charge. It was said that he never left the works for a single night, living and sleeping in a cottage just within the perimeter. It was built for him by the works carpenter, a Mr Rose. With wry humour, in the context of its environment, it was called Rose Cottage. Here again Gordon Adam slept every night during another world war and was ready when the German bombers struck. He led his firefighters with such courage and resource that much of his works was saved from almost certain destruction and hazarded his life on several occasions. For that night's work he was awarded the George Medal.

It was only when the danger had passed, and he would never have to sleep in Rose Cottage again, that he married and decided to retire to a house and small estate in the north of Scotland. His departure was planned with characteristic attention to detail. There were to be two, or possibly three coaches standing in a siding nearby, to be attached to the Aberdonian, or so I heard, if that were possible, and ready to accommodate livestock and gun dogs, furniture and other possessions. Three hives of bees were placed in a meadow nearby. Their owner deemed it only just when an errant swarm took possession of a fourth hive standing empty alongside and, being quickly confined, joined the others in their pilgrimage to pastures new.

Some time before announcing his retirement Gordon Adam had started to provide for a successor by promoting two of his younger men to head up the tar and ammonia sides respectively. He now recommended L.W. Blundell on the tar side to succeed as Superintendant, and I had no hesitation in submitting his name to the Court.

Beckton Products Works

The Beckton Products Works was capable of processing 200,000 tons of tar a year, covered 87 acres and employed 1,000 men. Its output was about one tenth that of the entire UK tar industry. By any standard it was probably the largest tar works in the country. It also processed all the ammonia liquor produced in the company's 14 gasworks, arriving by barge and pipeline at the rate of 100 million gallons a year. Those of us who can still recall what a tarworks looked like in the days of pot stills, open pitch beds, hand-stoked furnaces burning spent oxide, huge chamber acid plants to convert the sulphur dioxide in the furnace gases into sulphuric acid, and other manifestations of bygone technology, would agree that the view from Rose Cottage, where I was lunching with Gordon Adam on my first visit to Beckton, was unlikely to be inspiring; it was not. But I would say right away that no blame attaches to past managers. There being no provision for depreciation in gas companies' accounts (this was long before Sylvester), any renewal of plant at the tarworks had to come from the surplus on the trading account of the gas company. Towards the end of the century the trend was downwards, the company had to raise the price and the tarworks had to wait yet again for the money to renew its ageing plant and equipment.

The gas consumers were well organized in those days and would take any opportunity that arose to voice their protests. A dispute flared up at Nine Elms where a railway yard had to take its supply of gas from the Gas Light and Coke Company and the South Metropolitan Gas Company from their respective statutory boundaries at opposite ends of the yard. Boundaries and prices were both involved but some sort of peace was patched up. By 1898 the gap in prices had widened to 2s 3d per 1,000 cu. ft. in the South Met. and 3s 0d in the Gas Light. The Gas Consumers' Protection League was incensed and a public enquiry was called for. The Government responded with the Rankin Committee, before which George Livesey of the South Met. appeared. 'He made a vitriolic attack which spared the Gas Light, its Management and Directors nothing. Much of what he said was only too true, over-capitalization, inadequate engineering skill, incompetent buying of coal – all this was valid and damning criticism' (S. Everard's *History of the Gas Light and Coke Company*, Benn 1949). Almost thirty years later, when I joined the Gas Light and Coke Company, the two companies were still hardly on speaking terms! With that searing experience fresh in their memory the Court was more than ever reluctant to spend money at Beckton, rating it a poor investment with an uncertain market for its output.

By chance, in the middle of these regrettable events the Court had scored one success: they appointed a young barrister from Edinburgh to the post of Assistant to the General Manager.

What the future Sir David Milne-Watson thought of it all history does not relate. Soon his actions would speak where words might have failed him. During the next forty-five years no department could consider itself safe from his keen scrutiny, and no person either. Autocrat yes, in the old tradition of management, but not capricious in the exercise of power. To that end he was untiring in his efforts to safeguard the company's markets by setting up trade associations for sulphate of ammonia and for sulphuric acid and encouraging others to do the same for tar products. It does not seem that he was quite as enthusiastic when it came to authorizing the large sums that would have been required to modernize the works; much of which and the railway system that served it dated from the 1870s. It took the passage of years and a Second World War to bring that to a head.

As we walked round the works after the lunch in Rose Cottage, I was beginning to learn how much would have to be done before we could expect to operate profitably in a post-war world of competition in uncertain markets. Miles of railway lines were criss-crossing the whole area; made-up roads were few and far between; and eighteen small locomotives, each with a two man crew, were busy moving raw materials and products into, out of, and between the several sections into which the works was divided. Maintenance of locomotives and tracks was already a heavy drain on revenue: the ever-increasing cost of maintaining an antique infrastructure was likely to swallow up any reduction in costs to be gained by the replacement of obsolete plant. That was my first, and rather discouraging, impression of the Beckton Tar and Ammonia Products Works.

I talked to Falconer Birks. His advice was that something would have to be done. He was planning on the basis that a 10 per cent increase per annum was possible in the near future and tar and ammonia would have to be disposed of, if possible profitably; if not, then at least loss to the company. He thought that modernizing the infrastructure was a first priority and being a one-off operation it would be wise to use a firm of engineering consultants for overall planning and detailed civil engineering and structural work. He agreed it would be best to use our own staff for the process aspects of our planning. An outline plan and provisional estimate of cost should be prepared and presented to the Works and Products Committee without delay. He pointed out that provision for depreciation in the company's accounts had left between £8 and 9 million of reserves at the end of the war. It was being swallowed up rapidly by replacement of war-damaged plant. I should work fast before it was all gone. That was the kind of advice I was very ready to take.

The many other desirable improvements on the process side would have to wait until the layout of the infrastructure was finalized and the work well advanced. The engineers had already staked their claim in a first instalment of post-war reconstruction and expansion at the company's gasworks costing £7 million. I thought it prudent to stake a claim as advised by Birks and we went to the Works and Products Committee with a bid for £1.25 million. It was real money then; you could multiply by 50 to get some idea of what the same thing would cost today. To my relief it was approved in outline, subject to detailed submission of each major item. With some regret I had to leave the continuation of the task to Blundell and his team, when three years later, I left to cross the river.

The coke trade

Marketing in a situation where the input is not under the control of the sales manager can be an uncomfortable business. There had been a disastrous period between the wars when, it was said, some of the best roads and hard standings on many a gasworks were where surplus coke had been steam-rollered in because there was nothing else to do with it. The story was still being told of how, in the very short time it took to load a steamer bound for Hamburg with coke, the price had dropped several pounds and by the time it reached its destination the coke was unsaleable and had to be dumped out at sea. But meanwhile there was rationing and control, and whenever there was a shortage of the politically explosive 'house coal' Ministers and their officials expected the gas companies to fulfil all demands regardless of cost and disruption of works routine. The 'perambulator trade', the traditional sale of 28 lb of coke (off ration) into the customer's container at the works gate, reached new heights on Friday afternoons and again on Saturday mornings. Powerful reinforcements came from hundreds of school children with everything from a soap box on four discarded roller bearings to a perambulator that had seen better days with a nursemaid in the park, together with a sprinkling of taxis from Kensington and private cars from the suburbs. Ministry officials, snug in their offices, exerted all the pressure they knew how, on behalf of the municipal councils, to have us order our delivery men ('Impossible!' 'Then persuade them.') to carry 1 cwt bags of coke up four or five storeys of flats, whose landlords (the same councils) had failed to provide a lift. Nye Bevan had summed it up:

> This Island is almost made of coal and surrounded by fish; only an organising genius could produce a shortage of coal and fish at the same time.

Well, someone did and continued to do so, and it was quite a few years before conditions improved and we were able to return to our regular trade.

The Gas Light and Coke Company, in the person of Robert Foot, then the General Manager, had taken the lead before the war by bringing together the gas companies, large and small, in the south to form the London and Counties Coke Association. It had as its declared objectives to establish a sound marketing policy and to develop new outlets for coke. Foot was a skilful and persuasive negotiator. A market structure, based on zone delivered prices, was established before the war. It became a basis for maximum prices when rationing of coke came into force during the war, and continued after nationalization, until destroyed by that blunt instrument of Conservative economic theory, the Restrictive Trade Practices Act of 1957.

There was little I could do in this well-organized situation except attend the necessary committees and take the chair at meetings of the Technical Committee, the only one for which I was responsible. One thing I learned was that an efficient and single-minded woman can run circles round the members of a men-only committee, as were most, if not all, in those days. Miss Wooster was one such and not above using feminine wiles when she suspected that there might be trouble ahead. The Annual General Meeting of the London and Counties Coke Association was treated to a rather special new hat, outdoing those others which had served for lesser occasions throughout the year. But let no one be mistaken: beneath that gorgeous confection was a steely resolve to have things done her way, and a grasp of the facts and the figures to support the Chairman in dealing with any intervention from the floor of the meeting.

Sylvester's desire to see some form of statement which would define the profitability or otherwise of the by-product side of the company's activities was embarrassing, to say the least. It was committed to my care and I was quite certain there was no answer. In the present state of the art, gas could not be made without producing by-products, just as in our sister industry coke ovens could not produce coke for the steel industry without producing gas as a by-product. They used gas to heat their ovens: we used coke to heat our retorts, and we both sold what was left over for whatever it would fetch in the market-place. The real difference was that our main product, gas, was sold in a monopoly market, and therefore subject to rigorous scrutiny and generally under conditions of public control. The by-products were free of any intervention until the war brought controls of the price and destination of coke and rationing; all of which was competently administered by Miss Wooster and her staff.

Preceding wars had seen the price of coal rise sharply – on each occasion the ensuing peace saw prices revert to just about where they were before. This time there was no respite, and between 1939 and 1960 the price of carbonizing coal doubled every five years. This became our principal concern and, with the other by-products making so little contribution to the recovery of costs, we had to do what we could with our coke. The commercial market, consisting of large blocks of flats and offices, had been carefully cultivated but now was defenceless against oil, equally smokeless, requiring no stokers and becoming relatively cheaper all the time. We could not even appeal to patriotic sentiment, for when national policy had decreed that home-based refining should be encouraged their products were home-produced even if their crude oil had to be imported. It left only the domestic market, which required so much care in the selection of coal, in the control of carbonization and in the handling of the somewhat fragile product, that if all the costs had been fully evaluated and charged I am sure we would have given up in despair. The simple fact was that if coke had to be sold at what it really cost to make it would not have been sold at all, and if sold at what it would fetch the gas was too costly to be competitive with other fuels. It was hardly surprising that in the post-war years several million paraffin heaters were sold and captured a market that was not recovered for gas for some fifteen years. However, I am anticipating, as for the time being all fuels were scarce and all could be sold, even if not always at the price we hoped.

When J.W. Field retired in 1903, last of an old generation of accountants and managers, going back to the 1830s, the appointment of David Milne-Watson as General Manager began a new era of effective management and administration with clearly defined lines of responsibility at all levels. The increasing power and influence of the General Manager was reflected in a dinner he gave at the Savoy on 28 June 1904 'To meet Mr Corbet Woodall'. The guests included men prominent in associated industries and some neighbouring gas companies. Also Dr Hastings, presumably the same who in 1926, now Sir George and still the company's Medical Officer, passed me in as fit for service, before hurrying off

Harriet Smith, daughter of Sir Harry Burrard, my great-grandmother

Captain James Murray RN, brother of Harriet Smith

Mary Louisa Hamilton, my grandmother

Father *(right)* with hounds at Dooria in the 1890s

Father *c.* 1909 as Captain Assam Valley Light Horse

Mother *c.* 1900

Aunt Harriet with the family at Lochar House

Corpus Christi College 1924. *Ringed l-r:* Mowat, Case, Plummer, Grundy, Schiller

'The Front Quad was our Common Room', Summer 1925. *Top row l-r:* Clauson, Couratin, Curwen/Gott, Bakhle/Boas. *Bottom row l-r:* Brooks, Rees, Barnaby, Aldridge/Hutton

Sir Cyril Hinshelwood FRS

'I met a young lady', August 1925

Science applied to gas engineering at Kensal Green

Composite picture of the balloon barrage over London (Imperial War Museum)

A trainload of hydrogen cylinders (Imperial War Museum)

Part of a barrage of 2000 balloons flown in defence of London (Imperial War Museum)

One of the many flying bombs brought down by the balloon barrage (Imperial War Museum)

Lord Ridley, Director of Hydrogen Production at the Air Ministry

Dorothea *(left)* on war work for the Women's Legion in the Docks

Sir Edgar Sylvester *(right)* first Chairman of the Gas Council, visits coke ovens

Liquid oxygen tank adapted for Channel crossings

Sir Harold Smith *(left)* and Lord Mills at the Isle of Grain

The Rt. Hon. Richard Wood, Minister of Power *(centre)* at the Isle of Grain

William Wood Prince, pioneer of the ocean transport of LNG

Methane Pioneer arrives with the first cargo of LNG, 1959

Signing formal documents for LNG in Paris in 1961: Philip Drew and Michael Milne-Watson

Signing in Paris: Sir Henry Jones and M. Truptil

Ben Bella *(centre left)* at Arzew for the inauguration of the LNG complex

Crowds at the inauguration. *Foreground:* Drew, Wood Prince, Milne-Watson and F. R. Darling

Seismic survey: launching the cable

Seismic survey: the charge is detonated

Sir Denis Rooke CBE, FRS. Chairman of British Gas plc

At Buckingham Palace with Dorothea and Ann for my investiture, 1962

from his rooms in Albany to his duties at Ranelagh as Chairman of the Polo Club. Corbet Woodall, one-time engineer of the Vauxhall Works, was brought on to the Court in 1898 'at the request of members of the Court'. He was clearly destined to be Governor, when the long-serving Sir William Makins passed on in 1906. The partnership heralded by that dinner ruled unchallenged and dragged the Gas Light and Coke Company, only mildly protesting, out of the nineteenth into the twentieth century. That was how it was when I joined as a research chemist in 1926, on one of the lower rungs of the ladder of promotion.

Director of the Gas Light and Coke Company

This appointment was a truly astonishing situation and quite unforeseen by myself and those around me. The speech from the throne at the opening of Parliament in October 1946 had already cast its shadow before:

> A Bill will be laid before you to bring the gas industry under public ownership in completion of the plan for the co-ordination of the fuel and power industries.

The Conservative Party led by Brendan Bracken was preparing to use every sort of delaying action to drag out the proceedings until the end of the session and the life of the Parliament. We were sustained by the hope that it might not after all happen to us. Then came the event which set in train the steps by which I was to be elevated to the Court of Directors one month later:

> The announcement on December 20 of the retirement of Mr A.E. Sylvester from the position of Governor of the Gas Light and Coke Company came as a complete surprise to the gas industry. He is succeeded by Mr Michael Milne-Watson, who thus becomes the youngest Governor the company has had since its inception 134 years ago. The reason for Mr Sylvester's retirement is that he is acting on medical advice. (*The Gas World*, 28 December 1946.)

I was to take a seat vacated by Henry Woodall, the longest-serving Director and a Deputy Governor since 1926. He was a son of Sir Corbet, and his going severed the last link with the partnership which had created the company as we knew it. Naturally I was aware of what was being proposed. Michael Milne-Watson before he accepted the governorship had told the Court that he wanted me to be available to share the burden of events foreseen in the next two critical years, and nothing could have pleased me more.

The official notification when it came was conveyed in person by Brian Wood, the Company Secretary. He was of our generation, having succeeded an almost legendary predecessor, Wm. Lyle Galbraith, holder of that office from 1917 to 1937, who had a welcome for every person newly appointed to the staff, with a 'Come in, dear boy' from an office crowded with documents and family portraits. He had the inestimable quality of being able to lower the temperature raised by the not infrequent outbursts from the Governor, as I once observed. I was waiting my turn to enter into the Governor's presence to be told of the salary increase granted that year to those whom the Gods had looked on with favour. I happened to be the last in line at that particular session. Through the half-open door of the Governor's office came a roar of rage or frustration, followed almost immediately by the stately figure of the Secretary proceeding at something well over a brisk walk and waving a file. 'Wrong file, dear boy' he said as he passed, and 'So much to do and so little time' as he returned at a more regular pace. According to Everard, he left the impression of a Scottish gentleman with a mane of white hair, and his private notes and memoranda were written in ancient Greek, but there was little he missed about a man at the most informal of interviews. The new Secretary's business was short and to the point. The Court had that morning appointed me to be a member of the Court of Directors and a Managing Director of the company. That was the good news: what followed was not quite so good. It was required of every Director that he should be the holder of £5,000 of shares in the company. It may not seem so very much today but it was not the kind of sum I kept about me looking for a home. A telephone call to the bank in Edinburgh produced a reassuring telegram in reply and I was then able to take my seat at the next Court.

Sylvester remained on as a director. The only one of the directors whom I had not met before was Major the Honourable Gwilym Lloyd George PC, MP. He was the last Minister of Fuel and Power in Churchill's wartime administration. As the war drew to a close there was a fashion for post-war planning. He commissioned a Report on the Gas Industry, from a committee presided over by Mr Geoffrey Heyworth, later Lord Heyworth, a captain of industry and Chairman of Unilever, with these terms of reference:

> To review the structure and organisation of the Gas Industry, to advise what changes had now become necessary in order to develop and cheapen gas supplies to all kinds of consumers, and to make recommendations.

The Committee presented their report on 1 November 1945, by which time there was a new Minister, Emmanuel Shinwell, and a new Government with a socialist administration pledged to acquire for the people control of the commanding heights of the economy. As the Minister responsible for setting it up, Ll.G. must have been relieved to find that he was not required to implement it as well. The Committee had no hesitation in recommending that the whole gas industry should be taken over and reconstructed in public ownership. That surely was work best left to the socialists.

The main thrust of the Committee's report was that the industry should be managed by ten Regional Gas Boards financially independent of each other and with no central organizing or co-ordinating body. There was no capital structure as generally understood. They would probably be like municipalities, with access to the money markets for borrowing short-term on the lines of local authority bonds. The Greater London Management Board was to be made up of the Gas Light, the South Met., Commercial, Wandsworth, Croydon and all the other suburban companies. It would control at least one fifth of the whole industry and would have created more internal strife than any benefit that might accrue. However, it was not to be, and when the time came Reuben Kelf-Cohen, the Under-Secretary in charge, accepted the reality of the situation and made no attempt to join together those whom the forces of dissension had kept asunder for fifty or more years. The near-certainty of the nationalization of the industry, now imminent, never entered into our calculations. The size and coherence of the company in relation to the rest of the industry qualified us as a Regional Gas Undertaking in any future reorganization. We would proceed with a conscious feeling of superiority to our own private and special *Götterdämmerung*.

I had no ambition to go elsewhere in any future re-structuring of the gas industry. Falconer Birks was my senior by quite a few years. I could look forward to taking his place with its added responsibilities while I was still of an age to enjoy them. But sufficient unto the day. The Coke and Tar which were my special responsibility could soon be waking up from their long winter sleep under the blanket of governmental control. Sylvester had been instrumental in bringing together several national organizations, the most important of which was the British Gas Council, an amalgamation of several existing central organizations. It was to be presided over by Col. H.C. Smith, the Managing Director of Tottenham Gas Company. He took over the arduous task of keeping the Conservative opposition and Brendan Bracken fed with material to sustain their long-drawn-out opposition to the Gas Bill. Of more importance for the future of the gas industry was the work of a committee at Gas Industry House which during the first half of 1947 prepared a detailed scheme of regional boundaries and a draft form of organization to ensure the smooth development of the industry under nationalization. When the Gas Bill was published in 1947 it was seen to follow the industry's own plan rather than the Heyworth Report.

It was the work of Kelf-Cohen in his capacity as Under-Secretary at the Ministry of Fuel and Power. His abrupt and sometimes abrasive manner made no concessions to popularity. A dedicated socialist from his school days at Manchester, Wadham College, Oxford and first-class honours in history failed to cure him. A first in economics at LSE put him back on course if there had been any wavering. He viewed nationalization as a universal cure for all the nation's ills – that was, until he saw it in practice. I used to hear about him during the war from Sir George Evetts, my colleague at the Air Ministry, who was also an Adviser at the Ministry of Fuel and Power. Our paths crossed occasionally (and literally on Waterloo Bridge) as he bicycled from his home in Upper Norwood to his Ministry and I walked from my train to my office at the Air Ministry. Unlike the modern cyclist he made no concession to the weather, and I always associate him with the ubiquitous cycle clips which I was told adorned his desk. His magnum opus, *Nationalisation in Britain, The End of a Dogma*, shows him to be bitterly disillusioned by all that he had tackled with such enthusiasm. It was published in 1958, three years after he retired from the Ministry (he had never reached the highest levels which with some justice he may have thought were his due). He looks back over seven years during which he sees only meagre progress or failure. The gas industry was hard pressed to justify its existence, with continued calls on the Government to meet capital expenditure not justified by any increase in sales. Worst of all there was a steady decline in sales to the domestic sector on which the future of the industry depended.

It is too late to do more than give posthumous credit to the author of a constitution which was ideally suited to the problems which the industry faced at Vesting day. The twelve independent Area Boards were able to tackle the problems of rationalization and integration, in circumstances which they understood; unhindered by any intervention from a central authority. They were, nevertheless, ready when the time came to adjust to a centralized supply of North Sea gas and the whole operation was carried out with a minimum of delay and the absence of any friction. I feel sure that if Kelf-Cohen had been more closely in touch with those of us who were guiding the industry in 1958 he would have sensed a new confidence in its future. The Isle of Grain plant was coming on stream, making gas from oil drawn direct from the adjacent refinery. Many other Boards were introducing gas from oil plants in traditional gasworks. There was a growing consensus that we might safely sell gas appliances for heating the homes of our customers without too much danger of running on the rocks of the Peak Load.

Business as usual was the order of the day. When at the next meeting of the Court, the Governor asked if any Directors had plans for foreign travel I reported an invitation which I had received while still a Controller, from the Koppers Company of America. They were our leading clients for tar products, especially creosote for the pressure impregnation of railway sleepers and telegraph poles. Leave of absence was granted. The invitation came through Colonel Aitken, a partner in one of those specialist firms which handled overseas markets for tar products and a seasoned traveller. A cabin on the main deck of the Queen Elizabeth recently returned from war service and a suite at the Barclay in New York was no bad way for a first-time transatlantic traveller to learn the ropes.

While I had been away, a new Minister, Hugh Gaitskell, had taken the first step to involve the gas industry in its own demise. In a statement to the House of Commons in April 1948, he recalled the procedures in previous Bills where organizing committees of the industries concerned had been set up to assist the transfer of the Bills into action. He went on to say that the circumstances of gas were rather different. He had decided to secure the advice and assistance of the prospective Chairman and Deputy Chairman of the Gas Council. Mr A.E. Sylvester and Col. H.C. Smith had accepted his invitation to become Chairman and Deputy Chairman respectively of an as yet non-existent Gas Council.

It took them most of the rest of that year to sort out those from within the industry with a claim to preferment as area chairmen while leaving space for the injection of persons from outside who might be thought to add to our managerial skills or to represent socialist and trade union interests. I was approached quite early in the process. Knowing by then that Michael had been assured of the North Thames, the offer of South Eastern made good sense and we were able to discuss the situation before giving our individual answers to the ministerial envoy. The break with the old Gas Light after so many years was made easier by the hope that as Chairman of the South Eastern Gas Board I might work towards bringing our two Boards closer together. From purely selfish motives, I would not have the trouble of moving home during the critical early years of the new Board's existence. In the event, the staffs whom I thought might resent the arrival of a member of the rival Company north of the Thames were friendly and co-operative. The only real trouble that I had to face was to come from an unexpected quarter, as I shall recount in Chapter 10.

The final stage of my severance from the Gas Light and Coke Company came when I retired as a Director and my seat on the Board was taken by Brian Wood. I had been given the facilities of office, secretary, car and chaffeur until such time as I could make other arrangements at a destination as yet unknown, somewhere south of the river.

10
The South Eastern Gas Board

For forms of Government let fools contest
Whate'er is best administered is best.

Alexander Pope

Sunday the first day of May 1949 was Vesting day; when the entire British Gas industry, Company-owned and municipal alike, with all its Undertakings, numbering more than 1,000 in all, had to be transferred to its new owner, the Welfare State. The Socialist Party in its fifth year of power was still intent on capturing yet another of Herbert Morrison's 'commanding heights of the economy'. The twelve Area Boards created by the Gas Act 1948 were to be independent self-accounting bodies directly responsible to the Minister of Fuel and Power. Clause 1 of the Act leaves the Gas Council to the last, almost as if an afterthought. The Heyworth Report of 1945 which influenced the Gas Act 1948 in many respects had not included a central or overseeing body in its recommendations. The Gas Council had only two specific responsibilities assigned to it, research and industrial relations, together with a general responsibility for the creation and issue of gas stock to finance the capital requirements of the Area Gas Boards. Hugh Gaitskell, who replaced Emmanuel Shinwell as Minister of Fuel and Power following the disastrous breakdown of energy supply in the winter of 1946/7, was a realist. If there had not been a Gas Council in the Gas Act he would have felt it essential to create one.

Gaitskell's first step in putting the Gas Act to work was, as we have seen, to appoint a Chairman and Deputy Chairman designate of an as yet non-existent Gas Council. He delegated to them much of the task of finding twelve Area Board Chairmen and assessing the claims of those put forward by other interests, a process which occupied most of six months. We met as a Council for the first time on 25 November 1948 after the Council had been constituted by a minute signed by the Minister:

In pursuance of the powers conferred on me by the Gas Act 1948, I hereby appoint the undermentioned to be members of the Gas Council, subject to the provisions of the said Act and the Regulations made thereunder:

A.E.Sylvester Esq., FCA, Chairman
Colonel H.C. Smith CBE, DL, Deputy Chairman
Sir Andrew Clow KCSI, CIE
E.Crowther Esq., M.Eng., MIGasE
Colonel W.M. Carr OBE, MIGasE
Dr Roger Edwards
Henry F.Jones Esq., MBE
Mervyn Jones Esq., MA, LL.M.(Cantab), LL.B
Sir John Stephenson CBE, JP
M. Milne-Watson Esq.
W.K. Hutchison Esq., BA, BSc, MIChemE
O.R. Guard Esq.
C.H. Chester Esq., OBE, MIMechE, FCA

Dated this 25th day of November, 1948.

(Signed) Hugh Gaitskell
Minister of Fuel and Power

The appointments of the Chairmen of the twelve Area Gas Boards became effective at the same time. My first business as Chairman of the South Eastern Gas Board was to find a Deputy. I had first to be sure of the approval and support of the Chairman of the Council for my candidate. It was readily forthcoming when I proposed R.S. Johnson, Solicitor and Controller of Services of the Gas Light and Coke Company and he was duly appointed. That accomplished, we had to find four suitable persons to be part-time Members of the Board. I proposed K.W. Hickman a member of the City firm which had financed the South Eastern Gas Corporation and Tom Brown, the former Managing Director of the South Suburban Gas Company. From the Minister came the name of Dame Vera Laughton Mathews, the war-time Head of the WRENS and from the Unions Andrew Dalglish, retired Secretary of the Transport and General Workers Union. The Board was then constituted by minute signed by the Minister on 7 January 1949, and we held our first meeting at the Grosvenor Hotel on 11 January 1949

R.H. Sandford Smith, the Secretary of the South Eastern Gas Corporation, a holding company housed and fostered by the Gas Light and Coke Company, came to us as Secretary of the Board. The four of us, my Deputy, the Secretary and myself, with Mr Stredwick, the Chief Accountant of the Wandsworth Gas Company, seconded to the Board for the time being, constituted a working party to plan the takeover of the Undertakings in three months with a target of completion by Vesting day.

The office in which we had been planning the takeover was situated at Vauxhall on the upper floors of a one-time industrial gas showroom of the South Metropolitan Gas Company. The company offered it as temporary headquarters on 7 January 1949 when it was known that the Board had been formally incorporated. The gesture was much appreciated after the years of strained relations that had existed between our two companies. I think we owed it to Dr E.V. Evans, one-time Chief Scientist and a Managing Director of the company. He had opted for retirement and his pension and was offered and accepted a seat on the Board of the North Thames. I had intended to sit in with our working party at the conclusion of its task, but an epidemic of 'flu had taken its toll and only Stredwick and myself were present to deal with all or any problems which might arise; there were none. I went to lunch while Stredwick made some telephone calls and failed to collect a single complaint.

Our meeting marked the end of three months of hectic activity on the part of the Secretary and the Chief Accountant. They had to terminate on that day the powers of the owners or administrators of sixty-one Undertakings supplying gas in the Board's area, and replace them at midnight by a single authority being that of the Board. The fifty-three Gas Companies ranged in size from the South Metropolitan which supplied one third of all the gas sold in the area, with a highly developed central organization, a by-products works, a central laboratory and many other activities; down to ten small Undertakings, each with less than a thousand consumers; ending up at the Charing and District Gasworks Ltd., with only one hundred at the last count. Two Companies had statutory rights and obligations to supply both gas and water: Canterbury divested itself of its water while East Grinstead came over with both. The Gas Undertakings of five local authorities were vested in the Board. They were managed as departments of the local authorities and they were all agreeable to making interim arrangements until we were ready to take over. There were two undertakings in the hands of other nationalized Industries; no problem there. We acquired two Holding Companies owning undertakings in other areas. The only difficulty was the division of the 'spoils', being the excess of the assets over and above the assets of its Undertakings. There being no guidance in the Act, we negotiated a formula which satisfied both parties without recourse to the law, the Ministry or the Gas Council.

Our quarters at Vauxhall were conveniently placed although

accommodation was limited. Vesting day was a quiet, almost secret, operation, unnoticed by press and public alike. The Gas Council had minuted at its February meeting that 'while it might be advisable to have statements in the showrooms and local press, the Council should not engage in publicity for vesting day by way of advertisements in the national Press': in startling contrast to what went on in the process of returning the gas industry to private enterprise thirty-seven years later. I had arranged with the North Thames to take with me my chauffeur, Charles Rider, and my secretary, Elizabeth Frazer. Both were agreeable and Dick Johnson was able to make similar arrangements. With our respective cars that just about completed our new establishment.

Organization

It will be recalled that when I returned to the Gas Light and Coke Company after four years away at the Air Ministry, Edgar Sylvester was putting the finishing touches to his plan for the reorganization of the company. It took account of a number of personal and geographical factors which might have earned for his work the epithet 'pragmatic' in today's jargon. But it worked, which was the crucial test, and I had no hesitation in applying my experience in the Gas Light and Coke Company to the organization of the South Eastern Area Board.

London south of the Thames together with its suburbs had nearly three-quarters of the gas consumers in the Board's area of supply. The four largest of the gas companies were chosen as headquarters of four London Divisions: in order of size they were: South Metropolitan, Wandsworth, Croydon and South Suburban. Greater responsibility for administrative matters in the early years remained with these Divisions than in the Gas Light and Coke Company on which the organization was modelled. This was a passing phase and disappeared when our new central administration developed at the headquarters. Eight smaller gas companies in the suburbs were attached to the nearest London Division.

The 41 gas companies outside London were divided between the counties of Sussex and Kent in about equal proportions. Both counties were characterized by the concentration of consumers in the coastal fringes and the many small undertakings inland at great distances from any possible headquarters and from each other. The sensible solution was to depart from the 'London' plan and create two 'County' Divisions each with a General Manager, responsible directly to the Board. In Sussex there was a natural headquarters in the Brighton Hove and Sussex Gas Company. In Kent there had been some degree of integration through the activities of the South Eastern Gas Corporation. This holding company came into being as a defensive move, fostered by the Gas Light and Coke Company and financed through City interests, to circumvent the ambitions of an American group intent on gaining a foothold in the British gas industry. The holding company was vested in my board. After we had handed over all papers and records concerning the several companies vested in the North Thames Gas Board, it became the Kent County Division, with an office at Tunbridge Wells reasonably accessible to its undertakings.

Most of the appointments at Headquarters and down to divisional level had been made before Vesting day. The top executives of the larger companies had exercised their options to go and be compensated under agreements pre-vesting date or had retired to take their pension; there was no provision for Directors without specific contracts. We had sufficient talent to fill the posts at Board Headquarters and in the six Divisions. I was well satisfied with the quality of the senior staff available for promotion or redeployment as and when opportunities might arise. There had been little or no recruitment from universities or technical colleges to fill future vacancies; not surprising in view of the threat of public ownership hanging over the industry for so long, added to which there was the public image of gas as a rather over-age survivor from the previous century. There was an exception to prove the rule: at the Board's Tar Works at Ordnance Wharf they had recruited just before nationalization as Assistant Mechanical Engineer, a young engineer who had read mechanical engineering at University College London and after war service had returned to University College to qualify also as a chemical engineer. He is now a familiar figure in the news as the Chairman of British Gas plc, Sir Denis Rooke.

Difficult decisons had to be made before we could present to the world at large our top management team in its final form. The Chief Accountant was already functioning in the run-up to Vesting day; one would normally go on to appoint the Chief Engineer and Commercial Manager, but there were some complications and I had to leave them to the end. All the functional posts, those which service the industry (Controllers in Sylvester's hierarchy), could be filled with able specialists from the companies: Coal, Coke, Tar, Stores Control and Purchasing;

then Personnel with two representatives to give recognition to the special circumstances of the co-partnership element in the former South Metropolitan Gas Company, and the Chief Technical Officer, who was to play an important part in the development of the future policy of the Board; then, just below the line, four service officers, the Architect and Surveyor, the Solicitor, the Publicity and Information Officer and the Chief Medical Officer.

The two appointments which rated as equivalent to Managing Directors were the Chief Engineer and the Commercial Manager, heading up the two main streams of the Board's activities. When the General Manager of the Croydon Gas Company exercised his right to resign, with ample consolation under a written agreement, confirmed by a hearing before an arbitration tribunal, it cleared the way for V.W. Stanton, the Commercial Manager of the South Suburban, to be uncontested first choice for Commercial Manager. He had strong support from the former Managing Director of his company, Tom Brown, who was now a part-time Member of the Board.

The first place you might expect to find a Chief Engineer would be in the Metropolitan Division. The holder of that post was too near retirement and would certainly have refused if asked. His Deputy, Clarence Stott, was an experienced chemical engineer, but he was half way through a multi-million-pound reconstruction of East Greenwich, the Beckton of the South Bank as I secretly called it. There was no one to take his place if he were to be taken away to deal with all the paper work and administrative trivia of a Chief Engineer's office. There were some young and ambitious Divisional Engineers who would have plenty to do putting their respective houses in order. So I made my choice and shook the establishment by seeking out the Managing Director of the Brighton and Hove Gas Company, Raymond Prince. He was a qualified gas engineer but essentially a businessman with a keen sense of order in all that he undertook; unflappable and with a well-controlled dry sense of humour. I feel certain he would much rather have stayed on at Brighton, but he worked hard and loyally with a small staff. Then when three years later increased accommodation became available at the new Head Office at Croydon he was joined by Stott, as Deputy and Chief Constructional Engineer, and supporting staff. They included Denis Rooke as Development Engineer on his return from 'the Methane Venturers' (See Chapter 11).

The Commercial Manager was having a difficult time and regrettably, since most of the sales were cookers and they were more efficient than the obsolete models that many of them were to replace, the success of the salesman's efforts did nothing to revive the sagging sales of gas in the domestic sector. Had it not been for some success in the industrial and commercial sectors, we should have had to put a very bold face on our prospects for the future of the Board in our first Report to Parliament. In our Fifth Report I had to admit to a decrease in overall sales of gas, at 1.7 per cent below the previous year. I came to the conclusion, like Admiral Beatty at the Battle of Jutland in 1916, that 'there was something wrong with our guns'. It was *gas* we should be selling, not hardware, and with much of our success in selling being in new cookers using less gas, to replace old ones, we should look to selling in new fields which could lead to increased sales of gas.

Co-partnership

I mentioned earlier that our first senior staff appointments included two Personnel Officers. Henry Lesser as Service Secretary of the South Metropolitan Gas Company had been in charge of industrial relations since 1927. He had unique experience of how co-partnership worked in practice when applied in accordance with the intentions of Sir George Livesey, Chairman of the Company for over twenty years until his death in 1908. His funeral was attended by numerous workmen and the procession passed through miles of streets lined with mourners and spectators, to the cemetery in South London. Co-partnership was the outcome of a late-nineteenth-century attempt to avoid strikes and disputes in industry by providing for profit-sharing and worker-participation in management. In many other companies which adopted co-partnership in the cause of good employee relations it had become little more than a bonus scheme with some annual get-togethers thrown in. The unions had seen to it that the Statutory Joint Consultative Councils, which were to replace Co-partnership Committees where these existed, were not to be part of the negotiating machinery. They met their match at the Old Kent Road, not least because wage rates, three old pence per hour in excess of the national, had been negotiated through the Co-partnership Committee and also because the Board had three Directors elected by the co-partners, two from the manual workers and one from the Staff. The Conservative Opposition made rather a thing about co-partnership as leading to industrial peace and prosperity. That did not wash in debate during the passage of the Bill through Parliament, although Gaitskell gave way to the extent of allowing the bonus to continue for two years. Co-partnership Committees where they existed would then give way to Joint Consultative Committees, to be set up under procedures agreed with the unions.

Bob Bulbrook, a Trench Inspector from Old Kent Road, led a vocal minority of those who would not accept the olive branch. He electrified the Conservative Party Conference at Earl's Court on 14 October 1949 with his 'working man's' attack on nationalization. Lord Woolton and Mr Eden congratulated him and hundreds of copies of his speech were sold. He was selected as North Kensington's Tory candidate from a list that included barristers and former candidates. He was in demand as a speaker all over the country (*Evening News* 10.1.52). For a time he was better known than anyone else in the South Eastern Gas Board. His fame was rather shortlived and his Tory affiliations distanced him from most of the workers. I cannot now recall whether he was ever at the Co-partnership Committee; certainly I never encountered him when I was in the chair. The meetings were on the lively side, with vocal protests led by Co-partner Golding, who when ruled out of order asked me go outside after the meeting ended, when he looked forward to 'knocking my block off'. Not then but a year later when the last meeting was held, he did make a point of looking for me outside, shook my hand and said, 'Well, you've won after all, Guvnor.' It was not my doing but the foresight of (Lord) Tom Williamson, the General Secretary of the NUGMW that finally brought peace. He saw that things were getting out of hand under his pleasant but not very forthright Local Secretary, and sent Jack Cooper, later Lord Cooper of Stockton Heath, to take over, which he did most effectively.

The Croydon affair

In retrospect this crisis of the winter of 1951/52 was a stupid and unnecessary piece of political shenanigan aimed at those who were seen as traitors to the capitalist establishment by going over to the other side. It was not to be taken lightly: only two years before, the Chairman of a Nationalized Board had been handed down a six-month sentence by the Lord Chief Justice for a breach of the building regulations at Scarcroft, his Board's headquarters. To begin at the beginning, our search for a Board headquarters had quickly homed in on a new and only part-finished head office for the Croydon Gas Company. Construction had begun in 1939 and was suspended when war broke out. Although the outside shell was completed, parts of the inside were left unfinished and could not be used until floors, walls and ceilings had been provided. By completing the unfinished building we could make room for our staff of approximately 120 in addition to the 240 employees of the East Surrey Division. Most of the work would require to be authorized by the Ministry under Defence Regulation 56A.

The authorizations – there were more than one – came in standard format with a description of the work to be carried out and authority to carry out that work on the face of the document and an estimate of the cost on the reverse. I have little doubt that it was being monitored outside as the work proceeded. On 27 November 1951 the Member of Parliament for Croydon put down a question to the Minister, asking for the amounts spent against the authorizations. Sir Herbert Williams was a former Chairman of the Public Accounts Committee and knew his way about. The Press was soon on the trail and, if not exactly guilty yet, we were under grave suspicion. The figures in the cost sheets had not been segregated as between items that required authorization and those that did not and would have to be analysed as a matter of urgency.

I secured an interview with the Permanent Secretary, Sir Donald Fergusson, and told him how matters stood. Meanwhile on the advice of Dick Johnson, my Deputy, himself a solicitor, and Roy Huxtable, the Board's Solicitor, and in accordance with my own inclinations, we went on 20 December 1951 for an opinion to Michael Rowe of counsel, in conference first and written later. It was very encouraging. He began with theatrical effect by holding up the letter of authorization. 'On the front I see a description of the work which is authorized to be done. I turn it over and see, not as part of the authorization but purely descriptive, an estimate of what it will cost to carry out the work that is authorized.' After some further advice on how to proceed, he suggested that we could put it all behind us and enjoy our Christmas holiday.

The written opinion did not depart in material particulars from what we had been told in conference. Under the general guidance of the Chief Accountant all expenditure since work began was analysed and recorded under headings of work subject to 56A and other work, all subject to counsel's advice and final decision. The conclusion was that the expenditure on work subject to 56A was within the amounts quoted in the authorizations. That it appeared was not enough, and at the Board meeting on 29 February 1952 the Secretary reported that more information was being requested about classes of work done under different authorizations and departures from approved standards. All they asked for was supplied and always as approved by counsel. Until then I had been feeling confident about the outcome, but the stream of questions seemed to be designed to trap us into an admission of wrong-doing. I took the precaution of negotiating a mortgage of £3,000 as a fighting fund if, in spite of all the evidence, I had to face a criminal charge. I would if necessary go down with all guns firing.

The Member for Croydon put down a question on 10 March to which the Minister of Fuel and Power, Mr Geoffrey Lloyd, replied that the work carried out had been referred to the Director of Public Prosecutions and he referred to 'arrangements he had made following the "Scarcroft inquiry".' I knew that would really hit the headlines: I was guilty before trial. I rang up Dorothea at home; she had already heard from some kind journalist who wanted to be first with the news and a photograph of my return in my chauffeur-driven car. She would take the family Vauxhall round to the garage where my official Daimler was kept and drive me home. The Press photographers surrounding my gates were mortified and went off in pursuit of easier prey. Copies of the analysis of the type and cost of work on the building were settled by counsel and sent to Chief Inspector Stevenson who was conducting inquiries for the DPP. He duly called and, after obtaining a statement from the architect, said he had completed his investigation and would report to the Director. And now the sequel:

Minutes of the Board Meeting 25 April 1952

> The Chairman reported that he had seen the Minister of Fuel and Power and Sir Donald Fergusson who had informed him that the Report received from the Director of Public Prosecutions disclosed no grounds to warrant prosecution; the Director had also found no ground for suggesting that anyone concerned with the work done at the Board's Headquarters had not acted in good faith or that the work was not substantially in accordance with the specifications which were approved from time to time by the Ministry.

It is said of the Irish that they will forgive but never forget. The Irish half of me was unwilling to do either for quite a long time: not on my own account, I was quite happy to fight my own corner, but because of the method chosen to attack us. The Parliamentary question hits blindly where it can most hurt, at own's own family. Ann was at Oxford reading Chemistry, and saw the headlines before we could warn her of what the Press would be printing and give the reassurance that things were not as bad as they seemed.

With these two problems behind me I could give my undivided attention to a situation which threatened not only the future of my

Board but of the whole gas industry. It could be summed up in a few words. After four years of strenuous effort to improve the efficiency of our operations we had been just about holding our own. In the fifth year the warning signals were clear to be read. Sales of gas were down by 1.7 per cent on the previous year, with sales in the domestic sector down by 2.8 per cent. This was, and would continue to be, the principal market for gas in the south east. Boards in the north and midlands with lower capital charges, access to cheap by-product gas from coke ovens and a buoyant industrial load were better placed to compensate for adverse factors which were eroding the market for gas in the domestic sector. However, it seemed to me that the writing on the wall was there for them also.

The Institution of Gas Engineers

My year as President of the Institution of Gas Engineers 1955/56 would provide opportunities and a platform from which to advertise my convictions about the best way to reverse the trend. When in 1929 new by-laws were approved as a condition of the grant of a Royal Charter, the President explained that owing to a *necessarily narrow* interpretation of the word *engineer* they (the by-laws) had to be amended to exclude from corporate membership those engaged on the supply side of the industry or as chemists; they would, however, be admitted as associates. I suppose it all depends in the last resort on what you want. I for one was quite satisfied to be qualified as a chemical engineer practising in the gas industry.

I had, however, been elected to the Gas Engineers in 1943 while still at the Air Ministry. When my old friend Falconer Birks at the end of his year as President suggested that I should stand for election to the Council I had a fairly shrewd idea of what was expected of me. The way to the Presidency requires a degree of unanimity among important Members and past Presidents, so I asked no questions. In the third year on the Council you stand for Vice-President and, there being no opposition, are elected for two years. In year 2 as senior Vice-President the pace hots up with requests to stand-in for the President and as chairman of certain committees. At the end of that fifth year, provided you have not committed any of the more serious crimes in the calendar and with a show of reluctance as unfit for this high office, you will allow your name to be included in the ballot list which will go to all members for the election of a President in the coming year.

I was fortunate that, in combining my duty to the Board of South Eastern Gas with what turned out to an exceptionally eventful year in the Institution, I had the support of J.E. Davies, my Chief Technical Officer. As time went on I grew to depend on him for wise assessments of the forces which might one day determine the future of the gas industry. He was as I recall one of the two delegates from the South Met. who came to Kensal Green to inspect my new benzole/sulphur plant at Kensal Green, (Chapter 5) and recommended its adoption at his company's works. He worked amicably with F.J. Dent the official research chemist to the gas industry and that opened a door that had always seemed to be closed in my time at the Gas Light and Coke Company. Davies went with Dent in 1937 on an inspection of the first commercial Lurgi installation for the total gasification of brown coal, serving a German town of 60,000 inhabitants. He kept in close touch with Dent's later work on the hydrogenation of coal under pressure, which began when facilities became available at Bournemouth, at a hydrogen plant which had previously supplied the Balloon Barrage.

My Presidential duties included visits to the several districts of the Institution and the Irish Gas Association, with a speech to be delivered at each. It was useful and stimulating to find that we all seemed to be be sharing the same problem of getting the industry going again. The arrangements for the Annual General Meeting, for which we had secured the new Festival Hall on the South Bank, were to include a visit by His Royal Highness Prince Philip, Duke of Edinburgh. He had indicated his desire to attend and to receive his scroll of Honorary Fellowship and would agree to address the meeting. I had secured a paper on liquid methane by James Burns, Chief Engineer and Leslie Clark, both of the North Thames, which was guaranteed to arouse a great deal of interest. William Wood Prince, whose company, Union Stockyards of Chicago, had founded the liquid methane project, was also present; otherwise it had to be much of the mixture as before, except that we had the new Minister, Mr Aubrey Jones, promised for lunch and a speech.

My Presidential address was to be an affirmation of the eventual resurgence of our industry. I based my case on reasonable assumptions as to what might be possible if we were ready to make use of all the resources already to hand and any others that could reasonably be foreseen. The root cause of our problem lay in the policies of the Coal Board. Effectively the sole supplier of our raw material, coal, they were in active competition in the market for our principal by-product, coke, and had not hesitated to use this situation to their advantage. The price of carbonizing coal had increased to five times its pre-war figure, and that of domestic coal to only three times pre-war. There was a time when coal had been bought on its value as raw material for gas manufacture: the new coal price structure made it clear that those days were unlikely to return. The coke market was well-organized but with little or no control over the price on which the economics of gas manufacture were dependent. As one way of lessening that dependence I mentioned complete gasification of coal, with the Lurgi process in mind, and the gasification of oil at gasworks or at 'more specialized works operated in connection with a refinery to receive such products as might be available': a reference to the Isle of Grain project which was at the stage of preliminary discussions with BP.

The New Jersey Gas Company in the United States had not hesitated to take on the highly variable whole-house heating loads, with winter temperatures as low as 6°F, and were rewarded with average annual sales of 1,000 therms per consumer. Here at home, with average sales of only 100 therms, we were even so having to meet some at least of the peak load. A recent survey had shown how 25 per cent of households visited had used the gas oven to keep the house warm in a cold spell. I concluded with a hypothetical study of 100,000 in an average mix of domestic, commercial and industrial consumers. The outline in my address was fairly sketchy. What did emerge was a 40 per cent increase in output overall, which would permit the introduction of a tariff for the large consumer competitive with alternative fuels. In short it should be our aim to provide an adequate service to the public for whole-house heating at a price they could afford and it could and should be done. The proposed increase in supply could best be achieved using modern techniques for making gas from oil. If I cannot claim any immediate enthusiasm among my colleagues for the merits of central heating as a market for gas I did at least convince myself.

I became a member of the Oxford University Appointments Committee in about 1947. The Committee decided to pioneer the idea of courses to bring scientific thinking to bear at the level of middle management. They were to be called the Oxford University Business Summer School. I thought at once of a suitable candidate for the first course, who could tell me if it was worthwhile, and nominated Denis Rooke, who was then still at the Tar Works. One unexpected outcome was a telephone call from someone I happened to know in one of the larger organizations. He said that I had a man on the course who would be very welcome in their organization if we didn't want him. I assured him that we did.

A.G. Higgins was the Assistant Secretary at the Institution of Gas Engineers. I had some useful talks with him about the possibility of middle management retraining to be sponsored by the Institution. He suggested that a good way of doing this would be to organize a course at one of the Oxford or Cambridge colleges during the Easter vacation. There would have to be experts with a wide choice of subjects for lectures and much of the time should be devoted to syndicate discussions. I said I thought that was a good idea and offered to write to my old college to see whether it could be arranged there. I received a rather cool reply. 'The College was well endowed and hitherto had not found it necessary to embark on such schemes.' Higgins made some further enquiries and was told that the best venue for sixty people for a week was Pembroke College, Oxford. It was just the right size to accommodate sixty comfortably.

Dr Haffner, Chairman of the Education Committee of the Institution, gave us the invaluable support of his committee. He also made a most useful contribution to the success of the courses by prevailing upon the Southern Gas Board to release the lecture theatre at their Oxford showroom. It was only two minutes' walk from the College, and there were all the proper facilities for presentation on stage and screen. The 'Pembroke Courses' had very good support from all the Area Boards and from the manufacturers of gas plant and equipment. The first course was initiated in April 1961 under Dr Haffner's direction. I see from a copy of the programme that I not only 'opened' the course but presided at the morning session. In 1986 they celebrated the twenty-fifth anniversary of the founding of the Pembroke Courses, so the time I spent in 'selling' the idea to the Council and to the Institution had not been time wasted.

Whole-house heating

My immediate problem was to promote the idea of a market for whole-house heating. Many of my colleagues were still obsessed with the problems of the peak load. It had been highlighted by Falconer Birks in 1947 in a paper read to the Fuel Luncheon Club. His observation that gas demand did not increase proportionately to declining temperature as measured by degree days but to the

1.4 power can be explained. At that time much of the gas equipment in people's houses, especially the ovens of gas cookers, was pressed into duty for the purpose of heating the house, but then only in extreme conditions. My conclusion had been that if gas were used for all purposes the effect of temperature on load would be more nearly linear. John Davies had obtained data from America, which I quoted in the Presidential Address in support of my contention.

In an industry so dominated by the engineer's ethos, the first essential was to convert the salesman before you could hope to convert the customers. In one district in the South Suburban Division there was a salesman who had been successful in selling central heating. In another district of another division I met a salesman who was reluctant to sell central heating 'because his customers could not afford it'. I let it be known that it was not for the salesman but for the customer to decide, provided that the salesman was strictly accurate in estimating the cost involved. Nevertheless progress was slow. The oil industry had gone in first with attractive prices and oil tanks were to be seen in many back yards. The industry as a whole would not support central heating as an objective and my old company, still much under the influence of its engineers, was reluctant to take on what they saw as an uncontrollable peak load. So I decided to go it alone and in 1959 there appeared our first advertisement for central heating in a national journal. I was told that it produced more responses in the North Thames than in my own Board!

Although progress seemed slow, it was gratifying to have a visit from the Chairman of De La Rue, owners of Potterton's, with the message that for the past year my Board had taken half his company's total output of central-heating boilers. That did not mean that other Boards were neglecting the heating load; some like Wales were selling large numbers of the new and more efficient gas fires, which recovered heat otherwise lost up the chimney. Another approach to whole-house heating was that of Wates, the builders, who in a new development were installing warm-air heating under the 'Halcyon' trade mark in new houses. Norman Wates was one of a new generation of house builders, who could build down to a price while maintaining quality in all its essentials. We gave warm support to an advertising venture at the Savoy promoting the sale of 'Halcyon' heaters, while slightly regretting that that this was not linked to water heating with its summer base load, as with normal central heating based on pipes and radiators.

In 1959/60 10,000 central-heating boilers were sold, together with 3,000 warm-air units. The pace of development can be seen from the fact that these figures had risen to 18,000 and 8,000 respectively in 1960/61, with some 25,000 and 17,000 in 1961/62 confidently predicted at the Harrogate Gas Sales and Service Conference towards the end of 1961. That conference itself proved a turning point in the industry's attitude to its future.

Oil gasification

Even before nationalization one of the South Eastern Gas Board's forerunners, the South Metropolitan Gas Company, had been experimenting with the production of town gas from oil fractions. A plant was constructed at the Sydenham gasworks using what came to be called the 'SEGAS' process and started production in 1953. A pilot plant had first been designed and built at Old Kent Road to prove the feasibility of a gasification process based on the catalytic gasification of heavy fuel oil. Results were encouraging and the full-scale plant was designed in collaboration with the Power Gas Corporation. This process was successfully tried with a wide range of feedstocks from light distillates, which were then becoming increasingly available, to heavy residual oils. Its flexibility provided the foundation for negotiations with British Petroleum for the use of whatever fractions became available as by-products from their refinery on the Isle of Grain.

On 30 August 1955 I signed an agreement with British Petroleum, represented by John Pattinson, Deputy Chairman, under which an oil gasification plant was to be built on a site adjacent to their refinery on the Isle of Grain. I had already met Pattinson as the Managing Director of the Abadan refinery during the war. The agreement provided for us to make town gas from a wide range of oil products at the option of the oil company. Site preparation began early in 1956 and the plant came into operation in the summer of 1958 to produce 20 million cubic feet of gas a day for supply to London and North Kent. We planned to quadruple output in two succeeding stages by 1964 to supply a wider area.

This was a period of very rapid change in the technology of oil gasification. Scarcely was each stage completed than it was rendered obsolete by a radically different process. When the International Gas Union met in New York, I took the opportunity of going privately with Davies down to Memphis to inspect a new development by Texaco. It used a wide range of oils, which were partially oxidized at high pressure in an atmosphere of pure oxygen in a single-stage process. The gas so produced is rich in carbon monoxide and has to be further treated to convert the carbon monoxide to hydrogen. To complete the process it needs to be mixed with a rich gas, which could be produced if necessary by the SEGAS plant or, better still, bought as refinery gas across the fence. A Shell version of this process was used in the second stage of the Isle of Grain development. There was a mounting oil industry surplus of the light petroleum fraction variously known as virgin naphtha or light distillate. We negotiated a variation in the contract for feedstock in the third plant to employ ICI externally heated catalytic reformers, which could only use virgin naphtha. They were already widely coming into use in other Area Boards. It should be emphasized that the first two plants had been installed with this change of feedstock as a possibility and were able to change over to naphtha without major conversion, as provided for in the 1955 contract.

Intermission II

On reaching the age of fifty you begin to give some thought to what the future will hold. You know now that the ordered way of life provided by office, profession or armed service will cease abruptly in five, ten or fifteen years' time. The pension which seemed like an unnecessary precaution in the ambitious thirties now begins to look like a prudent investment. The near-certainty that inflation could erode it towards the poverty line within the statistical life of the pensioner is not yet a pressing consideration. During my last two years in the South Eastern Gas Board I had come to the view that the sensible thing would be to leave when I was sixty. I could then look for other activities which would hopefully be more rewarding financially than working for the State. If I chose wisely these new activities need not be less interesting. After all some of the excitement was gone from the business by 1959. I had established to my own satisfaction at least that there was a future for the gas industry; we would have to be prepared to sell the heating load and find engineers able to design and construct a supply system geared to the seasonal variations which this entailed. We had shown the viability of a total concept of gas-making based on oil at the Isle of Grain. Even if all the other Boards did not agree with these policies we could always go it alone. By 1963 all this should be demonstrable and that was my target date for when I would be sixty and not too old to start again. That was how it looked in 1959.

Then came the invitation to be Deputy Chairman of the Gas Council, after Henry Jones had been nominated to succeed Harold Smith as Chairman from 1 January 1960. It would be for me a limited objective. Now 56 and three years older than my Chairman (who seemed in excellent health), it was most unlikely that I would ever succeed to his office. I would have to step down from the authority of a Chairman. I knew that in public estimation the Area Board is a lower formation: the decision was not in the end taken on logical grounds and I simply decided to take the job. My successor was to be Nigel Bruce, a one time associate and friend from the Fulham days who had returned from his war service in the Middle East at about the same time as myself, and had been Deputy Chairman of the North Thames Gas Board since 1956.

11
The Methane Venturers

Following a chance meeting on the liner Queen Elizabeth, W.A. Iliffe, Assistant to the President of the World Bank, handed a report entitled 'Liquid Gas for the United Kingdom', based on proposals by W.M. Morrison for Union Stockyards of Chicago, to Gordon Roach, a director of William Press & Company. His firm had many connections with the gas industry. A joint company with Demolition and Construction, D.C.-Wm. Press, was formed to examine new projects. It took an early part in the exploitation of Liquid Natural Gas, or LNG for short. Roach handed a copy of the report to Michael Milne-Watson, Chairman of the North Thames Gas Board. At the next meeting of the Gas Council, on 4 July 1954, the Chairman, Sir Harold Smith, reported approaches from Shell Mex-BP as to possible use of imported natural gas. Michael reported that the North Thames was examining a similar proposal from the International Bank.

I could have been the only one of the Council Members present who had a special reason to believe that this was something more than just a possibility. At the Air Ministry in preparation for D-Day we had modified some of the road tankers used by BOC to distribute liquid oxygen, to enable them to be ferried across the Channel or the southern North Sea in all weathers. They were to safeguard supplies of oxygen to the fighters and bombers during the advance through Europe into Germany. Then when I was getting ready to ship an oxygen plant to Okinawa, and rebuild it there for the planned attack on mainland Japan, I learned that the US Air Force intended to rely on liquid oxygen ferried several thousands of miles across the Pacific. I could see no insuperable difficulty in the plan to bring liquid methane across the Atlantic.

I had some informal talks with Michael, which amounted to this. Our two Boards, North Thames and South Eastern, both with access to the Thames Estuary, were well placed to receive the liquid methane tankers if the plans for importing LNG succeeded.

North Thames was the better situated of the two. They had a large tract of land at Canvey Island and a foreshore with deep water close by. Also he had a well established Board, successor to the one-time Gas Light and Coke Company, with considerable technical resources while I was still putting mine together. All in all it seemed clear to me that his Board was the one to take the lead. The Gas Council had no staff or facilities even to carry out a feasibility study. At the Council Meeting on 4 August 1954 it was resolved that our two Boards be 'asked to conduct on behalf of the Council an investigation into the technical aspects of the receipt, storage, handling and supply of natural gas imported in liquid form'. It was not what we wanted but I was prepared to leave it at that for the time being. As yet none of us had met Wm. Wood Prince, President of the Union Stockyard and Transit Company of Chicago, and the originator of a scheme that was creating so much interest: I had not long to wait.

One September day in 1954 I was standing by the lift in the hall of a slightly old-fashioned building in Victoria, where the joint enterprise of D.C.-Wm. Press had its headquarters. A small group of interested parties had been invited to meet Wood Prince and hear about his plan to deliver natural gas in liquid form to England. I guessed that the athletic figure also waiting for the old-fashioned elevator was indeed the Racquets Champion of the USA, and President of Stockyards of Chicago, the man we had come to hear. As an opener I complained about the slow speed of elevators in England; he responded in kind and then admitted that he would be addressing us soon. He began by claiming that as a mere meat-packer from the Mid-West he had some hesitation about addressing expert Britishers on a subject of such complexity as the liquefaction of methane and the transport of LNG to the UK. His initial plan was for the shipment of liquid methane on barges from the Gulf Coast to Chicago where it would be used both as a fuel and as a source of chill for the meat-packing plant. From experience with this it should be possible to advance to the shipment of liquid methane across the ocean to Britain. He quickly convinced us that the plan he had outlined with such clarity and so concisely was a worthwhile proposition. It was good news at a time when we had failed to find natural gas on-shore and were rapidly running out of competitive strength in the fight against oil and electricity. Michael was on leave in Corsica and as soon as I could get back to Croydon, I telephoned his office and asked his secretary to arrange a meeting with Wood Prince: he was reported to be returning through London at the end of a tour of his

European interests. Their meeting was a great success and led to a good understanding which was vitally important to the success of the Methane Venture.

A small group was assembled, consisting of Leslie Clark, Development Engineer of the North Thames, Andrew Morrison, and Donald Holmes, both I think from D.C.-Wm. Press. They spent seven weeks in the USA contacting in all some fifty organizations, and reported in December that the scheme was technically feasible, that practically all the special plant and machinery could be manufactured in the UK, that there was no reason to suppose liquid methane to be more dangerous than petroleum spirit and that suitable vessels could be designed and built (albeit at a cost two and a half times greater than oil tankers).

The November meeting of the Gas Council gave formal assent to the arrangement discussed informally between Michael and myself. The North Thames took over responsibility for progressing all further studies of the LNG project. From now on I am the Historian with an inside track to where the action was. For the next year and a half there was nothing to report, for the adequate reason that the first design of the tanks in River Barges constructed for use carrying liquid gas up the Mississippi from the Gulf had failed to survive endurance tests. They were constructed of steel, lined with balsa wood. The cooling-down process went well and there was no reason to suspect any weakness in the design until the tanks were allowed to warm up for inspection. The heavier natural gas fractions trapped as liquid in the pores of the balsa burst out with almost explosive violence and shattered the insulation. It was the old story of 'back to the drawing board'. There emerged the concept of the 'double barrier' which was used in the next generation of methane carriers. The liquid methane is carried in free-standing tanks of suitable cold-resistant metal, in our case aluminium. The tanks, one or more, are located in a steel balsa-lined hold which is part of the ship's structure. There is a gap at the side of fifteen inches, which serves several purposes. Normally filled with nitrogen gas to prevent the chance of explosion, it can be purged to permit visual inspection. In the event of a failure of the tank it would contain the contents until other remedies could be effected.

With this difficulty surmounted Wood Prince was ready to put the project on a sound commercial base. A joint venture company was set up in the summer of 1955 by Union Stockyard and the Continental Oil Company. Not well known yet in this country,

Continental was one of the fastest-growing and most progressive oil companies under the direction of its brilliant and imaginative Chairman L.F. ('Mac') McCollum. Constock, as the joint venture was called, was owned in equal shares by the two founders, with Continental providing the senior management. E.F. Battson, a Senior Vice-President of Continental, became President, with John Murphy as Vice-President. We never had reason to query their judgment in the years that followed. I have heard since that 'Mac' was taking a close interest and was monitoring all the recommendations. The rest of 1955 and most of 1956 was occupied with testing the redesigned barges. I would surmise that a great deal of time was spent also in the office of J.J. Henry, a rising firm of consulting naval architects in New York, solving the problems offered by this new cargo. 1956 was also my year of office as President of the Institution of Gas Engineers. I invited a paper from Jim Burns, Chief Engineer, and Leslie Clark, both of North Thames, who had done so much to push the LNG project along. Billy Wood Prince was an honoured guest.

Research continued throughout 1956 in the US, and in December Michael was ready to write a letter to Harold Smith outlining the steps required for a trial voyage using a converted oil tanker carrying 3,000 tons of liquid methane. Constock had a provisional contract for the supply of large quantities of methane in Venezuela. It was suggested that British interests should join with Constock to form a company for the purchase and transportation of the gas. An estimate of £7 million was given for a 30,000 dwt ship carrying 18,000 tons of LNG. The price envisaged for methane delivered to Canvey Island would be about 6d per therm. Provisional clearance for the landing of LNG had been obtained from the Ministry of Transport, the Home Office, Lloyds Register of Shipping and the Port of London Authority. Since the quantities involved would be greater than the North Thames could take in its own area, the Gas Council decided that a conference should be held to consider the importation of LNG as it might affect each Board individually.

In March 1957 the Chairman reported to the Gas Council that he and Milne-Watson had met Wood Prince and discussed proposals now being submitted. Michael was authorized to inform Constock that the gas industry in Great Britain was prepared to take such quantity as would be carried in a 30,000 ton dwt ship subject to trials in a 3,300 ton capacity ship being satisfactory and to the consents of the Ministry and the Treasury and subject to the terms of the contract being satisfactory to the Gas Council acting on behalf of any Boards concerned. These proposals were never in fact discussed and would have run on the rocks for several valid reasons. The Treasury would be unlikely to give unqualified approval for a large amount of hard currency dependent on tests which they were not qualified to judge. The approval of the Minister would at the relevant time be a matter for the incoming Minister, Lord Mills, of whom as they say, more anon, and finally the Venezuelan agreement was still in the air and in fact never came down to earth. On 3 July Michael was able to report, following a visit to the US accompanied by Dr Burns, agreement with Constock on the presentation of a new proposal. It was for a joint company to buy, transport and sell methane in the UK. Constock had agreed to set aside the long-term features of the March offer, if the Gas Council would join them in a company to buy and convert a tanker to carry 2,200 tons of LNG.

The Methane Pioneer

Ministry of Power approval was given on 26 July 1957, after fresh representations had been made following the visit to the United States. The Minister, Lord Mills, made it quite clear in his letter just what he was approving. His approval was for a plan whereby the Council, jointly with Constock, would buy and convert a second-hand tanker to carry liquid methane. The cost to the Gas Council was expected to be in the region of £715,000 for the tanker and its conversion and £300,000 for the shore installation at Canvey. 'It would be clearly understood,' he wrote, 'that even if the experiment proved successful the Gas Council would remain absolutely free on its conclusion to decide whether or not to enter into any further contracts for the supply of liquid methane.' Ministerial approval had been preceded by the issue of the Petroleum (Liquid Methane) Order 1957. In effect this provided that a vessel carrying liquid methane and so labelled, might load and discharge its cargo at any harbour having installations constructed for the purpose.

It was now a time for action and an ex-Liberty ship, the *Normarti*, a type C1-M-AV1 Liberty ship, was purchased by Constock on 25 November 1957 in Nassau. Conversion to carry 5,000 cubic metres of LNG was to be to the designs of J.J. Henry Co. Inc. of New York who had been preparing their studies since 1954. The work was to be carried out by the Alabama Dry Dock and Shipbuilding Company at Mobile on the mouth of the Alabama River. The firm were specialists in conversions and repair and work began there on 2 December 1957. Construction of the aluminium tanks was undertaken by McDermot's of Morgan City in Louisiana, two hundred miles west, to designs by Arthur D. Little Inc. The aluminium was supplied initially by Reynolds Metals Inc., but certain components had later to be obtained from the Aluminium Company of America. The important work of designing and fabricating the insulating panels of balsa wood with hardwood facings and trim was carried out by Gamble Brothers at Louisville, Kentucky. The formalities for renaming the ship *Methane Pioneer* with British registration in the Port of London were in hand. Stephenson Clarke, a long-established firm of ship-owners and managers, were appointed ship's agents, dealing with crewing, victualling, bunkering and all else besides.

Meanwhile the administrative structure was being established. Subject to Treasury approval, the Gas Council authorised the payment to Constock in November 1957 of half the purchase price of the *Normarti*. Heads of agreement were signed on 20 January 1958 by Sir Harold Smith, for the Gas Council (with Ministerial approval) and by William Wood Prince for Constock. These provided for the formation of a joint company, named British Methane Limited, with equal shareholdings by nominees of the two organizations. The heads of agreement covered two stages:

(1) A pilot scheme.
(2) A joint venture to import liquid methane into the United Kingdom in specially constructed tankers.

The company was registered in the Bahamas for tax reasons and this required that a majority of the Directors had to be nationals of that country and Board meetings had to be held there. Michael Milne-Watson was nominated as the Gas Council representative, with myself as alternate, and E.F. Battson represented Constock. Hugh Wright, a banker and Chairman of the Bahamas International Trust Company, who looked after our finances, was elected Chairman at this first meeting and with two Bahamian nationals, the Hon. Godfrey Higgs and Mr L.C. Higgs, made up the requisite majority of Resident Directors.

For practical convenience an advisory committee was set up which was able to have its meetings closer to home, though still by law outside the UK. The Gas Council nominees were Sir Harold Smith, Michael and myself, with F.R. Darling of the North Thames as Secretary. Constock was represented by Ed. Battson and Wood Prince. The Committee met regularly, usually in some well-favoured capital, and was quite an effective means of keeping progress under review. Any advice it tendered to its parent in Nassau was, needless to say, given due consideration in the boardroom there.

Constock purchased a site on a loop of the Calcasieu River near the town of Lake Charles in the State of Louisiana, about 185 miles west of New Orleans and 150 miles east of Houston. It was conveniently placed for a supply of natural gas from a four-inch high-pressure pipeline from the East Moss Lake Field of the Texas Gas and Transmission Company. The gas was 85 per cent methane and contained carbon dioxide and sulphur compounds and other impurities. The liquefaction plant was designed to separate out the heavier fractions, to be used to fuel the power plant, and to remove the impurities. The whole complex was built on a barge self-contained as to steam and power. It was towed into position in a specially cut and dredged inlet next to the storage tank and the ship loading facilities. Work was well under way when Leslie Clark visited the site in April 1958 to inspect and report on progress.

Denis Rooke, by this time the Deputy Manager of the Board's Tar Works at Ordnance Wharf, had been seconded in 1957 from South Eastern to the North Thames group at Canvey, working on design and construction of the terminal. He was appointed to represent the Gas Council on site in the USA. Conversion of the tanker and other construction, all of which centred on Lake Charles, was being carried out at several different locations, some hundreds of miles apart. Work was proceeding steadily with just a few unusual obstacles. Serious difficulty was experienced in the production of flawless welds on the aluminium tanks for LNG. Denis found that, to speed up the work, welding was continuing well into the humid Louisiana night. The welding flaws were traced to water condensing on the metal to be welded. With simple precautions welding continued and passed the tests. At Canvey Island the gas reception facilities were being completed. They included an existing jetty to be adapted, and two insulated tanks each to hold 1,000 tons of liquid methane. The liquid was to be regasified by simple heat exchange with water (more sophisticated methods were to be used later), before transfer along a high pressure line to join the Board's Shellhaven pipeline for delivery to Romford. Here it would be reformed to produce a gas compatible with town gas.

By early 1959 conversion of the *Methane Pioneer* was finished and sea trials undertaken, together with tests of the loading system. The minutes of the meeting of the Gas Council on 7 January 1959 record the following: 'The Chairman reported that, as authorized at the last meeting, arrangements had been made for Mr Milne-Watson and Mr Hutchison to visit the USA in order to give approval to the sailing of the *Methane Pioneer* on its first trial voyage.' I suppose that if I had known then as much as I have learned since about 'unlimited liability without fault', I might have suggested an indemnity, but we were carefree and happy to be in at the beginning of the end of a long trail that began for me five years before, waiting for a lift in a building in Victoria.

We flew to Lake Charles, accompanied by Dr Burns to give some extra technical support to our decision. We took our duty very seriously and, observing that the LNG tanks were purged and the manholes open, we all descended into the 30-foot depth to inspect the structure and the dye penetration tests of which the evidence still remained. Our guide was Denis Rooke who had led the team responsible for the minute inspection of every inch of every weld in Tank 4. I took time off to look round the liquefaction plant, which I had noticed was designed round an expansion turbine. The principle of this elegant machine was perfected by the brilliant young scientist Piotr Kapitza who took Cambridge, and even the great Lord Rutherford, by storm in the 1920s and was prevented from returning in 1934 while on his customary vacation in his native Russia. He accepted the inevitable and among many other interests in Russia set out to improve oxygen production. His novel radial axial turbine had a much higher efficiency than the conventional impulse type. I have been wondering if the early liquid methane storage installation in Moscow was inspired by Kapitza and Cambridge.

Following our inspection, and in full agreement with Constock representatives, we signed the release note. This was confirmed by Captain Gibson who was in command. The *Methane Pioneer* sailed from Lake Charles on 28 January and soon encountered severe weather and Force 10 was logged, with twenty degrees of roll and seven degrees of pitch. Taking the southerly passage by way of the Azores, *Methane Pioneer* came in out of the mist on a bitterly cold morning to dock at Canvey on 20 February 1959. For the record, here are the names of the intrepid mariners who undertook this first voyage:

J.W. Hunt, Constock, Team Leader
D.E. Rooke, Gas Council, Watch Keeper

F. Brooks, A.D. Little, Watch Keeper
P. McIntyre, Gamble Brothers, Watch Keeper
J. Kenney, Constock, Instruments
P. Arthur, Stephenson Clarke, Marine Engineer
C. Ritter, Constock, Rep. of Management

It was a formidable load of extras for a small cargo ship, and even the sick bay had to be pressed into service for normal accommodation. 'Mr Therm's Tanker arrives' and 'Londoners Cook by Texan Gas' were among the headlines from a generally enthusiastic press. Unloading proceeded without delay and *Methane Pioneer* returned for another cargo, completing seven return voyages and delivering about 12,000 tons of methane in the year. Denis Rooke took part in one round trip. The cost to the Gas Council at £206,000 was well within the estimate. Later the vessel had some profitable charters for other liquids to set off against the cost of the trials.

Conch International Methane

The outstanding success of the first transatlantic crossing by the *Methane Pioneer* was sufficient to satisfy most reasonable critics that the transport of liquid natural gas was a feasible proposition. The success of the six extra voyages helped to convince any remaining doubters that it could be a commercially viable proposition as well. Shell Petroleum had been interested from the beginning and had made some studies in their tanker division. A downturn in oil prices had determined them to put the work aside for the time being. Anxious to catch up on the two lost years, and probably feeling that we were so far ahead that they should await the outcome of the *Methane Pioneer*'s voyage, they negotiated to examine the ship during the warm-up for inspection after the first voyage. Satisfied with what they had seen they entered into an agreement with Constock to set up a new organization to be known as Conch International Methane for future operations and capitalized at 40 per cent each by Shell and Constock and 20 per cent by Stockyards. There would have been substantial compensation for all the work that had gone into the project in preceding years.

On 1 January 1960 Sir Henry Jones became Chairman of the Gas Council in succession to Sir Harold Smith, who had retired, and I succeeded Henry as Deputy Chairman. It was during my first week in office that the Council heard of an impending merger of the LNG interests of Royal Dutch-Shell and Constock. Michael Milne-Watson reported that the discussions had reached a stage where both parties wished to have the general approval of the Council before finalizing the merger. This was readily given subject to the usual safeguards, and Conch International Methane became the supplier of LNG and our partner in British Methane Limited. Tom Grieve of the Gas Division, with Philip Drew, later Peter Coppack, to head up the project, were our contacts. Six months later Michael told the Council that proposals would be submitted in the near future for the importation of LNG on a large scale. Henry proposed that he, Michael and myself as the Council's representatives on the British Methane Advisory Committee should be authorized to consider the proposals, discuss them with Conch and submit to the Council a scheme for importing liquid methane.

After considering a number of options, Shell had come down firmly in favour of Algeria, then still a French colony where France was intent on continuing to develop her interests. These included large reserves of high-grade natural gas. The Advisory Committee of British Methane, meeting in The Hague in April 1960, heard reports on prospects in Nigeria and Libya. I had the impression that it would take quite a long time to bring these alternatives to fruition. Then, early in 1961, Conch submitted a firm proposal for a fifteen-year agreement to import Algerian gas. The scheme was based on two 167,000 barrel ships to deliver 86 million cubic feet per day of gas from the Hassi R'Mel field. This field, some 280 miles south of Algiers, was third in size only after the Dutch Groningen and Texas Panhandle fields. A hierarchy of French companies was involved. In particular, Conch would have a 50 per cent stake (later 40 per cent) in the company which would own and operate an ocean terminal at Arzew. It was the Cie. Algerienne de Methane Liquide (CAMEL) and would sell the liquid gas f.o.b. at Arzew to British Methane Limited, who would deliver it to the Gas Council at Canvey on a c.i.f. basis.

Soon after I went to the Council I sensed the need for a Committee to provide a forum for the discussion of technical matters relating to the production of gas. The prospect of a centralized supply of natural gas lent force to the arguments in favour and the Production Policy Committee met for its first meeting on 2 August 1960. The Gas Council had already set up a working party of the Area Boards involved to consider the distribution of the gas they were to receive. Denis Rooke was available in the newly established post of Development Engineer (see p. 210); in time to take part in the planning and execution of this the first stage of a fully integrated gas supply to all the independent Area Gas Boards. The gas would be delivered to Canvey as liquid under arrangements made by British Methane Limited and regasified there for delivery to seven, later eight, of the twelve Area Boards. It would have been uneconomic to extend the supply system beyond these eight at this stage. Our recommendation that there should be a single uniform price for all gas delivered was agreed by the Council. It was helpful to have this precedent during the next development of gas supply when there was enough gas from the North Sea to satisfy the demands of all twelve.

The Conch proposal was equivalent to one tenth of the output of the entire gas industry in Britain at that time. The c.i.f. price at Canvey would be about 6.5d per therm. The tankers were to be owned by British shipowners and chartered under the British flag by British Methane Limited: their joint cost would be £9.75 million. New tanks and a new jetty would be required at Canvey at a cost, to include pipework, pumps and control gear, of some £3.5 million. The Council could not itself purchase gas and contracts provided for each Board to be responsible for its own purchases through the common user pipeline network. Each Board accepted responsibility for the pipelines to be constructed in its area to specifications laid down by a working party of the Production Policy Committee.

Algeria's future was beginning to seem rather insecure: however, limitation of Gas Council investment to the UK, association with powerful and wealthy partners, and the availability of alternative uses for the tankers together with other sources of supply, made the risks acceptable. In the spring of 1961 I went with Henry Jones, Michael Milne-Watson and Leslie Clarke to visit the Saharan oil and gas fields and meet representatives of the French administration. The Rt. Hon. Richard Wood had succeeded Lord Mills as Minister of Power in 1959, though the latter with a seat in the Cabinet as Paymaster-General retained an overlordship for the energy industries. Although he had authorized the first experiment and it had been a success as the seven voyages of the *Methane Pioneer* demonstrated, Mills was definitely not in favour of the further plan to import liquid methane in bulk. So, even if we had a more sympathetic and accessible Minister, we faced the risk of effective opposition at Cabinet level.

Much time was spent on refining the initial agreement to the point at which binding contracts could be exchanged. There were lengthy negotiations on detailed pricing down to the finest fraction of a centime. Agreement could not be reached and the final meeting in Paris was adjourned. As we left to go Wood Prince caught my eye and we went to have a drink at an establishment more suitable perhaps for those looking for a night out. We went over the arguments once more and came to a figure in Francs which we thought was just about right and which Billy noted down on the inside of a glossy book of matches advertising our meeting place. He told me later that it took some explaining away next morning, when he found he had left it on the dressing table of the Ritz where he and his wife were staying. The story has a happy ending, because that was the price agreed at the resumed meeting. So finally on 25 May 1961 Michael was empowered to initial, on behalf of the Gas Council, a provisional agreement with Conch and British Methane to import liquid natural gas into Britain.

The Minister of Power had been kept informed of the negotiations and the final proposal was submitted to Richard Wood on 30 May 1961. Approval was announced in the House of Commons by the Minister on 3 November 1961. This bare account leaves out much of the political tension surrounding the issue. Opposition continued in the Cabinet right up to the last minute. Lord Robens, Chairman Designate of the National Coal Board, made some effective sallies in the committee room of the House of Commons and at the Ministry. The late Sir Martin Flett, Deputy Secretary at the Ministry, had given us all support in his power, but always came up against strong opposition from Lord Mills, when Minister of Power and later as Paymaster General. I have heard that we were on the point of losing our case altogether in Cabinet when support came from an unexpected quarter in the person of Rab Butler; perhaps just another case of politics being the art of the possible. The formal ceremony, requiring signatures of almost everyone present, took place on neutral ground in a house in Paris hired for the occasion; with lawyers and advisers present on both sides and photographers recording every detail.

Methane Princess and Methane Progress

The signing of the agreements marked the conclusion of the first phase of the methane operation. It was still necessary to maintain close liaison and agreement between the parties on such matters as the construction and delivery of the ships, standards of construction generally and arrangements of all kinds with public and other bodies. This was after all the first venture of its kind anywhere in the world. A joint service company, Methane Services Limited, was set up with Directors Michael Milne-Watson, Philip Drew of Shell and Chuck Filstead of Constock and Roy Huxtable, who had come across from South Eastern Gas to be Secretary of the Gas Council, as Secretary.

The heads of agreement provided for the Gas Council to finance and build the methane tankers for charter to British Methane Limited. It was a whole new world of finance where none of us had experience or expertise. David Robarts of Robert Fleming, merchant bankers, was consulted and came up with a plan. Out of a list of possibles, Houlder Brothers and Conch were selected and agreed to take responsibility for one ship each. The tankers were to be built to Conch designs supplied by the Gas Council and constructed in a yard of the charterer's choice. We left it to Michael Milne-Watson to seek agreement as to how the contracts for the tankers were to be allocated. Tenders were invited from three yards and it was decided to place an order for one vessel each, from Vickers Armstrong at Barrow-in-Furness and Harland and Wolff at Belfast. Because of the novelty of the design and its special features, Vickers were appointed to be the lead shipyard and to receive the designer's drawings first and process them for use in the yards. Although aluminium was coming into use in some of the smaller warships to save weight, there was no experience at either yard of what was involved or the precautions that would be essential in the fabrication of aluminium tanks for LNG. The design specified three separate cargo holds, insulated by means of balsa wood panels fixed to the sides and base. Each hold was to have three free-standing cargo tanks, free to expand and contract and constrained by carefully designed hard-wood keys at top and bottom. All this had been tested and tried in the *Methane Pioneer*. A new feature was that each tank was divided into two by a liquid-tight centre line bulkhead, designed to give added strength against the effect of rolling and minimize 'slosh' in empty tanks. It is reported that this added feature just about reached the limit of the design capability of the computer in the J.J. Henry office. They had to await delivery of a new and yet more powerful computer to solve the next problem. It was to develop designs for the tanks in the bow and stern to conform to the narrowing profiles of the ship's bow and stern sections, with a gain of a few valuable percentage points in the cargo capacity.

The *Methane Princess* was launched in June 1963 and named by

Mrs Wood Prince, followed by the *Methane Progress* in September, named by Lady Jones. Both ships had the balsa wood insulation already in place but the decks were only temporary to permit the tanks to be installed at the fitting out berths. The Belfast yard completed the fitting out and delivered the *Progress* to enter service on 26 May 1964 one month ahead of its Barrow-in-Furness rival. Having less experience of specialized work they had followed implicitly the instructions and advice of the Constock experts and avoided the difficulties experienced by the lead Yard.

The French experience

The French, though late starters, were not far behind Constock and Conch at each stage of the race to be first with full-scale operation. Quite properly denied access to Constock know-how, except so far as it had to be disclosed in a multitude of patents, they entrusted development to a consortium of shipbuilders, each pursuing its own preferred solution. Gaz de France held a watching brief, and it seems there were no secrecy barriers between the participants. The outcome was the conversion of a wartime Liberty ship to carry three experimental insulated LNG tanks. Two were made of aluminium and one of nickel steel. With widely differing configurations, all three used variants on the theme of PVC foam blocks and perlite for insulation. Conversion began in March 1961. Named the *Beauvais*, the trial ship was ready for sea in March 1962. All the shipyards had access to the results and were encouraged to acquire first-hand experience by sending their representatives to sea during the six months that the trials lasted. The final outcome was a ship of about the same size, speed and cargo capacity as the *Princess* and *Progress* to fit in with operating schedules at the port of loading, but with a totally different concept of the cargo containers. There were to be six vertical cylindrical tanks, with space for a small experimental one in the bows. The tanks were constructed of 9 per cent nickel steel and the bottom and top were adaptations, for these special purposes, of the classical dish ends of regular engineering practice. This was to meet a specified requirement that the tanks had to be capable of being discharged by gas pressure in an emergency.

Named *Jules Verne*, the French ship entered service in 1965 and, like *Princess* and *Progress*, served the fifteen years of her contract without major incident. I have been indebted to Roger Ffooks for most of the information about the French developments. His book *Natural Gas by Sea* is a comprehensive and well-documented record of the subject. He concludes the chapter on the first commercial LNG ships with this assessment: 'In summary, therefore, it can be said that most of the problems experienced by the early – and even later – LNG ships to date have been due to the conventional parts of the ship developing faults or to careless operation.'

The port and the LNG plant

My first sight of Arzew was in March 1961 when it was just a typical Mediterranean harbour. Although large in area it appeared to be open to gales from most northern quarters. There was a sloping beach up which the fishermen could haul their boats to safety. Their cottages clustered round the harbour, while on the higher land above and to the west were some superior dwellings, probably the summer homes of the well-to-do from Oran. A good-sized estaminet *La Fontaine des Gazelles* and a Total filling station just about completed the scene down at the harbour. On a hilltop dominating it all was a large fort still occupied by legionnaires, and a life-size statue of the Virgin Mary on a high pedestal.

We had come to Arzew by air from Algiers, calling at Ghardaia, a beautiful and restful oasis town, and Hassi R'Mel, a typical oilmen's encampment in the middle of the desert. What the last lacked in the luxuriant foliage and palms of the oasis, it made up in the comfort of the quarters. We were most hospitably entertained at a dinner calculated to make the Frenchman feel at home and the visitor wish it was always like this. *Loup de mer flambé* was just one of the surprises of an evening spent nearly 300 miles from the sea. Meanwhile the flares at the well heads indicated that testing and development were essential preliminaries to all that was being planned at Arzew. Our next stop was at Oran to meet the Departmental Chief Engineer of the *Ponts et Chaussées*, that most respected and successful national organization responsible for roads, bridges and harbours and some of the most beautiful and dramatic lighthouses anywhere to be seen. As we drove down to Arzew our host of the night before pointed to a rocky outcrop with some high hills beyond. 'There,' he announced, 'is your new harbour.' It was a small abandoned quarry which he proposed to attack with all the resources of the modern civil engineering profession, to supply the thousands of tons of graded rock that would be required for the breakwaters giving shelter to the new port, also foundations for the new piers and infill for the large area of foreshore on which the new liquefaction plant would be built. Being a realist, our host was already planning for his return to metropolitan France, and had his eye on an appointment which included maintenance of the motor race track at Le Mans. I can only suppose he was a keen follower of the sport.

I hope he got what he wanted. It may have come sooner than he expected: on 3 July 1962 De Gaulle signed an instrument giving independence to Algeria. At the meeting of the Gas Council on 2 August Michael reported that work had not yet started on the harbour. There was as yet no formal constitution for the new state, and power rested with the revolutionary *Bureau Politique*. Ben Bella, then a member of the Bureau, appreciated the importance of the LNG project to the economic future of the newly emerging independent state of Algeria. He announced his intention of going to Arzew on 14 September to inaugurate the start of work on the port. From then on the signals were all set for full speed ahead. The ceremony was attended at short notice by Michael and Henry. It was an impressive demonstration of the popularity of the new regime and it came as no surprise when Ben Bella became President under the new constitution. His next (and last!) appearance at Arzew was on 17 September 1964 when he formally inaugurated the production of LNG and the commencement of deliveries. The *Methane Princess* was lying alongside the new pier for the preliminary cooling of its tanks. It was an event on the grand, even imperial, scale. A cavalcade of eighty cars and buses escorted by motor cycle outriders brought official guests, the diplomatic corps and Algerian officials from Oran. There was a long oration by the President and lunch in the fort, now an empty relic of an imperial past. There was one familiar figure on our side, this time an honoured guest: Michael Milne-Watson had resigned from the gas industry at the end of March to join the steel industry (not yet renationalized) as Chairman of Richard Thomas and Baldwin. Regular deliveries of LNG to Canvey began on 12 October with the arrival of the *Methane Princess*, and the second cargo by the *Methane Progress* on 27 October 1964.

I do not recall any interruption in the delivery of methane through the pipelines after the whole system had settled down and that did not take long. There was a small preliminary hiccup when, in spite of routine draining and swabbing of the pipelines, methane hydrate, a white solid, looking uncommonly like snow, built up and blocked the northern section of the pipeline from Canvey. Careful manipulation of the pressures persuaded it to return to the nearest 'pig-trap'. There to the astonishment of the onlookers it was demonstrated that snow could be set alight and continue to burn. Several hundred gallons of methanol injected at the right point cured that problem. Unlike the *Pioneer*'s cargoes, very little of the imported methane had to be reformed to produce town gas directly. The steam reforming process developed by ICI to produce hydrogen for making fertilizers came to the rescue of the gas industry in 1960, just when most needed, using as feedstock a light petroleum distillate, surplus at the refineries and in plentiful supply. The gas produced did however have to be enriched by the addition of one or other of the 'rich' gases available: refinery gas if convenient, or propane or butane (at a price) or methane made by one or other of the processes developed in the industry's research laboratories. Imported methane available at the turn of a tap to the eight Boards connected to the pipeline was the preferred choice but there was room for all in a rapidly expanding gas industry.

In retrospect

There was one threat to a continuing place for LNG in the gas industry's plans for its future. In Chapter 14, entitled 'North Sea: Prospecting', I tell how the Gas Council went into the North Sea to look for gas and in Chapter 15, 'North Sea: Discovery', how we found it. When regular deliveries of LNG began in October 1964, we had completed the second year of a seismic survey in association with other American partners. The results were most encouraging: very large structures were located at considerable depth, which if they contained gas, not water, could revolutionize our industry. We did not even know if the rock was porous or plain solid; but nor did anyone else and the strictest secrecy was observed on all sides. Licences to search for gas and to retain what we might find 'to the exclusion of all others' were issued in September 1964 to the ritual cries of disappointment and favouritism; we knew we had not done too badly. It so happened that Shell were involved in two of our prime prospects and presumably knew as much as we did. There was a general shortage of drilling rigs and none forthcoming until 1966. Consumption was rising at 8 per cent per annum and the deliveries from Algeria were already pre-empted. In this atmosphere of uncertainty it seemed reasonable to examine a scheme put forward by Conch for a supply of 100 million cu. ft. per day of natural gas from Nigeria.

A party including myself and Denis Rooke for the Gas Council and Peter Coppack and Chuck Filstead for Conch left for Lagos on 22 August 1965. Our main objective was to be assured of adequate supplies of natural gas and a suitable site to process and load it on to tankers. They were expected to be twice the tonnage of their predecessors owing to the longer passage from Bonny Island to Canvey. We aimed to secure Federal Government support for the scheme, with pioneer status and authority to export; from the Regional Government of the Eastern Region access to land for purchase and other facilities on reasonable terms. A consortium of Shell and BP had been responsible for exploring and producing oil and gas since 1937, mainly in the Eastern Region. They were flaring in excess of 200 million cu. ft. per day and had located considerable reserves of 'dry' gas. Supply seemed to be no problem. The Federal Minister of Industries and the Federal Minister of Power were both well briefed and questioned us closely on many aspects of our proposal. I think they were reasonably satisfied, and prepared to grant pioneer status and export licences. Our interviews at Enugu, the capital of the Eastern Region with the Prime Minister and the Minister of Town Planning, were on a more relaxed note, but with a firm intention to secure a square deal for Nigeria, and sufficient gas left to establish a petrochemical industry.

Bonny Island at the mouth of the Bonny River, part of the River Niger Delta, had some surprises in store. Approachable only by river launch or helicopter, it had a substantial Anglican cathedral, a native school founded on English public school lines, several quite large houses gently decaying away, and a large burial ground segregated on strict racial lines. Yellow fever had taken its toll and it was sad to read the names of so many young men who had died within a year or two of arriving to seek fame and fortune. They were commemorated by cast-iron gravestones, sent out with the next shipload of young hopefuls. Two sites suitable for a liquefaction plant were inspected from the air; road access was almost impossible. There was ample room and depth of water for methane tankers. Our conclusion was that it did not seem impossible that a first stage could be commissioned within two and a half years of the signing of a contract.

1965 was a bad year for the North Sea prospectors. Two drilling rigs were found unsuitable for the conditions in the North Sea. Out of ten holes drilled or abandoned, only one was a producer. That was the first well drilled on BP's West Sole Field. It was significant as a pointer to the hoped-for outcome of drilling into the much larger structures further south. In 1966 our highest hopes were fulfilled and halfway though the year we knew that there was no case for a second LNG, at least for another twenty years.

As I write this the twenty years have passed. The gas industry has grown and expanded to five times its 1960 size, has for all practical purposes outgrown its own resources, has been importing in bulk from the Norwegian side of the Median Line, and will have to go on doing so, whatever Ministers may say; that is if it is not too late already with Europe having grabbed all there is for sale. The contribution of LNG I may seem small beer compared with the billions which keep surfacing in any discussion of the future. It did however come at a time when the whole industry was poised to expand at a rate of 10 per cent for as long as anyone cared to predict. There was no sign yet of any shortage of light distillate at a very attractive price; reformed and blended with methane to town gas standard this represented some 25 per cent more gas available for sale. Then when deliveries from the North Sea made inevitable the conversion of all gas using appliances to use natural gas LNG served an additional function as a convenient storage of gas against the seasonal demand. Several large storage tanks were installed at Canvey for the purpose.

Postscript

In the summer of 1969, sailing with Lord Runciman in his yacht *Bondicar* and other friends down the coast of Spain bound for the Mediterranean, I saw in the space of twelve hours all three Methane carriers, which at that date represented 97 per cent of the world's LNG fleet. The *Methane Princess* was proceeding south in the last of the twilight and the *Methane Progress* was going north. Twelve hours later the Watch called me up in Homer's 'rosy-fingered dawn' to witness the *Jules Verne* bound for Le Havre. I felt happy to have been in at the birth of a new idea and to have such convincing proof that it was alive and well.

12
Research, Development and Design

The origins of research in the gas industry

At Vesting day the Gas Council became responsible for the industry's research. For the first two years the Boards were too busy putting their own houses in order to be receptive towards any proposals that might come their way. There were two research organizations qualified to undertake corporate research for the gas industry: the Gas Research Board, founded just before the war to take over and extend research previously carried out at Leeds under the aegis of the Institution of Gas Engineers, and the research organization of the Gas Light and Coke Company which dated back to 1924. It was in two parts: Watson House, whose research activities covered all the fields of domestic and industrial utilization of gas, and the Fulham Laboratories, responsible for research into all aspects of gas manufacture.

Sir Edgar Sylvester recognized the responsibility of the Gas Council for research, but he retired before he could get much beyond setting up a Research Advisory Committee. He did, however, establish a precedent whereby the Chairman of the Gas Council was Chairman of the Committee and Harold Smith took over from him.

Sylvester used to ask my advice occasionally, but it was really Sir Harold Smith, as Deputy first and then Chairman, who was responsible for the decisions taken, and he used to consult me fairly regularly. I felt it was too soon to think about a central organization in overall charge of research but that we should build on the firm foundations of what we had. I thought that we should involve the Area Boards in the aims and objectives of the research programmes and suggested that we should plan to have three main centres, London with Fulham and Watson House, the Midlands with a relocated Gas Research Board covering gasification and industrial gas, and a third station to be located somewhere in the north, either Scotland or in the area of the Northern Board, with objectives yet to be defined.

I was beginning to feel that there was too much emphasis on a chemical approach to research. Sylvester with his keen accounting outlook pointed out that if the gas industry had to replace its distribution system, much of it sixty years old at current cost, we would be bankrupt. But the engineers were not yet ready to visualize a place for research in a scene they had dominated for a century, and we did not press the case for a third research station, leaving it to develop naturally when the need could be seen to arise.

From an early date I was able to recommend that the Council should give further support to the work that Dr Dent, as Assistant Director of the Gas Research Board, was doing to advance the knowledge and practice of coal gasification processes at high pressure. The Board HQ was at Beckenham in South London. Dent had a base at Bournemouth where he was making good use of one of my wartime hydrogen plants, at the Poole gasworks. It was taken over by the Gas Company at close to scrap value when Balloon Command was stood down and the hydrogen plants were being disposed of. It helped Dent in his early work that here was a virtually unlimited supply of hydrogen at a pressure of 3,000 lbs/sq. in. The other half of the Gas Research Board's work, on utilization of gas, mainly in industry, was sound but not impressive as yet.

The Gas Research Board had been funded as to 90 per cent by individual gas companies, most of which no longer existed, and by some far-sighted plant manufacturers. I agreed with Harold that we should discharge our duties under the Act by taking it over and funding it ourselves. The Fulham Laboratories, renamed the London Research Station, would in future be responsible directly to the Gas Council although they would continue to be administered by North Thames. As to Watson House, its research function should become the direct responsibility of the Gas Council, which would finance it. Its testing and approval function could become a cooperative effort funded by the Gas Boards.

Meanwhile Harold Smith had made soundings at the West Midlands Gas Board. The Chairman, George Diamond, was a perceptive supporter of research and thought highly of Dent's work at the Gas Research Board. He agreed to take over responsibility for housing the Board in new laboratories (eventually at Solihull) to become the Gas Council's Midlands Research Station and for its administration. Dent was appointed Director, with his main interest the programme of research into production of gas. The other part of the Research Board's activity could become the nucleus of a research body for industrial gas at the Midland Research Station.

The South Eastern Gas Board was heir to a relatively small but successful research laboratory at Old Kent Road inspired by the late Dr Carpenter. Under the direction of H. Stanier (Chief Chemist) and J.B. McKean (Chemical Engineer) it had brought to a fruitful conclusion the gasification of heavy oil in what became the SEGAS process and had other irons in the fire. I arranged for its continuation, on a contract basis, to carry out research to a programme previously approved by the Research Committee which would be included in the Council's own programme.

At Leeds research for the gas industry had grown up into a small research establishment within the University, supported by the Institution of Gas Engineers and under the direction of Professor Roberts, the Livesey Professor. It provided some of the personnel, including Dr Dent, who left to form a nucleus for the new Gas Research Board at Beckenham. Work was continuing at Leeds on a smaller scale. The Gas Council agreed to leave these arrangements unaltered and to finance them by direct grant from the Council. The Livesey Professor was to be a member of Sylvester's new Research Advisory Committee.

The Committee, presided over by Harold Smith, Chairman of the Gas Council, with Henry Jones as his Deputy, had as its members representatives at Board level from Boards responsible for administering research stations, the Directors of those stations and the Livesey Professor, with Dr Roger Edwards, Chairman of the North Eastern Gas Board, and myself as two Members of the Council with experience of research in industry, and three distinguished professors from the universities. They were Sir Cyril Hinshelwood FRS and Sir Robert Robinson FRS from Oxford and Professor Garner, the Professor of Chemical Engineering at Birmingham. The Committee was responsible for recommending to the Gas Council programmes of research and the research budgets.

From 1955 on, my contacts with the French, first through the IGE in my presidential year and then through the International Gas Union as a member of its Council, pointed to the increasing interest they were taking in transmission and distribution. It all came together in 1960, with liquid methane, high-pressure gasification, underground storage and the search for natural gas all pointing the way to a new technology to be explored and applied: the emphasis now on metallurgy and physics rather than chemistry and reactions. Sir Henry Jones was in full agreement with my thinking, indeed he had been suggesting for some time that there was great scope for research in the fields reserved for engineers. I could see the advantage of starting with a completely new organization. We settled for the original plan of a third research station in the north. The expedient of setting it up initially at Fulham saved time and gave an opportunity for people to get to know each other. I cannot now recall whether the ultimate objective of a new location was made clear at the time but it was never in doubt in my mind. And from then on things moved apace when Dr James Burns, by now Chairman of the Northern Gas Board, came up with the attractive proposition of a site in the New Town at Killingworth.

Sir Charles Ellis CBE, FRS

There was no Headquarters research establishment, any matters in that category being handled by the Gas Council Secretariat. As Chairman of the Gas Council, Sir Harold Smith had met Sir Charles Ellis, Director of Research at the Coal Board, from time to time to discuss matters of common interest and had a high regard for his ability. In 1955 Ellis resigned, together with all the other Directors of the National Coal Board, at the request of Mr Geoffrey Lloyd, the Minister of Power, 'to help in the reorganization following on the implementation of the Fleck Report'. Except for the Chairman and one other they were not re-appointed; nobody was told why. Harold seized the opportunity of securing the service of Ellis as (part-time) Scientific Adviser at Headquarters, and a member of the Research Advisory Committee. Sir Henry Jones recalls that Ellis took his responsibilities very seriously and that he brought system and logic to bear on the Council's research activities. He helped to focus attention on projects for coal and oil gasification and would point out those long-standing lines of research which appeared to have little prospect of success and should be discontinued.

The late 1950s was a period of grave difficulty in the gas industry; sales of gas were declining and there was a lack of confidence in high places about our ability to survive. It had been an industry based on coal for 140 years and the Coal Board was using its considerable influence to ensure that the gas industry continued to be so based. A majority of the Area Chairmen could see no future for coal even when gasified by one of the new processes then available, and were looking to oil instead. Meanwhile the Ministry of Power was concerned about the wisdom of spending any more money on research into methods of using coal as a raw material in the chemical and related industries. A Committee on Coal Derivatives was appointed under the Chairmanship of Sir Alan Wilson FRS, to investigate and report. I was a member of the Committee and will come back to that later. I do however recall with what care Ellis studied one submission in which I treated town gas not as a mixture arising from this or that process, but in the simplified form of a mixture of three components – methane, hydrogen and an inert gas as 'ballast'. The mixture had to conform to predetermined limits of calorific value, flame speed and specific gravity for the gas to function properly in the burners of the customers' appliances. 'Now I understand,' he said, 'what the gas industry is about.'

Renewal of the gas industry might be said to date from a submission by ICI to the Wilson Committee that their future plans were based entirely on the production of hydrogen from light fractions of oil; moreover they had perfected a process for reforming light distillate for the purpose and were ready to license it to any Area Board that cared to apply. The hydrogen would have to be enriched to town gas standard by bulk supplies of LPG (butane/propane) or, where available, refinery gas. The first demonstration cargo of LNG in the specially converted tanker *Methane Pioneer* had arrived at the Canvey Island terminal in February 1959. It was to be ideally suited for the enrichment of hydrogen to town gas standard after authority had been granted, albeit reluctantly, for full-scale development.

The Midland Research Station was soon ready with the alternatives of two new processes for making the rich gas component from light oil fractions. The new town gas was cheaper than anything that could be made from coal. Sales started to recover, reaching a cumulative 10 per cent annual increase by the middle 1960s. Ellis was delighted and appreciated the need to divert all available resources to the problems arising from such a rapid increase in demand, but he was concerned lest the Council lose sight of the necessity to revise its thinking about future research objectives. This led to the decision to establish a new 'Basic Research Group' alongside the London Research Station. It had a very broad remit to define and pursue the research objectives that it perceived as important for the industry's future. Dr John Gray was approached by Ellis and invited to apply for the post of head of the group. He was interviewed by Sir Cyril Hinshelwood and myself and appointed. The formation of the group gave new impetus to recruiting, with Ellis always insisting on the maintenance of high standards throughout, both in the appointments and in the performance of researchers; this was probably one of his most valuable contributions to the gas industry.

Engineering development had always been the province of the Area Boards. The appointment of Denis Rooke as Gas Council Development Engineer provided for the first time a coordinating influence, and at the same time indicated areas in which research was required; as in materials science, to meet the requirements of high-pressure and high-temperature technologies. The London Research Station became parent to the new Group, until it became the nucleus of the Gas Council's third research station at Killingworth, pursuing under its first director, the late Dr John van der Post, the high standards of recruitment and performance on which Ellis had insisted.

There were further changes when John Gray took over the London Research Station, merging it with his Basic Research Group. G.U. Hopton, the previous director, moved to Headquarters to deal with the administrative work formerly handled by Ellis and a small staff. Ellis was now able to relinquish his day-to-day duties while remaining a member of the Research Advisory Committee. From 1961 to 1968 he was Chairman of a new Programme Sub-committee responsible for formulating the overall programme of research to be put to the Research Committee and then to the Gas Council for approval. Planning procedures were set up for the first time, establishing a rolling five-year programme so that the research stations could plan ahead without being subject to change at short notice. Such changes, whether involving a decrease or an increase of resources, especially staff, are very difficult to accommodate without the adequate warning which such programmes supplied.

In 1969 Ellis relinquished the last of his activities, other than as External Member of the Research Committee, an appointment he held until his death. Great technological changes revolutionized the gas industry in Ellis's time: research and development played an important part and his enthusiastic support for a long-term strategy, and his insistence on high standards, made a valuable contribution to the technological success of the industry.

Frederick James Dent FRS

The rearrangements that followed the dissolution of the Gas Research Board after nationalization, when Dr Dent was appointed Director of Research at a new laboratory yet to be built, provided the opportunity he had been waiting for. He entered on his new responsibilities with the enthusiasm and confidence of an outstanding leader. His first venture outside the laboratory into the hydrogenation of coal under pressure took place at the Poole works. His interest arose from his earlier work on the Lurgi process, when he had hypothesized that methane produced under Lurgi conditions had come from the direct hydrogenation of coal, contrary to established opinion, and had gone on to demonstrate that this was so. It became clear after the autumn of 1944, when the Poole hydrogen plant became available, that a factor not allowed for in the extrapolation from laboratory to pilot scale was the exceptionally high rate of the exothermic hydrogenation reaction. A high-temperature wave passed down the vessel leaving a char that was unreactive at lower temperatures. This required a radical rethinking of the conditions necessary for the hydrogenation of coal. Dent turned to the fluidized bed technique to distribute the heat more uniformly and allow enhanced hydrogenation to raise the calorific value to town gas standard. The model worked successfully and the plant was assembled, comprising all the stages required for the complete gasification of coal. Before it could be commissioned events in the shape of North Sea gas overtook it and, although completed, the plant was never operated. This concept was applied in the USA in a new generation of gas from coal processes based on the principle of hydrogasification which Dent had pioneered.

Earlier work had demonstrated the feasibility of gasification at much higher temperatures when the process ash turns into a molten slag. Known henceforth as the slagging gasifier, a large pilot plant was built and equipped for operation at 20 atmospheres pressure and worked to everyone's satisfaction at the Midlands Research Station. Some years later a group of fourteen American companies financed a full-scale demonstration with a standard Lurgi gasifier at the Westfield works of the Scottish Gas Board, rebuilt to incorporate the slagging principal. The programme was successfully concluded and this remains as one of the most promising routes to synthetic natural gas when and if it becomes necessary to return to coal as a raw material for synthetic natural gas manufacture.

Only two Lurgi plants were ever built in Britain. From 1961 every Board was concentrating on the one-shot reforming process designed by ICI for reforming the low boiling fractions of crude oil to produce hydrogen. Variously known as virgin naphtha and light distillate or LDF, the feedstocks had in common a very low price due to market forces in a surplus situation which showed no sign of correcting itself. ICI was offering a new fully tailored, ready-to-use design based on the old-fashioned technique of externally heated nickel alloy tubes containing a nickel-based catalyst. The Area Boards had a choice of enricher – refinery gas for those fortunate enough to be close to a refinery, commercial LPG, and methane from the new LNG grid. Dent set out to find alternative means of enrichment, starting from the ever-plentiful supplies of naphtha.

Based on his experience with coal, he was exploring means of hydrogenating various fractions of oil using a fluidized bed of coke to stabilize the strongly exothermic reaction. Dent asked himself if there really was any need for the expensive fluidized bed when hydrogenating naphtha. All that was required was the 'thermal flywheel' effect which might be achieved by inducing gas recirculation within an empty reaction space without any catalyst. Model tests indicated that recirculation ratios of 20 or more should be possible, and a pilot plant was erected. The first test was a complete success. A rich gas was produced with stable reaction conditions which were fully responsive to control. Before the second run was completed one Area Board had ordered a unit to enrich the gas from an ICI reformer. The process was competitive with LPG for enrichment, and ultimately over 50 commercial units were built. While referred to in the earlier days as the 'empty reactor' it was later renamed, more appropriately, the Gas Recycle Hydrogenator (GRH).

Dent developed another extremely elegant and successful enrichment route in the Catalytic Rich Gas process (CRG). In this process purified naphtha reacts directly with steam over a nickel-based catalyst in a thermally stable reaction to produce methane. This may well be the process by which he will be best remembered. By 1974, Area Boards had installed 34 streams of Catalytic Rich Gas. But it was in the United States that the process had achieved its greatest success in the production of substitute natural gas. Fifteen very large streams were in operation or nearing completion by 1974. Together with prospective orders they represented a capacity of 2,000 million cubic feet per day of natural gas substitute. It may be observed that if all the prospective orders became firm they had a capacity twice as large as the whole British industry in 1960. All such processes were overtaken in Britain before long by natural gas from the North Sea. But in countries without surplus natural gas they continue to play a very useful role and may come to do so again in Britain when inevitably the output of the North Sea wells begins to fall off.

Dent received honours and awards at home and abroad and was elected Fellow of the Royal Society in 1967. Dr L.A. Moignard, who was Dent's longest-serving assistant, joining him in 1938 and remaining with him throughout his working life, has written an appreciation of Dent's life and work the full text of which appears in *Biographical Memoirs of Fellows of the Royal Society*, Volume 20 (1974), Frederick James Dent by Sir Kenneth Hutchison and Denis Hebden.

The London Research Stations

At Vesting day when the research activities of the Gas Light and Coke Company were transferred to the North Thames Gas Board it was accepted in principle that research should be directed and paid for by the Gas Council, but there was little change in the situation as it existed before nationalization. The Fulham Laboratory became the London Research Station of the Gas Council. Watson House remained as it had been in the past, part research laboratory and part testing and approving authority for the gas appliance industry. Dr Harold Hollings, my old chief at Fulham, had been appointed to be Controller of Research in the Gas Light and Coke Company with responsibility both for Fulham and for Watson House, and represented both at meetings of the Research Advisory Committee. I do not think he found this agreeable and I was not surprised when he exercised his right to voluntary retirement in 1951.

The London Research Station continued to align itself with the policies and problems of the North Thames Gas Board. Everyone settled down to a regime that differed only in detail from what it had been in past years. Research programmes reflected the persona of the Gas Light and Coke Company, and its successor the North Thames Gas Board.

According to Graham Cribb, who was made Director of the London Research Station in 1975 and has written a definitive account of '50 Years of Research at Fulham' with 155 references in the text, the change came in 1958: after that the London Research Station became more closely identified with Gas Council research policy. Its background of research in coal carbonization and related subjects had passed into history and the station was having to look for a new role. At the same time it was reorganized on a divisional basis under four headings: Analytical, Operations, Mathematics/Computing and Physics.

The Gas Council was becoming less interested in manufacture

and more involved in securing the supply of gas, first LNG and then North Sea gas. The London Research Station had a much larger field to operate in as the Corporate Laboratory of the gas industry, with a choice of expertise in most branches of science. The London Research Station could be said to have found its new role and was clearly thriving with its new Director, Graham Cribb. He was appointed following ten formative years with the Development and Supply Division under Denis Rooke, who was by then a full-time member of the Gas Council. The British Gas Corporation's research stations have since grown to five in number. They have entered into new fields with work on offshore exploration and production and with engineering problems of distribution. Besides the engineering achievements, the extensive work on mathematical and computer modelling undertaken at the London Research Station in the 1960s has paid off handsomely. It has strengthened the corporation's ability to manage complex projects and to model the structure and performance of gas and condensate fields.

Having joined the gas industry sixty years ago in what was then its largest research organisation, I find it gratifying to record how what began as No.1 Lab. Fulham has continued to grow and adapted to changing circumstances and has been ready to enter on a new life as the Corporate Laboratory for British Gas. As I write this, or to be exact, type these signals into the word processor, it has just been announced that there will be a complete new start at a fresh site away from London where it all began. It will be interesting to see how this develops, even if on strict actuarial grounds it seems unlikely that I shall be able to do more than witness the first sod turned in the chosen green field.

The Committee on Coal Derivatives

Towards the end of 1959, in my first year as President of the Institution of Chemical Engineers, Martin Flett, Deputy Secretary of the Ministry of Energy, invited me to be a member of a new Parliamentary Committee. The Chairman of the Committee was Sir Alan Wilson FRS, the Deputy Chairman of Courtaulds. He had left Cambridge after the war for a career in industry. The Committee was set up to review work in progress or projected for the conversion of coal into marketable products. Its full name was to be the Committee on Coal Derivatives. Martin made it quite clear that I would be there in my role as an expert and not as a pusher for the gas industry. I replied yes of course and he gave me a meaningful look. We both knew that Lord Robens would be pushing hard and with no holds barred to get what he could for the Coal Board. I had no idea that within a year I would be the Deputy Chairman of the Gas Council, but by then the Committee had nearly finished its work and I had no great difficulty in maintaining my claim to independence and dedication to the cause of science.

Our first task was to assemble facts, with examination in depth of the economics of each process. (Sir) Henry Benson was an establishment figure in the world of accountancy and full of common sense. Dr Holroyd FRS, a Deputy Chairman of ICI, remained suspiciously quiet through most of the proceedings until dropping the final bombshell as the Committee proceeded towards its conclusion. Maurice Banks of BP had played a leading role in our Isle of Grain project. He was a good spokesman of the oil industry. The case for coal was presented by H.E. Collins with firmness amounting to obstinacy but he had his Chairman to satisfy at the day's end. I mention these as members of the Committee who seemed most likely to influence its findings and took care in writing or forwarding reports to have in mind how they would receive them. I see from my records that I submitted in all some eight reports, three of which were my own work and the rest prepared for me by the staff at Croydon.

My first was a short account of how the Coal Board's new coal price structure with its premium on the cost of coal for carbonizing had damaged the gas industry. The price of carbonizing coal was now five times what it was pre-war while house coal was costing the housewife only three times as much. That was all right but the price of house coal was an important factor in determining the price at which gasworks coke could be sold. It was the net cost of coal arrived at after crediting the revenue from coke that entered into the calculation of the cost of gas and it was being squeezed at both ends. All such arguments fell on deaf ears at the Coal Board. That and Dr Holroyd's announcement of ICI's plan to base their future on the reforming of light fractions of oil rendered all such arguments superfluous, and not even of historical value. It would be like blowing on the embers of a dead fire.

The Committee's Report published in August 1960 falls back on the gas industry as probably the only customer left after the ICI process had taken its toll in the chemical industry. I raised no objection to the recommendation that we should study in depth the Coal Board's claim that large centralized groups of Lurgi plants, sited strategically near reserves of suitable coal, with transmission by high-pressure pipeline, could deliver the gas at centres of population at a price competitive with any alternative.

The Lurgi Joint Study

In November 1960 the Select Committee on Nationalized Industries entered the fray and began their examination of the gas industry, hearing evidence on the Lurgi process. Meanwhile the Coal Board proposed, and we agreed, that fresh detailed design studies should be carried out jointly. The Select Committee welcomed the decision since 'cumulatively there appears to be a good basis for looking at the possibilities of large scale Lurgi production'. The decision to carry out the joint study was taken in February 1961. It having been agreed that each side would be headed by a Board Member, the Gas Council's representatives were:

Sir Kenneth Hutchison, Deputy Chairman.
Mr R. Davis, Chief Accountant.
Mr D.E. Rooke, Development Engineer.
Mr C. Johnson, Coal Officer.

The Coal Board having contributed matching names the study group got down to work. It will be enough here to put on record the five phases as recorded in the full report which occupies 48 pages and spans a total of 2 years 9 months.

(1) Preliminary Studies. March 1961 to January 1962.
(2) Site Studies. Three site reports received, December 1961.
(3) Detailed Process Studies. Three contractors' reports based on the selected site received July to October 1962.
(4) Process Evaluation. To June 1963.
(5) Enrichment Studies. July 1961 to July 1963.

In Clause 14 there is a most important general disclaimer summed up in the last two sentences as follows:

> The Study Group have confined themselves to technical and related matters and have not attempted to draw general conclusions. They have not sought to come to any decision, or to advise, on the merits of constructing one or more Lurgi plants as a basis for an integrated national gas supply system.

By 1963 the ICI process was firmly established in the plans of the Area Boards on grounds of high efficiency, low cost of the raw material, no liquid or gaseous effluents, minimal ground space and, quite simply, the answer to the gas engineer's dream of what a gasworks should look like. By disclaiming any intention of advising on the choice the authors of the report had dealt the final and conclusive blow to any future for the Lurgi process in the UK gas industry for the foreseeable future.

13
The Gas Council

The Deputy Chairman's office was on the first floor of No.1 Grosvenor Place, Head Office of the Gas Council. It enjoyed what in my firm belief was the best view in London. Looking out over Hyde Park Corner there was never a dull moment as the traffic tried to sort itself out and frequently failed, after two sharp bends on what I believe was a recently introduced circulatory system. The view beyond took in the wooded acres of Green Park straight ahead and of Buckingham Palace to the right. I could listen every morning for the honking of the skein of Canada geese as they came into view at or about 10.30 on their daily flight from the Serpentine to comparative peace on the lake in the gardens of Buckingham Palace. If that sounds as if I had not enough to do it did indeed take most of a week to accustom myself to a new and very different regime. The daily duties at the head of a very active Gas Board had to give way to a few specialized activities affecting all the Boards and relationships on a regular basis with Ministers and Permanent Secretaries and many other matters as yet unspecified.

In the interests of continuity subjects which occupied a fair proportion of my time have been relegated to other Chapters. They are: Liquid Natural Gas in Chapter 11, and Research in Chapter 12, soon to be joined by Natural Gas from the North Sea in Chapters 14 and 15. I will also be turning back a page or two to pick up from Chapter 10 the story of how I became interested in the background of a successful sales campaign during my last year as Chairman of the South Eastern Gas Board.

First things first, and the successful trials of liquid natural gas transport by sea from America were to be followed up by plans for a commercial operation. This, unlike its predecessor, the voyage of the *Methane Pioneer*, would have to be a co-operative effort financed by those Area Boards which had agreed to take the gas. The Gas Council could by its constitution only aid and assist them in the execution of their plans. Towards the end of the previous year it had been agreed in principle to establish a Production

Policy Committee. It could not have executive powers, but if properly constituted with a representative at Board level from each Area Board, its recommendations were unlikely to be questioned by members of the Gas Council and would become binding on all the Boards.

In parallel with the establishment of the Production Policy Committee the Council decided to establish a Development and Planning Section as part of its own organization. It was to be responsible for the design and development to full-scale size of new production processes including those discovered at the Research Stations of the Council, and for preparing plans on a national basis for an integrated supply system. The Council appointed a panel of its members to interview candidates for the post of Development Engineer to head up the new organization. Fresh from his triumph on the first voyages of the *Methane Pioneer*, and after further passages had tested every feature of this revolutionary new concept of marine transportation, Denis Rooke was among the candidates. It was the unanimous recommendation of the panel that he be appointed Development Engineer from 25 July 1960.

Creative marketing

Three months after I became Deputy Chairman the figures which would go into the Annual Report of the Gas Council showed a further decline in the quantity of gas sold. It was only 0.5 per cent but it was a continuation of a trend which had started five years before. What I could not know or even hope for yet was that sales for the current year would be up by 2.8 per cent and would never look back from there.

As a first step to improving matters a conference of the industry's top commercial people was held in October of 1960 at Selsdon Park. Here we might have a good look at ourselves and our problems and lay some plans for the future. We agreed then on the need for an aggressive sales policy. I felt that one way I could help was to accept every opportunity that came my way to address influential groups of persons and especially those suitably softened up by a glass or two of claret at a luncheon club.

When an invitation came to address the Fuel Luncheon Club on 21 March 1961 it provided a platform from which to try out my own ideas for rejuvenating the gas industry. At that time few people in high places in government seriously believed that the industry had much of a future. To give me an opportunity to speak frankly and make bold claims, I assumed the role of an imaginary historian of the gas industry writing in 1980. My mythical historian found it convenient to begin his review of the industry at the year 1955. The output of electricity for the first time equalled that of gas on an equivalent thermal unit basis and continued to increase at 7 per cent per annum while gas remained more or less constant. The gas industry had remained for too long tied to traditional processes and to raw materials stated by the suppliers to be be their highest quality product and priced accordingly. (Everyone present knew that meant coal.) My historian went on to attack a lack of enterprise in the commercial outlook due to anxiety about the peak load and a desire to maintain a balance between the industry's two main products, gas and coke. The audience was quick to recognize attacks on some strongly held beliefs.

My historian pointed out that the Act that nationalized the gas industry was unable to define what it meant by 'gas'. The Wilson committee reporting in 1960 had shown how gas could be seen as a blend of three components, hydrogen, enricher and ballast. The ballast could normally be had free. The hydrogen was more expensive than the enricher, so why not just have the enricher? Why not leave out the ballast altogether? The full implications of these questions were realized in 1963 when liquid methane, the ideal enricher, became available in commercial operations following the successful trials of the *Methane Pioneer*.

> The problem that faced the gas industry [comments our historian] was how to satisfy a rapidly rising demand for gas on a seasonal basis. But the success that attended an all out attack on the whole house heating load by central heating, warm air and the individual room heater gave a new stability to the winter load. The final solution lay in the storage of gas in underground porous structures. The fact that the cost of such a system was related to the volume stored gave additional impetus to the search for means of producing methane rather than hydrogen to supplement the methane being imported in increasing quantities.
>
> During all this period of intense geological research it had been hoped that new sources of indigenous natural gas would be located. Although some minor successes were recorded, the final break-through was made possible only when the drilling rigs were taken off-shore. After some sharp international exchanges, it was possible for the Gas Act of 1975 to institute a North Sea Production Board with headquarters securely founded on the Dogger Bank.

The reception was so warm, friendly and excited that I knew the message had got through to the gas industry contingent who had come in force. It led to many invitations to address other luncheon clubs, to sing the praises of gas and attack with mockery or scorn any bodies or persons who might be standing in the way of the relentless march of gas to a rosy future.

In October 1962 I addressed the Electrical Industries Club on 'Why Gas?' and referred to an editorial in the *Electrical Times* headed 'Stronger Gas'. The article ended in these trenchant words of warning to all electrical salesmen, and I quote: 'But it is well to keep an eye on anyone with their backs to the wall.' What an engaging picture of the fourteen members of the Gas Council resolutely defending Murdoch House against hordes of savage tribesmen: 'Remember always,' cries the Chairman, 'do not shoot until you can see the whites of their eyes.' Kipling, thou shouldst have been living at this hour.

I went on quite seriously to outline the new advances in the gas industry which would free us from the tyranny of the new coal price structure and staked our claim to be able to compete in every field of service to the public that was open to us. The seventh Gas Sales and Service Conference was held from 6 to 9 November 1961 in Harrogate. This was a first-class opportunity to sell the idea of an aggressive sales policy based on new improved appliances to be backed up by publicity designed to eliminate the image of gas as an old-fashioned fuel. We prepared a simple handbook pinpointing those areas in which we might hope to stem the fall in the consumption of gas and turn ours into a new and expanding industry. The scale of the problem was starkly revealed in the first graph on Figure 2 with its picture of declining sales of gas and of therms per customer over the past ten years. It was relieved only by an increase in the number of customers. New cheaper sources of gas were becoming available but it was the salesman alone who could secure the share of the expanding markets on which our future depended.

At the conference there was dramatic confirmation of the coming revolution, when the East Midlands reported results which surprised even the South, and Port Talbot in Wales astonished everyone with a story of mounting consumption. The two load builders which everyone agreed were to improve the fortunes of the industry were gas fires and central heating. The second graph on Figure 2 shows two things: first, the large contribution that gas space heaters made to the recovery of the gas industry in the troubled years up to 1962, and second, how seriously the intervention by government in the form of hire purchase regulations had affected the industry prior to 1957/8. Figure 2 also shows the later trend in central heating sales. At the

Figure 2.

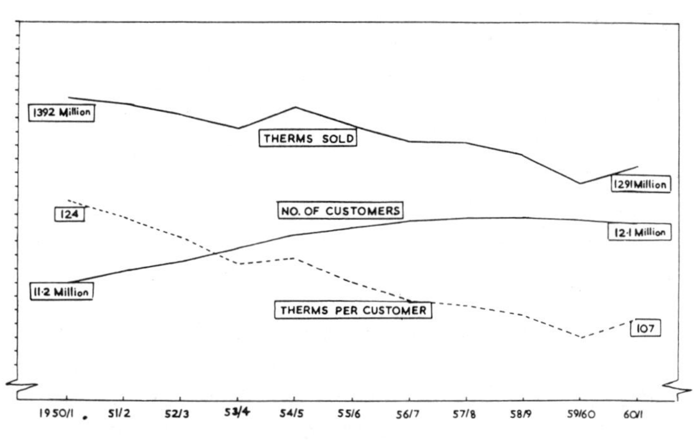

GAS SPACE HEATER SALES

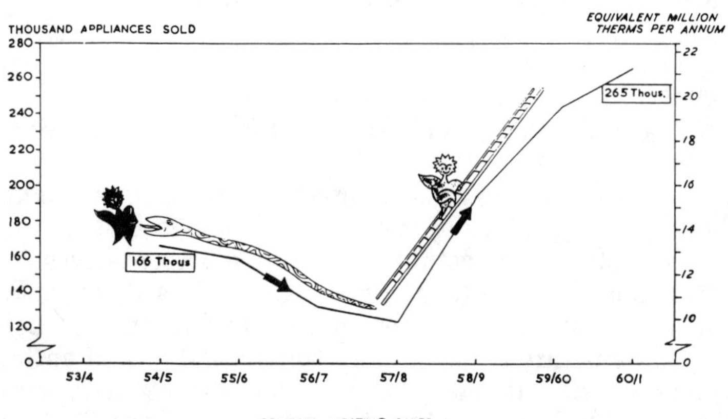

CENTRAL HEATING SALES

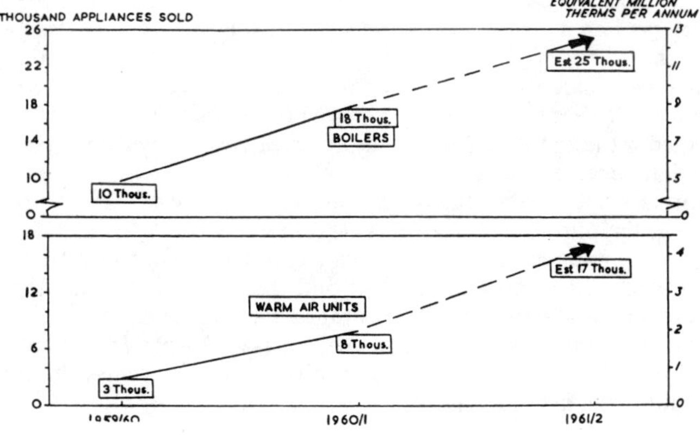

end of the conference it was, somebody said, 'as if everyone suddenly burst out singing'. The salesmen were elated and the engineers went away looking thoughtful.

Meanwhile, the groundwork was being laid for a national approach to improving the public's perception of the industry by changing its advertising image. In my last year as Chairman of South Eastern Gas I had found it disappointing that in spite of all our efforts to contain or reduce costs at every level and a pioneer effort in selling central heating we were still at a disadvantage when it came to meeting the customer. A.E. Tullberg, the publicity and information officer of the Board, came to see me and said there was nothing wrong with our prices or our selling effort: what we had not appreciated was the adverse factor relating to customer awareness of the product we were selling. He proposed that we carry out an attitude or opinion survey on a small scale and hire experts to do it. The results of that survey brought us up with a round turn to a realization that gas was no longer popular with a large and growing population accustomed to the cleanliness of electricity, the cheapness of oil and the comforting sight of an open coal fire. Recalling that experience I decided to set in train a similar but much larger-scale survey of customer attitudes in the whole country.

Hitherto the commercial affairs of the industry had been handled by a committee of commercial managers. A Commercial Policy Committee was established with representatives from all the Area Boards and its members all at Board level. W.N.A. Camp, an Assistant Secretary on the staff of the Council, was appointed Secretary of the Committee. His skill and enthusiasm soon made itself felt. He proposed that the attitude survey be entrusted to Dr Abrams of Research Services Ltd. The principal findings of the survey were:

> As a fuel gas had a weak image, and when it was not weak it was negative. Though the image of oil was also negative, it managed to be a commercial success. The image of coal, by contrast, was positive – it was homely and comfortable. The image of electricity was both positive and strong – it was clean, modern and convenient; cleanliness at present was an obsession, as was convenience.
>
> In contrast with the image of gas the fuel, there was a more favourable image of gas apparatus, such as cookers and water heaters.
>
> There were some groups who were less favourable than others to gas: the young, the middle class, and men. And in those days it seemed that it was the aspiration of all classes to be mistaken for middle class. The gradation up the social scale seemed to be; lower class – direct from solid fuel to electricity; middle class – from electricity to oil. It seemed in each case there should be a field for gas.

Soon after the results of these first surveys had been made known the Gas Council agreed to a recommendation to review the whole of its policy on national publicity. Hitherto this had been designed as an extension of the Boards' own selling efforts using national media, mainly press and magazines, in a series of co-ordinated campaigns, each directed to a particular type of appliance, such as cookers, refrigerators and water heaters. The Council set up a panel of four of its members to review practice and advise on policy. Its members were Michael Milne-Watson, Harold Leach, Pat Welman and myself; and William Camp, still in his capacity as Secretary of the Commercial Policy Committee, but soon to be appointed Public Relations Adviser.

In the federal system of the gas industry the panel provided a link between the constituents, i.e. the Area Boards, and their specialist advisers at Headquarters, and avoided the pitfall of trying to decide in full committee about activities which would inevitably involve a great deal of subjective judgement. The panel accepted the findings of the surveys and as an interim measure decided on central heating as a subject through which to display gas as a provider of comfort and a source of well-being for the whole household, and not merely as a kitchen convenience.

The advertisements were couponed in order to measure public response in terms both of media and of geography, but it must be emphasized that these advertisements were intended not only to sell central heating: of equal importance was the new image of gas that they would present. Meanwhile notice was given of the termination of the previous system of co-ordinated load and appliance advertising campaigns and it was decided to give effect as soon as possible to a new concept of national publicity directed from the centre.

There is controversy in advertising circles about the value of image advertising, and the supporters of the hard sell have been sceptical. The only serious objection I can see is the difficulty of measurement of results which may involve a time scale of months, even years, whereas in a hard sell campaign response can often be measured within weeks. The panel's recommendations were endorsed by the Council and this marked the beginning of a fruitful partnership with Colman, Prentis and Varley, the agency selected after lengthy consideration, with Cyrus Ducker at the head of the account. Pursuing their own independent enquiries the agency confirmed the view that it would be necessary to plan a long-term campaign in order to win the public over to the industry's point of view of gas as a modern, up-to-date fuel. From the start they contended that television advertising provided the most effective medium for this purpose and was capable of reaching the widest band of public at the lowest cost.

They put forward the idea that speed is the quality that distinguishes gas from its rival fuels and to advertise this they presented the claim which soon became familiar, High Speed Gas. Reinforcing it there is the flexibility of gas identified with the flame that can be turned up or down at will – in C.P.V.'s words, 'Heat that obeys you'.

As Cyrus Ducker put it in a recent letter to the author:

> Opinion research of various kinds among the users themselves began to reveal a significant picture. Although fairly discouraging in general the results displayed one thumbs-up sign of exceptional importance. Roundly criticised as 'dirty', 'smelly', 'dangerous' and 'old fashioned', gas was nevertheless regarded, particularly in the kitchen, as a more efficient and economical fuel than electricity. As one woman succinctly put it: 'Turn it on – and it's on! Turn it off – and it's off'! And another 'With gas, I'm in charge – the flame does what I tell it'. Electricity's claim to be the superior modern fuel for everything and everyone was evidently far from impregnable; and the hunt was now on for an advertising theme and style which, exploiting the major asset of gas's controllability, would lend a more modern air and some excitement to the word gas itself ...
>
> The amiable, innocuous figure of 'Mr Therm', around which the Gas Council's advertising had for many a year revolved, seemed too bland, too type-cast to take up such a challenge. The word gas itself must now face the limelight. Above all it needed a lively nickname, to express an innate quality.
>
> And so it was that HIGH SPEED GAS! made its bow one morning in the newspapers of an unsuspecting British public. Advertising headlines – WHIZZIGAS! – GETUPANDGOGAS! – HEAT THAT OBEYS YOU! accompanied by cheerful, cartoon-style illustrations – invited readers to realize how 'with it' they were to be using gas.
>
> The advertisements began to attract attention. Allusions to them by well-known comedians, cartoonists and politicians, referring to 'high speed' this and 'high speed' that, were not long in coming, and the preliminary aim of the campaign – to wake people up to the value of something they largely took for granted – began to look achievable.

Meanwhile various possibilities for television commercials were being investigated and, by the time the go-ahead was given in July 1963, the general pattern with which by then most people were familiar had evolved in the studios. Music in a modern idiom and the straight presentation of attractive young people in modern surroundings was the formula, putting over the message, 'High Speed Gas, heat that obeys you.' In order to give the impact that a new television campaign requires, we had to withdraw for a time from the national daily Press, except for a modest continuing effort in central heating, and from cinemas altogether.

There was nothing irrevocable about these decisions and the Press was used again to give effect to an industry public relations campaign. It was designed to impress on influential people the achievements of a resurgent gas industry in the scientific, technical and industrial fields using colour wherever available. The engaging picture of a field of barley ripening where a season before a pipeline had been laid down was found to pack a punch of unexpected power. The Electricity Generating Board was just then in serious trouble for placing its pylons in a beauty spot and remained convinced in spite of our protestations that we had done it with intent to score a point.

All publicity matter was pre-tested on sample audiences and tested again afterwards for recall. The choice of media was based on a balance of viewers and readers by class and geographical location, and throughout the campaign every effort was made to see that the money expended was put to the best possible use. There was positive evidence of a change in the public image of gas as measured by sample interviews carried out by an independent body. On the findings and results it is reasonable to assume that a very considerable part of the increase in sales was due to a public more in sympathy with the goods we had to sell.

On 28 November 1963 I summed up our experiences with an address on 'Public Image and Private Eye' to the Executive Association of Great Britain. The audience, I thought, must by now be sold on the new image of gas, but:

> I do assure assure you that it was not always so and about eight years ago some of us began to wonder if everything was right with gas. For the first time in history electricity was selling more in equivalent thermal units than gas and was continuing to advance while gas seemed to be suffering from what we had to admit in the privacy of our own offices was a very slight recession.

After summarizing our plans for producing more and cheaper gas, I went on to reflect on how we had found the unknown negative factor in gas sales, apart from the fact that electricity had the advantage of being connected in each new house while gas was almost on the point of having to pay to be allowed in, and I concluded:

> What we are trying to do in our national advertising is to change the weather. We are trying to create a new climate in the fuel market, a climate in which sales of gas and gas appliances will continue to thrive. We are not

> taking our present boom for granted. People are beginning to talk about a new look gas industry as if it had just happened. It hasn't *just* happened, but it is here and we are determined to see that it is here to stay. We have taken two themes where we know gas is superior, speed and flexibility, and are building round them a picture of a far smarter, far more 'with it' fuel than anyone ever thought gas could be ... I won't say that specific merit no longer counts – it does like anything. But you've not only got to be good, you've got to look good. We think we've learnt that lesson.

The impatience of Parliament

The Deputy Chairmanship brought me more than ever before in contact with the political environment of the gas industry and this led to serious reflections on the history and current nature of that environment, which are worth exploring here at some length in virtually the words I used in an address given at the Administrative Staff College at Henley-on-Thames on 14 May 1964.

Any situation of national monopoly provokes the desire of a democracy to curb the resulting power, without itself getting involved in the exercise of that power. The Royal Charter granted to the Gas Light and Coke Company in 1812 made possible a public development at limited private risk. The success of the experiment and the near monopoly conditions it created soon attracted the attention of Parliament and governments of all complexions. The Whigs under Lord John Russell in 1847 legislated for maximum price. The Tories under Disraeli in 1877 for the sliding scale (by which the dividend was governed by the price charged for gas). They overlooked, however, the expansion of the economy and made no allowance for inflation. The coalition under Lloyd George in 1920 introduced the principle of the Basic Price which provided in effect for a minimum dividend. All these acts represented attempts to curb monopoly while giving a fair reward to financial enterprise.

The outcome of nationalization as a political doctrine was not wholly foreseen at the time when the 'new Boards' were set up. I use this word to distinguish them from the older utility boards – these new boards were born in the fire of political controversy and were intended to represent the first flowering of a new socialistic democracy. Thus for a time they were referred to as Socialized, not Nationalized, Boards. But to a surprising degree they have reflected a way of life that has little resemblance to what the voters, at least in 1945, believed to be socialized doctrine.

Throughout his political life Herbert Morrison had seen the

dangers of state-controlled enterprises in what would for many years to come be a world dominated by private enterprise. He had as his ideal, state-*owned*, and only in the last resort state-*controlled* industries, answerable to the Government of the day for their overall strategy, and not answerable to Parliament for their day-to-day actions. They would be efficient, substituting ideals for sordid profit, and it would be sufficient if they were to 'break even' after making all proper provisions for depreciation, taking one year with another. They would not be subject to the scrutiny of the Public Accounts Office – they were to have auditors appointed from among those who customarily audit the accounts of public companies in private enterprise. Close study of the Nationalization Acts shows how light, almost delicate was the control that was available to the responsible Minister.

He would have to approve a general scheme of capital development – and having done so presumably find the money needed – he might give a direction – but only in the national interest – and then presumably accept the consequences of any failure to supply or other major crisis that might result. How was it supposed this would work in such a way that the Minister would take responsibility before Parliament, the Press and the Public for the actions of a Board that he had appointed?

The appointments to Boards were not considered 'career appointments', but the Government of the day avoided making them political ones. Of the first four chairmen, one was a Private Enterprise Baron, one was a Civil Service Knight, one was a Trade Union Leader (already knighted) and one was a Gas Industry business man, the only one chosen to lead the nationalized version of his own industry. All were duly honoured for their services.

The final blow to Parliamentary prerogatives was the confirmation of a ruling that private questions could not be put on matters which by statute were the responsibility of the Boards. This angered Socialist and Conservative back benchers alike – and not only at times when the political opponent happened to be in power. The PQ is the accepted vehicle for conveying a grievance past the entrenched defences of the civil service and into the public light of day, where, with the aid of a watchful press, justice can be seen to be done.

A partial solution was evolved which may not have commended itself to MPs anxious for public notice in the press but which satisfied many of them. Members were invited to write direct to Chairmen of Boards about any grievance or difficulty brought forward by constituents. It has always been the custom in the gas industry for the Chairman to deal personally with every matter raised in this way and to reply personally to the member; and if the matter was one lying within the power of the consultative council (e.g. consumers' complaints) to see that such matters were properly treated.

Select Committees

There remained a continuous undercurrent of feeling that Parliament – the watchdog of democracy – was being got at by a combination of autocratic Ministers and Minister-appointed tycoons. The remedy of parliamentary questions being ruled out, there remained debate; but the parliamentary system is poorly organized to deal with all the complexities of an industry's annual report, and nothing came of that. When in doubt one sets up a committee and some members, aware of the joyful witch-hunting that the Public Accounts Committee offers around the entrenched precincts of Whitehall, voted enthusiastically for a Select Committee.

The committee duly met in 1951, and finding itself up against the limits of the scope of the PQ, decided to establish a standing committee of the House to examine and report on the 'aims, activities and problems of the corporations'. I cannot speak too highly of the work of the Select Committee in its new form during the late 1950s and early 1960s under the leadership of its first Chairman, Sir Toby Low, later Lord Aldington. The atmosphere of hostility on the one side and definite mistrust on the other that seems to emerge from the findings of the Public Accounts Committee has been totally absent in the proceedings of the Select Committee. The investigation was close and searching, but not unfair, and I think it was the general feeling among those who had been investigated that the trouble taken to provide evidence and answers to questions had been well worth while.

The investigation of the gas industry occupied thirty-four sessions. The Select Committee produced its main report in August 1961 and there was a Second Special Report published in March 1964. The aim of the enquiry as defined in the report was 'to find out the present situation of the gas industry, the difficulties and opportunities of the future and the ways in which it is proposed to meet them'. The subjects discussed ranged from highly technical matters like those involved in the coal-vs.-oil controversy, to questions of motivation in the relationship between the Minister, the Boards, and the Civil Service.

Consumer interests were represented inter alia by a searching examination of the basis of tariff policy. The interests of the mining community were well to the fore (the committee contained representatives of all the parties). The merits of the Lurgi process and of the importation of liquefied natural gas were examined at length, even to the extent of hearing the views of the Coal Board in a special session. Financial policy came under review in relation to the standards of profitability. Organization was the subject of a recommendation that there should be a Thirteenth Board to deal with some aspects at least of production. Throughout the hearings there was keen interest in the relationship of the Minister to the Boards, especially in the kind of advice that falls short of a Direction under the Act, but which it would be hard for a prudent Chairman to disregard. The Committee was against it.

The investigation took place at a time when to an outsider it must have appeared that the fortunes of the gas industry were at a low ebb. But the Committee was able to point out the factors which would contribute to a renewed prosperity, and although after only three years some of the technical background was already dated, the revival which they had postulated had in fact taken place.

This was certainly accountability of a kind, involving all those responsible for the affairs of a nationalized industry in a fairly detailed review at relatively long intervals, but I am certain it was not what Members of Parliament had in mind when the matter was being discussed in the early days of the nationalized industries.

The corridors of power

We have now examined some of the more important facets of accountability – perhaps those which most often attract the attention of theorists – and it is time to see what lies behind it all. At this point I should declare my thesis to be that the accountability of a nationalized industry is inseparable from the source from which that industry draws its authority, and I believe that in practice and in fact an industry is accountable to the Minister who answers for it before Parliament, finds money to finance it, has sole power of appointment of the Boards, *and* even of the Consultative Councils who represent the consumers.

The basis of the control exercised by a Minister through his department is threefold. Section 1 (5) of the Gas Act of 1948 has a requirement for each Board to submit a plan for capital development for the approval of the Minister, which approval could only be given after consultation with the Council. Elsewhere, in Section 42, we find that no Board, nor the Council on their behalf might borrow without the consent of the Minister and the approval of the Treasury, and then only for carefully defined purposes. Finally the White Paper on the economic obligations of nationalized industry, although not having the force of law, established a code of financial conduct which could presumably in the last resort be enforced by a direction but was sufficiently binding without.

Capital development programmes were prepared in great detail once a year and examined by officials of the Ministry. Each programme was for a five-year period and was in effect a prospectus against which the Board received its right to borrow money from Treasury sources. The Council also received programmes, and its officials examined them so that the Council might be in a position to reply when consulted by the Ministry. The Select Committee seemed somewhat puzzled, even distrustful, of this procedure, suggesting that, as every Chairman of a Board was a member of the Council, open criticism might be stifled on the principle of 'Buggins' turn next'. It might indeed have been more logical for the programmes to be examined first by the Council and presented in unified form to the Ministry.

Another thing that bothered the Select Committee was the extent to which the Minister's wishes (conveyed privately and not in a Direction) might alter the profitability of a Board. The White Paper provided that any such advice must be made public and be taken account of in the financial targets. The White Paper regularized much of the relationship between a nationalized Board and a Minister. It became increasingly difficult for a Minister to interfere in matters of importance if he was thereby compelled to accept responsibility for any failure to meet the target.

Ministers of the Crown

When Winston Churchill won the 1951 Election with a small majority he found himself saddled with an election pledge to build 300,000 Homes for the People. He sent for Harold Macmillan to come down to Chartwell and offered him a new Ministry of Housing with a seat in the Cabinet. Macmillan knew absolutely nothing about the problem or what organization existed, nor did Churchill. He tells how in great doubt he went out to consult his wife who was walking with Mrs Churchill in the garden. His wife was in no doubt at all: he ought to accept, and he did. At his office he came to the conclusion that the only possible way to carry out the assignment was to return to the wartime structure at the Ministry of Supply and appoint a Director-General to take executive charge of the whole operation. He decided that the man for the job was Sir Percy Mills who had been the Machine Tool Controller at the Ministry during the war but had since returned to his old firm of Avery in Birmingham: they had remained on friendly terms ever since. Even so, the best Macmillan could do was to secure a one-year leave of absence and that was in exchange for a hand-written letter from Churchill to the Company Chairman together with a signed photograph! Both were delivered personally by the Minister. In his political memoirs Macmillan pays generous tribute to the value of the contribution of Sir Percy Mills to the ultimate success of the housing programme during his year of service; and thereafter by visits whenever he was asked to advise.

Not surprisingly, when Macmillan became Prime Minister at very short notice on 13 January 1957, to succeed the ailing Anthony Eden, he had already sent for Percy Mills to take on the appointment of Minister of Power. There were as ever potential troubles with the miners and many other problems in an area of which as Prime Minister he had no previous experience. So Percy Mills became Lord Mills of Dudley in the County of Warwick and a member of the Cabinet; and, although he did not know it then, he would have to make one important decision affecting the future of the gas industry. It was to approve the plan jointly with our American partners to convert a second-hand tanker to carry liquid methane. This he did, but with strict conditions designed to keep it an experiment and not to allow it to grow into a commercial operation. In 1959 he was succeeded by the Rt. Hon. Richard Wood MP as Minister of Power but remained influential in his capacity as Paymaster General and a member of the Cabinet. In Chapter 11 I have told how nearly our plan for commercial development came to being vetoed by the force of his objections when Paymaster General and a member of the Cabinet. I only met Lord Mills once, and that was when I was Chairman of Segas. He came down at his own request to visit the Isle of Grain works. It was the first to be designed and built for the sole purpose of making gas from oil. He was clearly interested in the unusual basis of our contract with BP whereby we took as our feedstock at the boundary fence whichever of the products of the oil refinery was in surplus at any one time and at a very favourable price.

The Rt. Hon. Richard Wood MP visited the Isle of Grain soon after becoming Minister of Power in October 1959. It was important to have an accessible and understanding Minister in the years that followed; when Henry Jones and I unrolled plans for the future of the gas industry that were certain to be opposed by the powerful oil lobby. We met not too formally in a room at the House of Commons. Only the Permanent Secretary and the Under Secretary of the Gas Division normally attended the meetings and on our side only the Chairman and myself, with perhaps the Secretary of the Gas Council to take a note. In these pleasantly informal conditions we could cover a great deal of ground and it was perfect for my plan to introduce the thorny subject of Gas Council participation in the great North Sea adventure.

Before going into that in greater detail I should mention that the Minister showed so much interest in the seismic surveys which were at the centre of our programme of exploration that we offered to arrange for him to join a survey vessel and see at first hand how the thing was done. Having regard to his disability, the consequence of being blown up by a land mine in the desert war, I thought it prudent to have him join the vessel in Immingham dock and waited confidently overnight in a Flixborough hotel. Then as ever the North Sea took over and gales were forecast. The survey vessel would be delayed and would almost certainly fail to arrive before the lock gates closed next morning. I rang Richard at his Yorkshire home and told him the only possibility would be to transfer at sea from a small service vessel which could lie afloat at the outer harbour wall and take us out to the survey vessel. He said, 'Splendid, Diana and I will be along in good time.' There was quite a heavy swell left over from the overnight gale and I was thankful when the whole party got safely aboard with the crew standing by to assist and Richard refusing all aid and relying only on a stout walking-stick.

In what follows I shall be relying as to dates on some notes that survive of our part in the discussions with Ministers of Power during my seven years at the Gas Council:

1962

Richard Wood Minister of Power since 1959.

23 May. At this the first meeting at which the question of North Sea gas was discussed I gave an account of a meeting in my office with C.F. Dohm, the President of Amoco. I explained that this was the overseas arm of Standard Oil of Indiana, one of the largest American Oil companies but having no presence in the UK as yet.

30 July. In reply to the Minister about co-operation with the BP/Shell/Esso consortium we said that BP had declined our offer to join their Consortium: we had been approached by Amoco before we heard of the BP consortium's plans.

8 October. We noted that two other American companies had joined Amoco in the seismic survey. I stressed the advantage to the Gas Council of our proposed participation.

4 December. The Permanent Secretary had suggested that we should consider Gulf Oil as a partner, with its long established British presence; we reported that efforts to persuade Gulf to join with Amoco in our survey programme had failed and Amoco were anxious to go ahead. We reiterated reasons for participating in the survey proposed by Amoco.

1963

20 February. Discussion of Gas Council's proposal to enter into an agreement with Amoco who had been joined by Amerada and Texas Eastern, both American companies, for exploration of North Sea.

(Agreement sent to Ministry 12 March, signed 21 March 1963).

24 June. I reported that the current survey would occupy all the summer months. Drilling was unlikely to start before next Spring.

21 October. F.J.Erroll succeeds Richard Wood as Minister.

24 October. We report on Council's association with Amoco group. Results of first year's work highly satisfactory. It was clearly worth continuing the prospecting operations. Discussion of need for early legislation and issue of licences.

1964

29 January. Discussion of gas industry's position in exploitation of natural gas (following on Second Reading of the Continental Shelf Bill the previous day). I reported the results of our seismic survey and the satisfactory experience of the working of the partnership agreements.

23 April. Discussion of scope of exploration licences etc. following the Royal Assent to the Continental Shelf Act.

16 October. Frederick Lee succeeds F.J.Erroll as Minister following Labour victory at the General Election.

1965

1 February. We reported that contract had been placed for a drilling rig. It was hoped to commence drilling early 1966. Meanwhile seismic surveys were continuing.

16 November. We report that the Economist Intelligence Unit had been commissioned to study markets for North Sea Gas. The Amoco/Gas Council rig expected to be ready for drilling April/May 1966.

7 December. BP discovery of the West Sole gas field.

1966

16 February. We report no agreement yet with BP on location of land terminal. I state that in future Council would insist on evidence of size of reserves on offer. Council's rig not now expected before August.

5 April. Richard Marsh succeeds Fred Lee as Minister.

23 May. Discussion of impact of North Sea gas on energy policy. Reference to White Paper on Future of the Gas Industry. Importance of planning and need for Government guidance on basic assumptions. Importance of adequate future pipelining resources.

22 November. I report joint study with CEGB (Gas for Power Stations). Also reports on latest Amoco Group strike and on gas purchase negotiations.

In this the last of my meetings with Ministers it seems that interest had passed from how much gas was there, and where, and how it was to be found, to the question of what shall we do with it and how much shall we pay. *Sic transit!*

Permanent Secretaries and others

Regular meetings with the Permanent Secretary accompanied by whichever of his deputies was handling our affairs were arranged to take place at intervals of two or three months. They were held in our office in the late evening after dinner, where no telephone or caller could interrupt. It had become the established practice to circulate to those present a fairly comprehensive note of what had been discussed. The meetings were for information not for action or decision, except as the participants might themselves decide later. I think that was as good a way as any to handle some quite contentious matters.

Sir Dennis Proctor was Permanent Secretary at the Ministry of Power for nearly six of the seven years that I spent as Deputy Chairman of the Gas Council. His career was rather exceptional in that, having reached the elevated status of Third Secretary to the Treasury, he resigned at the age of 45 to go into business, mainly shipping in Denmark. He returned eight years later to an appointment as a Deputy Secretary and from 1958 to 1965 Permanent Secretary at the Ministry of Power. Most agreeable company at dinner before our meetings, he did not hesitate to pursue with skill and vigour any matter on which he felt we might be falling into error. He came to our meeting on 2 October 1962 accompanied by Angus Beckett, formerly Under-Secretary Gas, in his new capacity of Under-Secretary Oil. Predictably it was not an easy meeting. It began with Henry mentioning how his request to join the group consisting of Shell, Esso and BP in their seismic survey of the North Sea had been summarily rejected by the Chairman of BP. We could, however, get the information we wanted by joining up with Amoco or Gulf or both. The arguments for and against went back and forth until we tacitly agreed to a policy of *reculer pour mieux sauter*.

That brings me to 16 January 1963 when it was noted, and I quote, if only as a masterpiece of non-information: 'The Chairman (of the Gas Council) mentioned that he had written a letter to the Minister on the 16th January on the lines of the discussion he had with the Permanent Secretary.' Not to be outdone, on 12 February Pat Murray (the Deputy Secretary) said a reply to the Chairman's letter could be expected very soon. He thought it would be satisfactory; until finally on 26 March it was mentioned that the agreement for a North Sea survey would be signed three days later, on Friday 29 March, subject to approval of the work programme and the budget.

The rest of the year (1963) was mainly occupied by the issue of licences and the Continental Shelf Bill, which received the Royal Assent on 15 April 1964. Then on 21 October 1963 in a Ministerial reshuffle at the accession of Sir Alec Douglas-Home as Prime Minister, F.J. Erroll became Minister of Power (later Lord Erroll of Hale).

In our discussions about seismic surveys we had argued that they were by their nature a research operation. By themselves they had no productive component and consisted only in the gathering of information by which future profitable discoveries might be made. They should therefore be a charge on the revenue of the Council whose finances were now in a healthy state. In 1963/64 the industry's estimated surplus would be well in excess of the £9.4 million for the previous year. (In fact it proved to be £13.3 million when the figures were published.)

So far so good, and we had established beyond all reasonable argument that seismic surveys were the sole responsibility of the

Council and not part of a Capital Development Programme to be authorized by the Minister. The going was not so good when it came to the matter of joining with our same American partners in a drilling programme. Dennis Proctor quite properly asked whether it was really necessary for the Gas Council to be involved once the survey stage was past. After all the Council would have the opportunity of buying all the gas other than what was permitted to be used under the Continental Shelf Act. We made the case that by being aware of the true cost of exploration we would be so much better placed when it came to the stage of agreeing a price. This was accepted and the way was thereafter clear for us to enter into the world of oil and natural gas production. These arguments were in private and public discussion only came later. It seemed an easy victory.

Each of the records of two later meetings in June/July 1985 uses a full page of discussion about the Council's participation in a drilling programme. We had negotiated a satisfactory base with a 10 per cent participation minimum and an option to go up to 50 per cent at some later date. It might cost up to £2 million a year for the 31 per cent share proposed. We had arrived at that figure as being the same proportion as that being claimed by Amoco, the largest shareholder among our three American partners. We considered that it was not burdensome in relation to the industry's estimated surplus.

The new formula with its options proved useful when Labour won an October election and we had a new Minister in the person of Fred Lee, and, within a year as it happened, a new Permanent Secretary in the person of Sir Matthew Stevenson promoted from Deputy. In a new round of licences we took cognizance of the declared interest of the Labour Party in participation and exercised our option to elect for a 50 per cent interest. Sad to relate, there were no discoveries comparable with those in the heady days of the first round of licences in the southern part of the North Sea.

Shortly before he retired Dennis presented me with a slim volume entitled *Microcosmographia Academia* by F.C.Cornford, a Cambridge don who had surveyed university politics with detached and cynical humour in 1908. It seemed, wrote Dennis, that I might find the book useful, having broken every rule in it including 'Nothing should ever be done for the first time.'

> The principle of the dangerous precedent [thus wrote Cornford] is that you should not now do an admittedly right action for fear you, or your equally timid successors, should not have the courage to do right in some future

case, which, *ex hypothesi*, is essentially different, but superficially resembles the present one. Every public action which is not customary, either is wrong, or if it is right is a dangerous precedent. It follows that nothing should ever be done for the first time.

Matthew Stevenson succeeded Dennis as Permanent Secretary and our meetings took on a more serious tone, especially in the matter of a price for the first delivery of gas from the North Sea as I have recorded elsewhere. Within the year and at short notice he was whisked off to take over from Dame Evelyn Sharp, Permanent Secretary at the Ministry of Housing and Local Government. She had given adequate notice of her intention to retire but nobody believed her, so she just went. That at least is the story as I heard it. From May 1966 we settled down to life with David Pitblado as Secretary, supported by Robert Marshall as his deputy, with interminable discussions about the price of natural gas, interrupted only from time to time by anxious enquiries about how our organization was standing up to the strain of these vast new quantities of gas. There were grave warnings as to the price we were expected to pay, with the Lord Balogh quoted as infallible and the edicts of the Federal Power Commission of the United States as the Gospel. I found it almost impossible to convince them that the probability of finding a second field as large as the Leman Bank had not been in any way increased by the finding of that field. (Alas, history records that I was only too right there.) Meanwhile negotiations dragged on and I was glad to hand over all such problems to my successor, Arthur Hetherington, when the time came that he was ready to stand in before taking over.

There were many other problems coming my way, mostly ephemeral in relation to the imminent revolution that would transform the gas industry. The one that gave me most satisfaction concerned the coke side of the gas industry's trade and led to the definitive statement of the view that I had long urged that the gas industry had no business making coke, except as an unavoidable by-product of gas manufacture. Here I will quote from our Annual Report 1963/64:

In May 1963 the Minister of Housing and Local Government announced that he was instituting an immediate review of current Clean Air arrangements in conjunction with the Ministry of Power. As part of that review the Minister of Power re-examined during the year the prospects of solid smokeless fuel supplies in consultation with the (Gas) Council and other fuel producers. The result was the publication of a White Paper 'Domestic Fuel Supplies and Clean Air Policy' (Cmnd. 2231) …

The White Paper stated … 'It has been suggested that the Government

> should intervene to slow down the movement away from coal carbonisation and so augment supplies of suitable coke. But this movement reflects radical changes in technology and raw material costs and it would, in the Government's view, be a mistake to undermine the economics of gas production, which is the main function and business of the gas industry, for the sake of a by-product. Such intervention would involve either subsidising the industry or increasing the price of gas and so reducing the important contribution which this fuel can make to clean air.'

A Christmas carol

The Coal Industry Society invited me to address them on the occasion of their Christmas luncheon on 11 December 1965. I asked myself and my audience whether it would not be more appropriate to fall in with the spirit of a Christmas carol. Or should I be more serious and attempt a grand design in which all fuels are neatly slotted to fit in with a predetermined rate of growth in the economy. But I hesitated to rush in where only planners and economists feared not to tread. Who was I to question their forecasts in the brave new economic world we lived in:

> This beautiful country called England,
> Land of the Rocker and Mod,
> Where Kaldor speaks only to Balogh
> And Balogh speaks only to God.

It would be better surely to stick to something I knew about and tell them all I knew about gas in one easy lesson, which brought me up to the prospect of finding gas in the North Sea. If, and I repeated if, natural gas was found on the scale of Slochteren in Holland the industry would rise rather rapidly to five or six times its present size. We would then have solved our present dilemma. Carbonization of coal was an excellent method of making coke but suffered from the disadvantage that, if gas was to be made at a price that was competitive with electricity, coke would be too dear to sell at all. I touched on our publicity and reminded my listeners how sales of gas had increased during the last four years. By then I thought they had had enough, for this was to be no lecture but a Christmas Carol.

Good King Wenceslas was about to address his page at the start of my talk before I had became involved in more serious matters. The page was in fact the Press and Information Officer to the Royal Court. 'Sire,' said the PIO, 'that is no peasant gathering winter fuel. It is the leader of a team of geologists working for the

Mogul Oil Company.' 'Where then is his dwelling,' said the King. 'A good league hence,' said the PIO. 'I sneaked in while they were out at the local and looked at the seismograms. And, Sire, let me tell you that this dump you call a palace is situated on the crest of one of the largest anticlines in Europe underlain by a deep bed of Rotliegendes sandstone.' The King was no geologist, but he knew what that meant. 'Bring me,' he said, 'a case of Bourbon and a pen and parchment.' Out they went together and returned with a contract which provided for 10 per cent royalties and 50 per cent profits for the Exchequer and an overriding 5 per cent royalty, for Royalty of course. The page, who had hoped to be cut in for a mere 1 per cent, was completely overlooked and had to return to Cracow where he became a Professor of Economics. His lectures were attended by oil men from all over the world. They included a statement known as Page's Law: 'Be sure to have a contract in writing before giving away valuable information.' The King, who was a kindly man at heart, arranged for all his peasants to have central heating (by gas of course) and composed a carol; and everyone lived happily ever after.

Six years that transformed the industry

Rather than leave this chapter on what may appear as a somewhat frivolous note, I will recall some of the changes of unprecedented depth and magnitude which in the short space of six years changed beyond recognition an industry with one hundred and fifty years of history and proud of it. The transformation was even more remarkable for the speed with which it was accomplished. In an outline of new plants completed or under construction at March 1964 the Gas Council Report records that every one of the twelve Area Boards was in the middle of a massive construction programme by which all existing gas-making plant would be replaced by oil reformers. The total capacity of reforming plant recorded as going into operation, under construction or on order, was calculated to produce just over 1,000 million cubic feet of gas a day or about half of the industry's total future capacity. In a human way, the replacement of ancient gas works by these gleaming examples of modern engineering practice had a most profound effect on the public's respect for the industry and on the industry's own morale.

1961/62 Report of the Gas Council: 'It gave members of the Council great pleasure when Her Majesty the Queen, in the New Year Honours of 1962, conferred a Knighthood on their Deputy

Chairman, Sir Kenneth Hutchison.' At the next meeting of the Research Advisory Committee, when Hinshelwood came up to shake my hand, I said I would happily exchange it for an FRS. He said 'Why not have both?' Four years later when he knew, but I did not, that I was going to be elected to the Royal Society he came up to me and said 'Now you are going to have both.'

14
North Sea: Prospecting

The gas industry's search for natural gas began with an agreement negotiated by H.C. Smith (later Sir Harold Smith), then Deputy Chairman of the Gas Council, and Sir William Fraser (later Lord Strathalmond), then Chairman of BP, which was signed in 1952. A productivity team representing employers and unions had visited the United States around 1950 and reported the extraordinary growth of the gas industry there.

At this time any discoveries of natural gas in Great Britain had been very small indeed and most were incidental to the search for oil. With a view to encouraging a renewed exploration effort the Conservative Government of the day nationalized all the petroleum reserves in the UK by the Petroleum (Products) Act of 1934. This Act incidentally set a pattern for much future legislation by requiring that any gas discovered should be offered first to the appropriate gas undertaking. Only if refused could the finder sell it direct, and then only for industrial purposes.

As yet gas could not be imported – the *Methane Pioneer* was still years in the future – and the reward for discovering gas on land would be very great indeed to a gas industry looking round almost despairingly for some way to improve its fortunes. The agreement with BP provided for a joint enterprise, in which, over areas designated as prospective for gas, the cost of drilling would be borne by the Gas Council and, whatever the outcome, any gas would go to the Gas Council and any oil to BP. Conversely BP would drill in areas designated as prospective for oil, and would hand over any gas they found to the Gas Council and keep any oil for themselves. To give the whole thing a start, two small discoveries made at Eskdale in Yorkshire and Cousland in Scotland were made over to the Gas Council for exploitation.

We searched vigorously and drilled two deep wells at Crowborough in Sussex and two more at Eakrigg in Yorkshire, spent quite a lot of money in exploratory work elsewhere without any tangible result and became rather discouraged. Our secondary objective of delineating areas suitable for the storage of gas underground became more attractive. The commercial success of development of domestic heating was placing ever greater demands on the flexibility of the gas supply system. Professor Illing FRS was called in to advise. He always thought that the chance of finding any worthwhile quantity of gas on the English mainland was minimal. He believed that our secondary objective, of storing in aquifers, was reasonably justified. We had spent upwards of a million pounds with nothing much to show for it. Suddenly all became clear when rumours of a major gas field discovered at Slochteren in the Netherlands were confirmed in 1959. The gas was said to derive from early geological strata, which could be identified with the great carboniferous fields whose existence just below England's green and pleasant lands had fathered Blake's dark satanic mills. We could discern a favourable pointer in the existence of the minute gas field at Eskdale which was being produced to supply a village or two in the North Eastern Gas Board's area.

My talks with Illing crystallized these ideas. That part of the Continental Shelf which had produced the great forests of the carboniferous era 300 million years ago on the land areas of Great Britain and Ireland had been uplifted during succeeding eras. Across the North Sea in the Netherlands it had been depressed and contained, under great depths of salt deposits and other sediments of the Permian and other eras. So in England we had coal at or near the surface and no gas, but in north Holland coal, possibly, but at very great depth, with gas trapped under the salt caps. If gas was what we wanted we should be looking for it under the waters of the North Sea somewhere between Eskdale in Yorkshire and Slochteren in Holland.

It is a long haul from a personal conviction to the final step of advising one's colleagues to spend money and effort on what could turn out to be the biggest flop of one's career. That is if you want your colleagues to remain your friends. My campaign began with the address to the Fuel Luncheon Club in March 1961, reported in Chapter 13. The *New Scientist* asked for a copy of my discourse, and it was published and would have reached a wider circle of readers, including oil companies at home and abroad.

Towards the end of 1961, it seemed that the time had come for some more positive action. I had a friendly relationship with BP, dating back to 1942, when I had most helpful cooperation in obtaining a supply of hydrogen for the RAF at Abadan. It continued through my time as Chairman of the South Eastern Gas

Board, with a jointly planned gas-from-oil plant at the Isle of Grain. I therefore wrote to their Deputy Chairman on 16 November, quoting Professor Illing's view as being firmly inclined to the belief that gas (and presumably oil) was much more likely to be found offshore in the North Sea, perhaps at best close to the shore in the northern part of England, and in conclusion:

> We appreciate how wide are the implications of such a search and how great would be the expense. Nevertheless we feel that the prize is so great that the whole project is worth discussing at some suitable opportunity, and indeed I think that Illing's view might be of considerable interest if, as I understand, you are already engaged in preliminary discussions with other oil companies.

The answer was non-committal: the discussions they had had with other oil companies with regard to the potentiality of the North Sea had been very tentative and exploratory. They thought it best to leave the matter at the possibility of an exchange of views between geological experts. On 1 June 1962, the Chief Geologist at BP telephoned the Council's Coal Officer to tell him that an announcement was to be made the following day to the effect that Shell, Esso and BP had entered into an agreement for a joint survey of the North Sea. Sir Henry Jones was out of town at the time and I was abroad, but our further enquiries revealed that the arrangement was exclusive and no new partners could be admitted.

My disappointment was intense, but there was one ray of light: on 10 May there had appeared in my room at Hyde Park Corner a person carrying a very welcome message. C.F. Dohm, the Executive Vice-President of American International, known I think at the time as Pan American, but now and henceforth Amoco for short, was a dynamic personality. He wasted no time on lengthy introductions, and in a few minutes outlined his proposals. Amoco were interested in exploring the North Sea and he wanted to know more about the procedure for acquiring a licence. I told him of our own interest and about how we had been searching, so far unsuccessfully, for gas onshore. Dohm then advanced the idea that the Council might be associated with his company in a search offshore. Amoco would be prepared if necessary to finance the search. He had received no encouragement at the Ministry of Power, who advised him that it might be several years before the legislative position would enable them to issue offshore licences. He left with me his company's interpretation, as it might be agreed under the terms of the 1958 International Convention.

The Convention had followed a number of unilateral declarations claiming what amounted to sovereignty over the Continental Shelf. The United Nations took up the matter at Geneva and finally in 1958 an international conference took place, which led to a Convention that was to come into force when twenty-two nations had ratified it. The Continental Shelf was here defined as being the sea bed and subsoil from the outer limits of territorial waters to a point where the depth is 200 metres or alternatively wherever the sea bed is exploitable. Thus depth and exploitability are the criteria, but the powers which the Convention confers are limited to exploration and exploitation.

As to the limits of possible competing claims, it was declared that in the absence of agreement voluntarily reached by adjacent states, these should be determined by application of the principles of the median line. This line is defined as a line, every point of which is equidistant from the nearest points of base lines, from which the breadth of the territorial seas of each state are measured. Normally, territorial sea is measured three miles from land, but there is provision for sea that is enclosed between headlands and between offshore islands.

At our own regular meeting with the Minister on 23 May 1962, then Mr Richard Wood, I reported my conversation with Dohm. I hoped to convince the Minister and his officials present of the importance of ratifying the convention and passing the necessary legislation. Angus Beckett, then Under-Secretary in charge of the Gas Division, was by training a geologist and had long experience in administration of oil matters. I noticed that he was showing a keen interest and it was not long before he was transferred back to the Oil Division, where he remained in charge throughout the North Sea development.

Professor Illing who had given me valuable advice in the early days of my interest in the North Sea was not willing to continue as consultant through the operational stages. I realized also that there was no prospect of persuading our partner in the onshore search to admit us as partners in a survey of the North Sea. Amoco was showing continued interest in an association for that purpose, so we authorized negotiations to begin between Walter MacDonald, the Manager of Negotiations for Amoco, and Roy Huxtable, the Secretary of the Gas Council (he had been with me in the South Eastern Gas Board). They were both resourceful and skilful negotiators and, not being surrounded by crowds of experts, the negotiations were brief and effective. They came up with a proposal for a jointly financed seismic survey of a clearly defined area of the North Sea. The Council's participation would be 10 per cent of the cost of the seismic survey but with the right retained for the Council to participate up to 50 per cent in any further development consequent on the results of the survey.

An agreement on these lines suited us well. The Gas Council wanted information almost as much as it wanted gas and they knew they were not likely to get much information from the oil companies. If the prospects in the North Sea were reasonably good, they would shape their future accordingly and start looking at what was involved in the high-pressure pipe lining and transmission of natural gas across the country. If the prospects were very good indeed and they were to receive a satisfactory allocation of licences and if the government would back up their efforts, the Gas Council might take up their option to participate as to 50 per cent in the development of what could turn out to be a highly profitable enterprise. A figure somewhere between 10 per cent and 50 per cent might serve to keep us in touch with developments at not too high a cost with the prospect of a modest profit in the end.

Amoco, on the other hand, were as yet unknown in this country, in spite of the fact that their parent company, Standard of Indiana, is one of the largest oil companies in the United States of America. At one time among the biggest operators in Venezuela, but without any overseas outlets for oil, they sold their interests during the depression, when they were prevented by legislation from importing oil into the United States. It was not until 1958 that they re-entered the international scene. Coming again so late, they may have found the going tough and to be associated with the 'Nationals' was a policy they had successfully followed in Egypt and Iran. If gas was the objective, why not join the gas men of the United Kingdom who, since Hell hath no fury like a woman scorned, were quite ready to take up with their new suitor.

A further approach to BP in September produced only another refusal, so we went ahead to draft the final agreement with Amoco which was sent to the Ministry on 12 March 1963 and signed on the 21st of that month. It had been indicated (informally of course) that, in the view of HMG it could not be said to be objectionable. Nor of course did HMG want to be involved in any responsibility if the whole thing was a failure. There would be no positive objection to including the expenditure involved among the debit items, which would eventually be borrowing requirements, etc. etc.

The legislation required to establish sovereignty over the oil and gas reserves of the part of the North Sea that lay on the United Kingdom side of the Median Line, was in preparation. We foresaw the possibility of having to lodge applications early in the following year. The United Kingdom was the 22nd and last to sign the Convention, in June 1964. The Convention then came into force and the Median Line as defined therein became the boundary of British interest in the North Sea. Meanwhile a Bill to give effect to the provisions of the Convention was passing through all its stages in Parliament and received the Royal assent on 15 April 1964. It gave powers for the granting of licences and reaffirmed the principle embodied in the 1934 Act by which Gas Undertakings, now the Area Boards, were to be given the first opportunity to buy any gas, except as required by the finder for his own industrial purposes, at a reasonable price; 'reasonable' in this context being nowhere defined.

Our Group was widened to include two other companies, as provided for in the draft agreement. Amerada, founded by the first Lord Cowdray, passed into American control during the war except for a 20 per cent holding by the British Treasury. Texas Eastern was a successful pipeline company, which had taken some interest in exploration for gas. Amoco were operators for the Group.

The seismic method used consists of a ship towing a cable, which may be up to a mile and a half long, with sensitive microphones strung out at regular intervals along it. Another ship tows an explosive charge located at the exact centre of the cable. The ships proceed at a uniform speed on a predetermined course. On reaching the required point cable is paid out at the exact ship's speed. It lies stationary on the surface for a few seconds while the parent ship by signal detonates the charge and activates a series of instruments which record the interval of time between the explosion and the reception of the reflected noise at each of the microphones. Interpretation of the data depends on the fact that a sound wave will be reflected and refracted at the interface of rocks of different kinds and results are still in milliseconds not in metres, so much remains to be done before the contour maps of the sub-sea surfaces emerge.

It is possible under favourable conditions to shoot as much as 60 miles a day and we had budgeted for a total of 3,000 miles for the first year, at a cost of about £120 per mile. We aimed to establish a ten-mile square grid over the whole of the initial survey area.

Shooting started in accordance with a first agreement in the spring of 1963 off the east coast of England and it was not long before the experts interpreting the seismic data were beginning to draw exciting conclusions about the deep underground structure of the rocks. It began to seem possible, even probable, that they would reproduce the conditions which had created the great gas reserves at Slochteren. The wisdom of the group's decision to act on Amoco's recommendation and use a long cable, at some extra expense, was demonstrated early on by its greater ability to penetrate and to record information down to 10,000 ft. and more. The Gas Council/Amoco Group was not alone in the North Sea and at one time as many as twelve survey teams were hard at work trying to catch up on the flying start by Shell, Esso and BP, before the expected winter gales would bring work to a halt. As every yachtsman knows, it is quite difficult to pinpoint a situation one hundred miles off land to within a mile or so, and it was necessary to be accurate to within fifty yards if the surveys were to be consistent and reproducible when plotted as a grid. This was made possible by a special Decca navigational chain.

On reviewing the results of the first season's survey, it became clear what extra information would be needed and there were indications also that the survey area should be extended north of the area included in the first agreement, which was modified accordingly. During the second season of 1964, the Group shot a total of 5,450 miles and became more than ever convinced that this northern area was worth exploring, although there was no prior evidence about the probable presence of gas. My own conviction was that the Council's best interest would be served by obtaining information over all and every prospective area in the North Sea. If we found oil and no gas, we could make good use of that instead in a new generation of gasworks.

The stage was now set for the issue of licences under the Continental Shelf Act, both to explore (which we had already been doing for three years without any such formality) and to produce gas under licences, which would be granted for blocks, each about ten miles square, for a period of six years at a rate equivalent to about $6,250 per annum. The rate was to rise steeply after the first six years, reaching a maximum in the eleventh year equivalent to $72,500 per block per year. The validity of the licence was to be for a period of forty years from the end of the sixth year. A list of the numbers of blocks on offer was published on 15 May and the applications were lodged on 14 July 1964.

The time had now come, when, under our agreement, it should have been necessary to nominate the percentage interest which the Gas Council wished to take in the further development. The

Ministry of Power, who would have to authorize the borrowing from public funds of the money necessary for this much more expensive stage of operations, were naturally anxious to know the extent to which they would be committed. The Council for its part was in difficulty about deciding on a proportion, until it knew what blocks would be allotted to them. Our partners in the Group agreed to meet us in this difficulty and to defer the Council's election as to the final participation, provided, however, that all the survey costs after 6 July would be re-allocated in proportion as the Council made its final decision. The award of licences was announced on 17 September and, after studying all the financial implications (the Group had been awarded 36 blocks and undertaken to drill ten wells, which might cost anywhere between \$5 and \$10 million), the Council decided to participate to an extent equal to the interest of the largest of their associates as follows:

Gas Council	40 parts (31%)
Amoco	40 parts (31%)
Amerada	30 parts (23%)
Texas Eastern	20 parts (15%)

We were somewhat disappointed with our allocation of 36 blocks, finding ourselves rather heavily committed with 12 of these north of the latitude of Berwick upon Tweed, where the prospects, though exciting, were less certain and the cost of exploring in deep waters so far from our shores would be much greater, and began to wonder too if we had been over-optimistic, when we saw how few other oil companies had applied for licences there. Some time later, when I met John Birkin of Shell, he told me that the Shell/Esso Group (BP had gone their own way after the surveys) had also been feeling rather exposed in these northern waters and had taken comfort from the thought that, if they had made a mistake, it was better to do so in company. This thought had occurred to us too. In fact, the area in question includes the southern part of the great Tertiary Basin, with large reserves of oil. The best of the gas proved unfortunately to be just on the other side of the Median Line in Norwegian waters.

There was strong competition for blocks in the southern part of the North Sea. This is in the area of Zechstein salt, which would provide the gas-tight cover for the gas fields we hoped to find. We had applied for 60 blocks and were disappointed at only being awarded 14. As will appear later, three of these included half the largest gas field in the North Sea and more than half of another one, and as things turned out there was really no cause for despondency.

Gas Council representatives took an active part in all the discussion that went on as a preliminary to filing our application. Our entire geological staff consisted at this time of one petroleum engineer, Peter Hinde, with Denis Rooke and myself as enthusiastic amateurs. Yet the technical information was presented with such extreme clarity by our experts, headed by Ian Macartney of Amoco, who had been in charge from the start, that none of us felt in any way excluded from the debate.

To complete the exploration story, there was a second round of awards in November of the following year, by which time there was a Labour Government in power intent on participation at the very least. The Group agreed with our suggestion that it would be politic for the Council to take a 50% share in the 16 blocks which were awarded. The Coal Board, who had not taken part in the original search, started exploration partnerships with Continental in the North Sea and Gulf in the west during 1965. A third round, after I had left the Council, introduced the idea of a forced union with the Gas Council or the Coal Board for the new territory to the west of Britain. It was an unnecessary complication in what had so far been a straightforward commercial venture, but was presumably a sop to the protagonists of a National Hydrocarbon Corporation, which some of its more dedicated supporters had hoped would take over all the North Sea operations.

The position of the Gas Council in all this was, to say the least of it, unclear, although our right to do what we did was never queried. While all this activity was going on offshore, the search for suitable geological structures on land as reservoirs for gas to meet the winter load was proceeding quietly under Illing's general direction. That was until we thought we had a suitable anticline not far from Winchester. Church and State rose in their collective wrath and drove us to take shelter under a Private Member's Bill in Parliament. The fury of our enemies drove us to withdraw it on a promise of a Government Bill in due course to legislate for in-ground storage. Dennis Proctor saw in this new Bill an opportunity to rectify a situation which would have to faced sooner rather than later. The Gas Act 1948 vested all powers to make and sell gas in the twelve Area Boards: the Council's function was mainly to advise and consult and to act where required on behalf of a Board or Boards. The Gas Act 1965 would give the Council powers to buy and sell gas, and the Minister to appoint three Members of the Gas Council additional to the Chairman and Deputy Chairman and the twelve Area Board Chairmen.

15
North Sea: Discovery

Connoisseurs of the oil scene from all over the world agreed that during the period leading up to the date set for the submission of applications, the London Hilton had been as satisfactory a setting as anything they had seen in Caracas or Bogota or Djakarta or Bangkok – you name it: they had been there. Now the talking was over and it was time for action and, following the issue of licences, there was great activity behind the discreet frontages of the offices of most major oil companies, each planning to be the first to announce a discovery. Added to the usual competitive urge, there were those who thought there might be an opportunity to drive a harder bargain for the sale of gas before the market was flooded. Amoseas (Standard Oil of California and Texaco) were first out in the North Sea and 'Mr Cap' started drilling on the Dogger Bank on Boxing Day 1964 but three months later abandoned its well. Ten more wells were started in the next twelve months.

Our licence obligations required the drilling of ten wells in depths of water which could be anywhere between 60 feet and 270 feet and the arguments favoured the jack-up type of drilling barge. These have three, four or more retractable legs, which can be lowered to support from the sea bottom the barge complete with its tall derrick, working machinery and living quarters for forty or more men and then, by hydraulic operation, raise it well above the surface of the water, where it rests clear of the highest waves.

The decision was to have a new jack-up rig built, which was to be leased on a three-year contract with the International Drilling Company, and *Orion* was launched or, to be more exact, commissioned at John Brown's Yard on the Clyde on 1 June 1966. It weighed 5,000 tons and measured 180 feet by 150 feet, excluding the helicopter deck, and was designed to drill in 250 feet of water and to withstand winds of up to 125 miles per hour and waves up to 64 feet high. It could drill to depths of 20,000 feet. The commissioning was performed by Dorothea at a very pleasant ceremony in the best tradition of launching a liner.

Activity in the North Sea during 1965 was limited by the small number of rigs available. Two at least of these proved to be unsuitable for the conditions in these inhospitable waters. Of the ten wells completed or abandoned, the only one of commercial potential was the BP discovery well on what became known as the West Sole Field, 45 miles east of the Humber. Mr Fred Lee, Minister of Power, had paid a visit on 8 November and stated, 'They are quite sure they are on to something big, and so am I.' If there were any doubters left, the sight of the test flare, which was lit on 7 December, was enough to convince them that this was indeed the bonanza. The *Financial Times* duly reported on the same day:

> On the Stock Exchange yesterday, oil shares moved ahead strongly in the afternoon on the rumours that British Petroleum was to start 'flaring' today, and prices improved further towards the close, following confirmation by the Company.

But the public were reminded of the real danger and difficulty of these offshore operations when, on 27 December, *Sea Gem* collapsed and fell over into the sea, with the loss of thirteen men.

The BP discovery was significant to our Group for two good reasons. It was reported to be in the Rotliegendes, the same sandstone which provides the reservoir at Slochteren, and we had secured three blocks lying on a line between West Sole and Holland. Also it was on a structure which our own seismic information had given as a first choice, and it was satisfactory to know that, even if it had not been licensed to our group, the advice of the experts had been proved sound.

The Gas Council, in its capacity as the buyer and distributor of North Sea gas, was keenly interested, and we awaited with some impatience an invitation to share the good news. The invitation, when it came, was for Henry Jones and myself to lunch at Finsbury Square, whither we repaired hopefully, returning more in sorrow than in anger. The proposition put before us was encouraging insofar as BP were prepared to offer 100 million cubic feet per day on the evidence of only one well, but as to price – this was to be the first shot in a long battle between producers, pressing for prices related to retail value, and the Gas Council wanting a figure based on cost plus a fair reward for effort and risk. It will be recalled that the relevant Acts had never attempted to define what was 'reasonable' for the price of gas, and the present area of disagreement turned out to be very wide indeed.

The Council, through Hedley Parker, our legal adviser, had

taken the precaution of studying methods used in the United States for controlling the price of natural gas. Federal control of gas prices dates back to 1938, when Congress passed the Natural Gas Act, without a single dissenting vote in either House. This had followed a report by the Federal Trade Commission two years before, in which the virtual monopoly of the pipeline companies was held to threaten the interests of the consumer. The Supreme Court has consistently upheld the right, indeed the duty, of the Federal Power Commission to prevent 'the exploitation of the consumer at the hands of the Natural Gas Companies'. So far so good, and the pipeline companies soon achieved the relative respectability of public utilities with limitation of dividends and avoidance of duplication of effort, for each new pipeline required a certificate of public convenience. Over and above all this there were certain obligations as to continuity of supply. At first sight, all this was uncommonly like the gasworks' clauses in our 1870 Act, even to the point where the Commission has power to prescribe a uniform system of accounting.

But the Phillips Petroleum case of 1954 gave a fresh turn to the screw, for the Supreme Court ruled that the Natural Gas Act applies to the sales of gas to a pipeline company, if such gas was intended for use in inter-State commerce, even though the Act had specifically excluded the producing and gathering of gas. The Court held that this was necessary in order to achieve the prime purpose of the Act, which was to protect the consumers. In another case, the Court ruled that the cessation of supply by a producer at the end of his contract is only possible if the Commission so orders. No wonder that one of our partners complained that the way things were going we might as well be nationalized and that to them was a fate worse than death.

We felt we could not be faulted for following the rules based on such high principles as those expressed in the Supreme Court of the United States, so when Henry Jones met J.E. Swidler, the Chairman of the FPC, at a World Power Conference, and received an invitation to view the working of the Act, we accepted with alacrity and Hedley Parker left for Washington without delay.

The FPC formula, which was to provide the basis for most of our thinking about price, was established in what came to be known as the Permian Basin Case. Since it had proved impracticable to cost every gas well individually, the price of gas was to be determined on an area basis, using average values for parameters which could be assumed to apply to a single geological structure. Thus the average cost of a well and its potential output based on a predetermined life of its producible reserves and the exploration success of the basin (being the ratio of discovery wells to the total number of wells drilled), together with some other cost factors, determined the bare cost. After adding a margin for profit and incentive for further exploration the FPC was able to announce a field price for the Permian Basin and a separate price for Louisiana. Note, however, that this was not a fixed imposed price. What the FPC said was that any agreements concluded at or below this price would be approved without further examination, but knowing how long it would take to conclude a hearing, most natural gas companies were prepared to settle at the field price. This was the cost-related basis, which conditioned the Council's views about the price that they should offer to pay for North Sea gas. There was no historical experience on which to evaluate an FPC formula, but using a success figure of one in ten, which had coincidentally been the experience of the first year in the North Sea, and the cost of drilling that had figured in the budgets, and applying these to the North Sea, prices suggested were of around 2d a therm for medium-sized discoveries.

The oil companies had their eyes on the price at which gas could be sold and had access to the detailed accounts of the Area Boards and the Gas Council. In 1954/55 the average industry revenue for gas was shown as 16.58d per therm. There was clearly a wide range for manoeuvre. Another pointer to a possible interim settlement was the price at which the Gas Council had been importing liquefied natural gas, on the argument that, if the gas had not been found, the Council would have had to import more. The cost of LNG had been discussed and argued about during the proceedings of the Select Committee in 1961 and was known to be about 5.5d per therm.

There followed some weeks of coming and going with only a slight narrowing of the area of disagreement to show for it, during which one felt that some impatience was being generated in Government circles and an expectant Press was dropping hints about the bitter quarrel which they hoped to be able to report in due course. The fact was that a great deal was at stake. If the Gas Council were to concede anything like the so-called market price and this became a precedent for all sales – or even if they conceded the price of the alternative material, liquefied natural gas – they could never hope to market successfully the large quantities of gas that they hoped to find. If BP were to accept the Gas Council's reasoning on prices, they would have sold the world oil industry into an FPC type of bondage.

The Government kept up the fiction that this was a matter to be freely negotiated between the parties as provided for in the various Acts. In a difficulty of this kind, the usual thing is to send for the Civil Service. Matthew Stevenson had succeeded Dennis Proctor as Permanent Secretary and could be described as a man of strong positive convictions. The meeting which he called to resolve the matter consisted of only three people and, so far as I know, we made no notes and kept no record of what was quite a lengthy meeting. But very soon after that we concluded an agreement with BP for 100 million cubic feet per day at a prescribed load factor for fifteen years, the price to be 5d per therm for the first three years; thereafter to be negotiated.

As I have said, there were no notes or report of our meeting, but I cannot pretend to have been left unaware of some important factors, which could decide our course of action. First, the gas industry was expanding at the rate of 10 per cent per year, a rate which showed no sign of slackening. Second, any repetition of the recent West Midlands failure of supply (in November 1965 and January 1966) would be most unpopular in high places. Third, the naphtha, which was used to make gas, was free of all excise duty, by what can be described as administrative decision and not by a clear statement of law. And fourthly, if the Council wanted to import any more LNG, they would certainly have to get permission from the Government and finance for the purpose. On reflection, these seemed to add up to a very compelling reason for accepting the Permanent Secretary's recommendation and arriving at a settlement on terms which would allow the first delivery of natural gas from the North Sea to proceed on a limited scale as quickly as possible and at no higher cost than the alternatives then available to the industry. The three-year term of the price recommended would not prejudice free negotiations towards what we hoped to be a more realistic price if, as was expected, much larger quantities of gas should become available.

BP have not revealed what was in their mind and may have been disappointed at the short term of three years for the 5d therm. They too wanted to get ahead with supplying gas and would soon be making an issue of millions of shares, so that any prior announcement would be, to say the least, quite helpful.

The Minister of Power, Mr Fred Lee, made a statement in the House of Commons on 5 February 1966, in which he referred to the fact that agreement had been reached with his 'advice and assistance to both parties in composing the ultimate difference between them'. He went on to say:

> with the permission of both parties I disclose to the House the main features of the arrangements between them. The Company undertake to deliver and the Council to accept at least 50 million cubic feet a day for 15 years from the commencement of supply. The Company will use their best endeavours to increase output to 100 million cubic feet a day during the first three years of supply, and will offer these additional supplies to the Gas Council, who undertake to receive them on a prearranged programme. The agreed price is 5d a therm, but this is valid only up to an average of 100 million cubic feet a day and for a period of three years from 1st July, 1967, or the date of commencement of the guaranteed supply, whichever is the earlier. Above the stipulated quantity in the first three years, and for supplies beyond the first three years, the price will be for re-negotiation.

He further went on to say:

> As far as price is concerned, this is a limited and temporary arrangement; and the agreed price is lower than actual import prices already being paid, and competitive with the price of authenticated offers of comparable gas in comparable quantities from overseas. The eventual economics and costs of production of North Sea gas cannot at present be measured: they will depend on the number of failures, the total quantity of gas obtained and the number of producing wells required to obtain it, the distance from the shore and many other factors. We must all hope that much larger quantities will be found than the minimum mentioned above and that the price can be significantly below the level adopted temporarily in the first case.

I have heard it suggested that the world oil industry was misled into believing that 5d was to be the going rate for all the gas found in the North Sea. If that is so, they must have failed to read the small print, and that in my experience is in no way characteristic of the world oil industry.

As for the Government, as 50 per cent shareholders in BP, they must have been pleased at the success of the stock issue, quite apart from the hopes generated about a relief to the balance of payments. Fred Lee was genuinely pleased for the sake of the gas industry, which he had defended stoutly when things went wrong in the West Midlands and much of the industry there was shut down for some days by the gas shortage already referred to.

Plans were quickly made to bring the gas into the new national grid system, which had been created to distribute the imported LNG, and the North Eastern and East Midland Boards undertook to survey a route and supervise the construction of a 24-inch high-pressure main from Easington on the Yorkshire coast, across the Humber and then by the shortest practicable route to a point just south of Sheffield. The 1965 Gas Act had regularized the functions of the Gas Council, who were thereby empowered to manufacture, find, distribute and sell gas. The Act had also allowed some increase in the number of members of the Council, and Denis Rooke was appointed a full-time member with responsibility for production. At that time his entire engineering staff numbered about 32 and the boards were fully extended with a massive production and distribution programme, required to meet the regular 10 per cent p.a. increase in demand. It was a great achievement to have the main completed and tested ready to receive gas when it was most needed.

There still existed in 1966 the general shortage of drilling rigs experienced in 1965 when only ten wells were completed or abandoned. The only discovery of commercial significance had been that of BP, and this had ended in the tragic loss of the rig. The French drilling rig Neptune was hard at work all year, but had only scored two dry holes so far and was now in January 1966 on location on what later became known as the Leman Field. Our seismic information indicated that, if Shell found gas where they were drilling, it was almost certain that our adjacent block would share in the discovery, so we judged it sensible to leave that one for the time being. Our hopes centred on two blocks just to the north east of Leman, where our seismic information indicated a large though very complex structure. Continental had drilled on the west flank and found gas and water in Rotliegendes sandstone: Shell had drilled to the east and found water only, but a good depth of Rotliegendes.

Our opportunity came when a consortium drilling in German waters decided to call a halt for the time being and the rig they had chartered, called Herr Louie, was likely to be free, but not for long. Amoco had a 10 per cent interest in the consortium and one of their negotiators was over in Germany at this time. After a few telephone calls I told him I was willing to pledge the Gas Council credit if he could get an option, which he did. Fortunately for us, both the Gas Council and our partners were ready to confirm this old-fashioned way of doing business. So Herr Louie became Mr Louie when it arrived on location of 19 March and was jacked up by the following morning, to start drilling on 4 April.

It was now a case of waiting with what patience we could muster for the results. With a three months' start Shell/Esso were first in with a very cautious announcement and the hint of more to follow. In fact, Hedley Parker, who had been put in charge of negotiations, told me that they had found several hundred feet of good Rotliegendes sandstone full of high-quality gas and would soon be ready to discuss quantities and prices. It would be a quite unbelievable piece of bad luck, if this were less than a very great find, although some step-out wells would be needed to prove it commercial.

Meanwhile, Mr Louie was drilling ahead and the news came that the Rotliegendes had been penetrated with shows of gas. By 4 June all the necessary cores had been extracted and the wells had been cased and perforated. The tests made were well up to expectations and we were confident that this was a commercial gas field, but the experts warned that the assessment of field capacity might be a lengthy process, since the structure was complex and probably faulted. We decided to move Mr Louie after completing the well, leaving it ready for future use as a producer, on to a site on our block adjacent to the Shell/Esso discovery. This was to fulfil the dual purpose of evaluating the total capacity of the Leman Field and to establish the interest that our group might have in its development. Unfortunately, Mr Louie was feeling his age and the metallurgist's report on the state of the structure supporting the legs made it imperative to retire him temporarily from active service for repairs in Germany. *Orion* was now on its way round the coast and was diverted to the well abandoned by Mr Louie. By a piece of most skilful manoeuvring, it was positioned accurately and was able to take over drilling of the same hole. The well was completed on 21 September and results exceeded all expectations with a substantial proved depth of good quality sandstone and a high deliverability on test. We could now be confident that Leman really was a major gas field and that we had a substantial share in it. *Orion* was moved across to continue the work on evaluating our first discovery, which was to be called 'Indefatigable', and soon proved that this field extended well over our two blocks.

So out of three holes drilled we had made three important discoveries and this induced a state of optimistic euphoria, which was quite hard to restrain at the Ministry and even at the Gas Council. World opinion was by now fairly convinced that the North Sea was an important petroleum prospect. If this was not enough, another group called Arpet, headed by Atlantic Richfield, completed a well in October further inshore, which indicated the near certainty of a fourth major gas field, later to be called Hewitt. This discovery was particularly interesting to the experts, because it was the first in which gas had been discovered in anything except Rotliegendes. The gas in Hewitt is almost certainly of the same origin as the rest, but for some reason has escaped past the salt cover into a later sandstone called Bunter. The discovery opened up new possibilities over the whole area, although so far nothing of commercial significance has yet been found in Bunter sands elsewhere.

Meanwhile what we hoped would be the first major discovery of gas on land had been made in Yorkshire. The Gas Council in partnership with BP had surveyed this area and drilled two deep wells without success. BP suggested that we should accept an offer of a farm-out to Home Oil of Canada, who were willing to undertake the drilling of a number of obligation wells as required by the licence. After several disappointments, they struck good quality gas at Lockton in a limestone formation embedded in salt. Under the farm-out agreement with Home Oil, the Gas Council became owners of half this reserve. (This turned out, in the event, to be a heavily faulted structure and the field was shut down.)

So in the second year with a total of three major offshore gas fields discovered and proved, the score to date was four from twenty-seven exploration wells drilled together with a number of possibles, none of which was likely to be large and most were not even commercial. The question everyone wanted us to answer (and in the absence of an answer there were plenty who were prepared to speculate) was not how many, but how much.

The size of a gas field is by custom expressed in trillions of cubic feet (this is the American trillion equal to one million million) of recoverable reserves of gas. In order to reduce such a figure to something which can perhaps be understood, we start by assuming a twenty-five year life of the field, so one trillion will produce 40 billion cubic feet a year or just over 110 million cubic feet of natural gas a day, if taken continuously over the years. In practice, there is a build-up period of about five years and the rate of production of gas at the plateau is likely to be about 130 million cubic feet a day. Since most contracts provide for some variation as between summer and winter, the winter rate would normally be about 200 million cubic feet a day.

In November 1966 I said in another address to the Fuel Luncheon Club that we could reasonably assume recoverable reserves of not less than 10 trillion cubic feet, with an upper limit of 20 trillion. The North Sea on this rating was less than a third the size of Slochteren, which had been reported as 60 trillion. Nevertheless, it was a large reserve of gas and in five years the gas industry might be taking 2,600 million cubic feet a day as a daily contract quantity from the North Sea. In 1960 the whole gas industry output of town gas was equivalent to only 1,000 million cubic feet of natural gas a day. So we could now foresee a gas industry growing to two or three times as large as it had been.

To complete the North Sea story in the first decade, after the end of 1966 only one major gas discovery was been recorded in the southern North Sea. Continental, who had drilled unsuccessfully to the west of our Indefatigable Field, took the Coal Board into partnership during 1965 and made a number of important discoveries, which added up to one useful gas field, which they called Viking. Some other small discoveries were recorded, but the cost of piping gas offshore was such that these might have to wait until a common pipeline system was established. However, the simple and perhaps unwelcome fact was that, in the area covered by the presence of carboniferous gas in Rotliegendes or Bunter sandstone, 85 per cent of the total reserves found within the first five years were discovered in a single period of twelve months. The next four years only increased the total by 15 per cent. This is not to say that nothing more will be found. What is certain is that several very good prospects failed to produce and it soon appeared that future finds would be much smaller and more scattered, and more costly to find and bring into production.

The area to the immediate north continued to be most disappointing. Further north again, in what can be called Scottish waters, the picture was far more exciting and the finds there and in the Norwegian sector proved as important to the economy of the country as all the gas finds of the first five years. The Scottish sector, it will be recalled, is the area in which Gas Council/Amoco and Shell/Esso found themselves almost the only believers in the first round of bidding. Interest grew when a consortium headed by Phillips made an important discovery of oil on the Norwegian side of the Median Line, approximately on the latitude of Aberdeen, and another group headed by Amoco also found oil there. These discoveries and other drillings confirmed our hopes that there would be great depths of Tertiary sediments. Several substantial discoveries of oil were soon reported on the UK side of the Median Line and it became clear that the major subsequent activity was to be in the north. Oil was far more valuable to the oil companies than gas, not only in terms of the money reward, but more importantly in the freedom to market it under their own control and usually through their own outlets. The associated gas was a vital addition to the sources available to the gas industry, whose growth by 1970 showed signs of exceeding the rate of discovery in the south.

16

The Future of the Gas Industry

At the beginning of my seventh year as Deputy Chairman I could see it was to be a case of now or never, for I would be 63 in October. Remembering all the gold watches I had handed out at Croydon to those with forty years' faithful service, I became sharply aware that this could happen to me also. On the first day of September 1966 a gold hunter watch suitably inscribed landed on my desk to mark my forty years' service – a present from old colleagues and friends in the South Eastern. Henry, but no one else, had known for some time of my intention to retire although I do not think he really believed it would happen. Our relationship had been friendly throughout, under conditions where strain could so easily have arisen; it had also been fruitful as the results showed. As to some of the more controversial actions of the time, like the killing of Mr Therm and his replacement by things like 'Whizzigas', he may not have been altogether convinced. Since the only way that the medium can produce results is by prodding the public into awareness of the message, quite a number of other people, including politicians, were shocked. There was inevitable official and public criticism, but we gave as good as we got.

When it became common knowledge that we were prepared to abandon coal as a basis for a future successful gas industry, it was he who had to face attacks in front of the Ministry. He had to give the vital evidence that swayed the Parliamentary Committee which urged the Minister to make a decision about the importation of liquid methane. He had to contend with a strong personal intervention by Lord Robens, who appeared in person before the Committee at his own request. Meanwhile I was free to continue in ways best suited to my own resources and inclinations, including a sort of general warfare with electricity and coal to establish our sphere of influence, indeed to show them we had a right to be there at all. The long-standing running battle with the Coal Board had come to a head at meetings of the Departmental Committee on Coal Derivatives (the Wilson Committee) in

1959/60. The basic issues (described in Chapter 12) were clearly defined and the Committee could but agree to the ICI decision to base its future plans on oil; or, to be more precise, light distillate of which there was a growing surplus. At the end of all our discussions and the joint study with the Coal Board, we were convinced that there was no case for the Lurgi process in face of the competition from oil and the expected resources of natural gas. It seemed also to convince the Coal Board for we heard no more of the matter.

The discoveries in the North Sea held out the promise of a cheap and plentiful supply of gas. The Gas Council's involvement technically and financially had given us a new feeling of independence; we could speak with authority. We would never again be subjected to control of the rival energy producers. Surely now was the time to go, undeterred by the inevitable argument that 'the time was was not yet ripe'.

> The Principle of Unripe Time [thus Cornford again in *Microcosmographia Academia*] is that people should not do at the present moment what they think right at the moment, because the moment at which they think it right has not yet arrived ... Time by the way is like the medlar, it has a trick of going rotten before it is ripe.

Encouraged by these thoughts the opportunity to make public my 'last will and testament' came with an invitation addressed to Henry, to deliver a paper at the annual meeting of the Canadian Gas Association. He was prevented by prior engagements and suggested to the Association that they might invite me, which they did. The gas industry in most of Canada had been fighting in past years a losing battle against the competition of hydro-electricity and oil. The discovery of great reserves of natural gas in Alberta, much in excess of what that province could use, led to the decision to construct the trans-Canada pipeline. Natural gas was now available in the centres of industry and population in Central and Eastern Canada. The Canadian gas industry was flourishing and expanding at the same sort of rate that the United States had experienced fifteen years before. They were interested to learn where we in Britain stood in the light of reported discoveries in the North Sea. For our part we could certainly benefit from their experience, and I was only too happy to accept the invitation. Once again, as often in the past, the task of writing a paper which would have to be understood by a large audience provided the opportunity for a critical appraisal of one's own beliefs. So I chose for my subject 'The Future of the Gas Industry in Britain'. The writing occupied much of my spare time in the spring of 1966. It was essential to my purpose that this should be a personal effort and not an assembly of facts, figures and forecasts produced by the growing specialist departments in the Gas Council.

Attitudes to forecasting are conditioned to excess by the sacred cow of the Trend. Unskilled and daring characters will go so far as to project a line joining two points onwards towards infinity. This of course is wrong. The scientific forecaster likes to obtain at least three points, and having evolved a formula which will fit them on a straight line declares that to be a trend. From there it is but a short step to predicting the future with every appearance of certainty; a procedure which has always seemed to me to owe more to predestination than to free will, or, to quote from *The Week-end Book*:

> There was a young man who said 'Damn!
> It appears to me now that I am
>   Just a being that moves
>   In predestinate grooves –
> Not a bus, not a bus, but a tram.'
>
> Anonymous

In 1955 when progress in the gas industry came to a halt there had been many in the ministries and elsewhere who, projecting a trend, could see no future for gas except as a stagnant part of the economy. During the next five years official forecasts were for a zero growth rate and many critics went so far as to see a decline as inevitable.

If we had accepted that as our fate we could easily have made it come true. Fortunately a true gas man is not easily disheartened. The successful trials of the *Methane Pioneer*, bringing natural gas across an ocean, convinced the doubters that, even if the future was not quite assured, at least it had some prospect of success. Our firm intention was to cut free from coal: coal entailed high cost and inflexible production. We would take advantage of any oil products which might be in surplus, and therefore cheap, and endeavour to use only the cheap and flexible production techniques associated with light distillate. We had acquired the mood of optimism which is essential to success in a selling operation. This began to spread as one after another of the Boards found a public willing to pay for the convenience that gas could provide in heating the home. The fresh start could be said to have stemmed from the 1961 Sales and Services Conference in Harrogate, where, as related in Chapter 13, it seemed as if 'everyone suddenly burst out singing'. For the first time in ten years domestic consumption had reversed its downward trend, and a slight but very welcome increase had been recorded, entirely due to success in selling gas for home heating. The industry's official five-year forecasts which provided the basis for capital authorizations had to be adjusted upwards each year, and even then failed to keep pace with increases in successive years running at the rate of 1 per cent, 2 per cent, 4 per cent, 8 per cent and now 10 per cent predicted for 1966.

Gas sales were increasing faster than electricity, and gas was winning back the loads which it had lost during the boom period of the kerosene room heaters. Our weakness was an increasing dependence on virgin naphtha or light distillate (alternative names for the same thing). I could see that the combined demands of the gas and chemical industries would probably overtake the supply. Prices were certain to harden. It would take several years to bring to a successful conclusion the processes being developed by Dent and his co-workers in Solihull (described in Chapter 12) for the gasification of heavy oil. The importation of natural gas from Holland by an underwater pipe had been studied and was known to be feasible. Other possible sources of liquefied natural gas were being kept under review. The first discovery of natural gas by BP in the West Sole Field, soon to be followed by Shell's Leman Bank and Amoco's Indefatigable, introduced a new dimension into forward planning. The projection of past trends became even more meaningless to the Ministry planners, who were under pressure to produce a national fuel policy and were becoming embarrassed, to put it mildly, by the near-impossibility of their task.

I was reminded of Gaston Berger who had established in Paris a school of forecasting technological changes based not on the projections of past trends but on the analysis of forward situations. This he called '*l'attitude prospective*'. Having established that one such situation is feasible and advantageous, you track back over time to arrive at your present situation by a series of tentative but feasible steps; the merit of the system being that it is free from the tyranny of present attitudes conditioned by past trends.

My plan then for the Canadian paper was to examine two situations which might exist some ten years ahead, assuming certain possible rates of discovery of gas in the North Sea, and test these for feasibility and financial viability. The paper represented one of the earliest public predictions on the size and structure of a new gas industry. It was published in full in the *Journal of the the Institution of Gas Engineers* (Communication 717).

Gas industry planning was based on the expectation that natural gas would play an increasing part among the feedstocks available. But the demand for gas was growing at a rate which exceeded the best firm estimates of new discoveries, after allowing for the time taken to bring them up to full production. A substantial number of reforming plants would still have to be built: fortunately, many of these plants were versatile and could be adapted to produce synthetic natural gas during the transition period.

The First Case Study

Case study no. 1 was based on what we could already see as the minimum outcome of North Sea discoveries estimated at a thousand million cubic feet a day. I thought that this would be absorbed by increasing demand. Natural gas would supply about half the total output of the gas industry, the rest being from naphtha reformers. The case for starting the conversion of the supply system from town to rich gas seemed to me to require no further justification. I also assumed that a second scheme for importing 100 million cubic feet a day of liquefied natural gas would be completed and that all the liquefied natural gas would be used to supply winter seasonal demand. Liquefied petroleum gas, LPG for short, was also treated as a supply on a seasonal basis, and refinery gas as a constant load. Coal gas and coke oven gas were assessed at a total of 200 million cubic feet per day at a constant rate throughout the year. Naphtha was assumed to be converted into gas (lean or rich) at a rate determined by seasonal demands.

I assumed that there would be no increase in the number of gas consumers in the domestic sector due to increased competition from other fuel interests, but that the introduction of natural gas would lead to a large increase in the quantity of gas they used. What emerged from this study was the magnitude of the problem of dealing with the seasonal load, for on this depended the future of the gas industry as a supplier of convenient heat. I had to try out many different solutions of the business of supplying economically a demand which could reach forty-four million therms a day in winter and fall to only nine million therms a day in summer.

A feasible solution consisted of aquifer storage (we were then optimistic concerning the outcome of searches by Professor Illing in Oxfordshire), bulk storage of liquefied natural gas, and peak shaving by LPG, together with the seasonal and varied use of naphtha reformers. A trial cost analysis suggested a possible reduction of about 20 per cent in the average cost of gas after allowing for the cost of converting customers' appliances to use natural gas and greatly increased expenditure on plant for production, storage, transmission and distribution.

Liquefied natural gas would require storage on a huge scale, involving twenty-five frozen-ground storage cavities of the kind then planned for the Canvey Island terminal, where four units, each of 21,000 tons were scheduled for completion in the near future. Its extreme flexibility gave this method an outstanding advantage. For example, I proposed that gas could be delivered at the rate of up to 1,000 million cubic feet per day. Underground storage in aquifers might make a greater contribution when more was known of the size and characteristics of suitable geological formations in the United Kingdom. LPG could be stored in refrigerated or pressure tanks at the point of usage, or in salt domes connected by a pipeline distribution system.

The initial price of North Sea gas was then still under negotiation with no end in sight. To avoid the appearance of being committed to any one figure, the price of Slochteren gas at the Dutch border was used in the calculations at 3.25d per therm.

Domestic tariffs yielding on average 20d per therm could be sufficiently promotional to achieve the proposed levels of consumption. The average large user would have a bill for heating and hot water of £72 10s 0d and the owner of a warm-air system would pay £36 per annum for heating, charges which should be within the means of the relevant income groups. Tested another way, the National Plan (then still current) assumed a growth in the rate of domestic consumption equivalent to £7,400 million if maintained for ten years. The 12 million gas consumers would enjoy £5,000 million of this, and the extra domestic gas bill of £200 million, representing 4 per cent of extra domestic consumption in the hands of consumers, seemed reasonable.

Commercial tariffs averaging 16d per therm should be sufficiently attractive to gain a good foothold in the shop and office business, and industrial gas could be offered down to 8d per therm for large-scale users.

This tentative outline of a future gas supply, implying a reduction of 20 per cent in the average cost of gas, assumed that the economy would continue to expand and that no non-market restraints would be applied to the expansion of the gas industry.

The Second Case Study

The second case study assumed that the North Sea would fulfil our more optimistic predictions and supply natural gas at an average rate of 4,000 million cubic feet a day, or four times that in the first study. By now all our customers would be converted to natural gas, and naphtha reformers would be used only to help meet the seasonal demand. This could vary between 122 million therms a day in winter and 26 million therms a day in summer. Storage of the required additional amounts of seasonal gas could be met by extension of the liquid natural gas storage and the further possible development of aquifers already mentioned, together with the drilling of more wells in producing fields (which, compared with USA and Canada, were located reasonably close to the main centres of consumption) and the sale of gas on an interruptible basis. The idea of creating storage by recharging working reservoirs was sound enough but was really a non-starter. It would have entailed renegotiating contracts which had taken well over a year of blood, sweat and toil to reach a grudging conclusion on both sides and could in no wise be tampered with thereafter. (Twenty years later the Rough Field was to provide flexible supply from one site on the required scale). The industry came to rely on interruptible loads, to be supplemented if necessary by the extended use of liquefied natural gas.

This was the first time that the great scale of the capital expenditure required to provide a natural gas system on a national scale had been disclosed:

	£ mill.	*mill. therms p.a.*
Assets employed by the gas industry in 1964	600	3600
Additional capital required for Study I	1235	7600
Additional capital required for Study II	1181/1838	18000
Cost of converting appliances	360	

This led to cumulative gross additions of between £2,776 and £3,433 million, depending on the proportion of the local distribution network that had to be replaced (in Study II), all spread over ten years.

These estimates, admittedly speculative at the time, were confirmed in the Gas Council's 1970 publication entitled 'Natural Gas in the 1970s', which forecast an expenditure of £2,570 million in the ten years to 1975.

Figure 3. The British gas industry's 1964-65 results and case studies I and II fitted to an exponential growth curve.

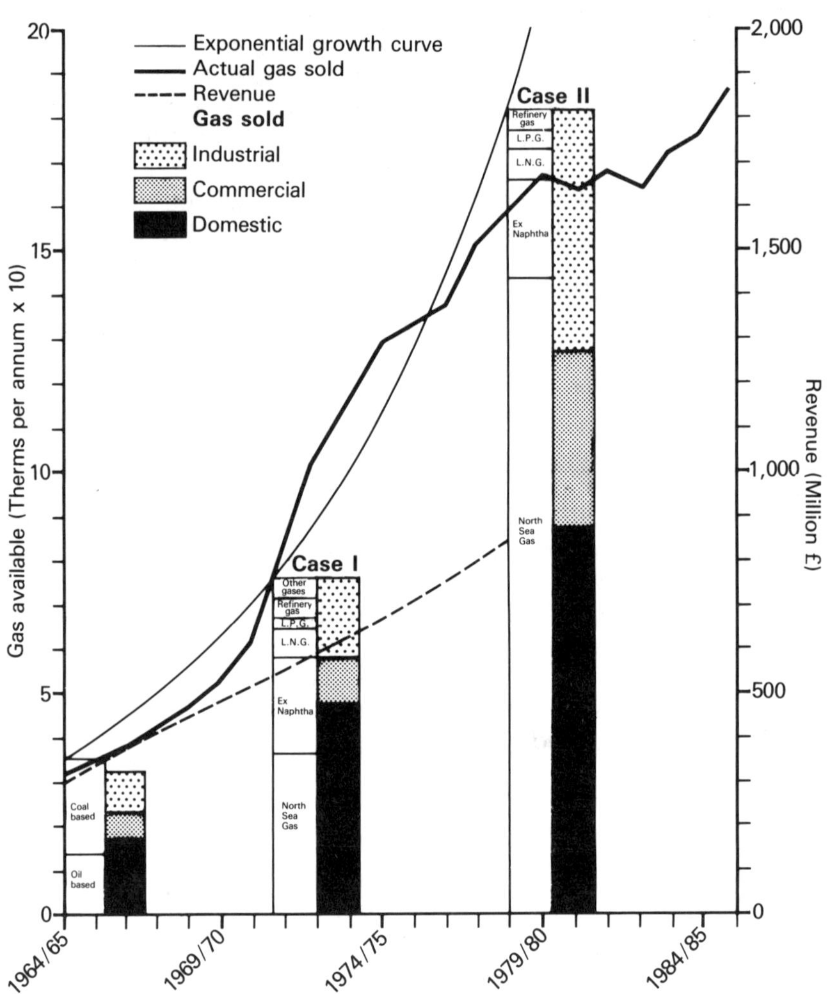

Growth rate of 12% p.a. is illustrated for cases I and II.

Figure 4. Gas and Electricity Supply, 1940-85 (Equivalent thermal units).

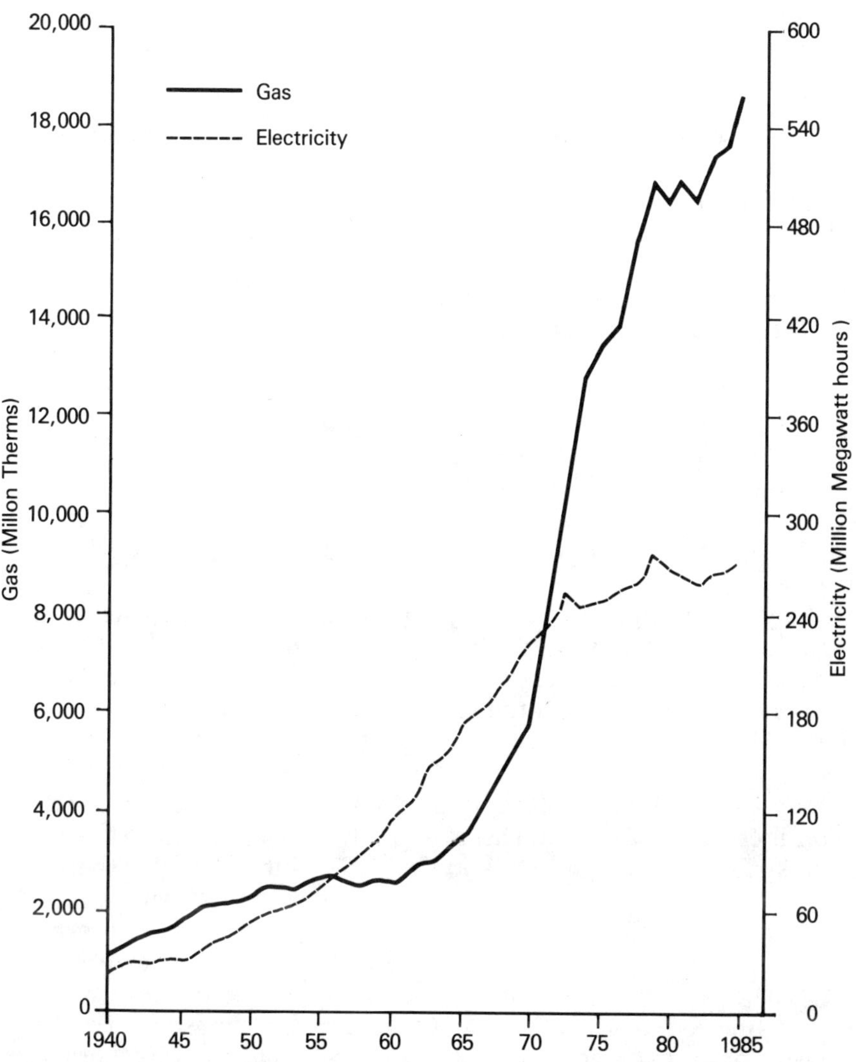

The price of North Sea gas in these larger quantities should be less than that used in Study I and a figure of 2.5d per therm was used, which corresponded to prices prevailing close to the Texas gas fields. It was assumed that all appliances had now been converted to use natural gas and that all the naphtha in the contracts was being converted to natural gas on a seasonal basis and that liquefied natural gas and liquefied petroleum gas were still available and being used for peak-load control.

The gas industry, always capital intensive on the production side, was now in process of changing to a condition where at least two thirds of its costs would be for the distribution of its product. However, the economy of scale would be very great indeed and Study II suggested a final cost of gas between 10.5 and 11.6d per therm. This was just about half the 1964 price of gas.

The proposed sales pattern was:

	mill. therm	*£ mill.*
Domestic	8,700 at 14d	507
Commercial	4,000 at 12d	200
Industrial	5,300 at 6d	132
Total	18,000	839

There was support for this projection in the accounts of the Peoples Gas Company of Chicago, an American utility serving over a million consumers with its own transmission and aquifer storage system, and I quoted results from their published accounts for 1964:

Domestic	1,177 mill. therms	48%	at	9.3d per therm
Commercial	213 mill. therms	9%	at	8.2d per therm
Industrial	456 mill. therms	43%	at	4.8d per therm (firm)
	629 mill. therms			3.6d per therm (interruptible)

In Chicago half the domestic consumers had house heating and consumption averaged 1,180 therms a year against 700 therms in Study II and 160 therms a year as it was in the UK in 1966.

The supply of 18,000 million therms per annum was equivalent to 45 million tons of oil, and would represent between 20 and 25 per cent of the total energy market by about 1980, comparable with that in the United States where natural gas already represented over 30 per cent of total energy resources, and Canada where it represented 18 per cent.

In Figure 3, the gas industry's 1964-65 results and the two case studies were fitted to an exponential growth curve and the subsequent actual results have been added as a continuous line. The scale at the bottom of the graph was originally given in years for the rates of growth of 10 per cent, 12 per cent and 14 per cent, but the outcome matches most closely the 12 per cent rate. Figure 4 shows the rapid pace of development of gas supply compared with electricity after 1960.

My paper caused no stir at Murray Bay down on the north shore of the Saint Lawrence estuary, where the Canadian Gas Association were meeting. After all it was doing little more than forecasting a situation which they had all experienced. In London it hit the headlines on 27 June: 'North Sea finds will slash your gas bill' and '6d off, that's the long range forecast for your gas bill'. The City editor of *The Times* reported 'Forecast of gas supplied at 6d a therm', stating that 'more detailed evidence of the Gas Council's unashamed, and so far unjustified optimism arising from the North Sea resources, has been given by the Deputy Chairman, Sir Kenneth Hutchison'.

It turned out that the predicted lower price of domestic gas, which is all the public knows and cares about, was not to be approached for some time to come, for there was another valid solution of the overall sales pattern in which gas is sold more cheaply to industry and in greater quantity, much of it interruptible.

The cause of this was the pressure to achieve rapid build-up of supply. North Sea discoveries came very fast and within a year reserves of twenty trillion cubic feet were demanding to be used. The Government wanted the speediest possible relief from the recurrence of repayment problems; and the oil companies wanted to maximize profit by securing the earliest possible return on their capital.

The result of these pressures was that the contracts as finally negotiated provided for a build-up period much shorter than the time required to create the market for domestic gas on the scale predicted in Study II above. The only solution in the time available was to sell gas to large industrial users, including one or more electricity power stations, at a price competitive with coal or fuel oil. Some would have to be sold on an interruptible or seasonal basis, at a price which would be substantially lower than for year-round consumers. In Chicago 60 per cent of the industrial gas was sold as interruptible or 'valley' gas, at just over half the price of the year-round supply. The effect of such a policy must inevitably be to increase the revenue which has to be recovered from domestic consumers, who are in effect paying indirectly for the storage problem which their seasonal demand presents.

By 1980/81 (towards the time horizon implied by Study II) some 51 per cent of all gas was supplied to domestic consumers compared with the 48 per cent of the study and the 48 per cent of Peoples Gas of Chicago. For industrial gas the outcome in the same year was 35.5 per cent against 39 per cent in Study II and 43 per cent in Chicago in 1964. The target demand of 18,000 million therms was approached in 1979/80 (16,864 m. therms in that year), but not exceeded until 1985/86. The figures for pricing were much affected by the intervening upheaval in energy prices, but the comparison is still interesting. The figures below are expressed in 1980 new pence (based on the 1980/81 British Gas Corporation Annual Report and using a 4.5 factor for inflation of the earlier figures):

Average Revenue from gas sold and used in pence per therm

	Study II	*1980/81 Actual*
Domestic	26.3	24.2
Commercial	22.5	26.1
Industrial	11.2	18.8

The relatively higher price for industrial gas reflects in part the general abandonment of interruptible supply after domestic heating expanded to fill the initial gap in demand.

These considerations concerned the future – it was enough for me at this stage to know that between wide possible limits of what the North Sea might hold the gas industry could progress and prosper. The technical problems were not insoluble and I was satisfied that I would not be leaving before my task was completed.

The most pressing single decision to be made during 1966 was whether, or when, to start converting consumers to natural gas and how fast. The technical problems were formidable, because almost all popular fires and water heaters had been designed round the non-aerated burner – popularly known as the batswing. This had the merit of almost complete silence, but they just would not convert – they had to be changed. The older type of aerated burner – the Bunsen burner of our laboratory days – as was used on cookers, was relatively easy to convert. Watson House, with my strong support, had tried for a year to find a compromise gas, which while still consisting mainly of methane would also contain enough hydrogen to burn successfully in non-aerated burners. No valid solution emerged and planning needed to start forthwith. A Conversion Executive, headed by Desmond Ellis the Deputy Head of Watson House, was established by the Gas Council in 1966 to co-ordinate the efforts of all the Area Boards, with a remit to rationalize the ordering of the millions of replacement parts that would be required.

Our second urgent problem in that year was to settle the terms and conditions of supply of gas by the companies to the Council, and to agree a price. Here we were up against an intractable problem. The first settlement following the initial and special West Sole case of 1965 was not reached until some eighteen months after I had left the Council. If this seems to be a long time to settle a simple matter, and public opinion inclined to this view, it should be remembered that the value of 30 trillion cubic feet of recoverable reserves was at least £3,000 million in the money of those days. When added to this the goods were to be delivered over a period of twenty-five years, any settlement reached at the time could well appear unrealistic towards the end of the contract. I felt then, and feel more strongly now, that it was a serious mistake in tactics by both sides to try to determine a single price and a rigid set of conditions for most of the life of the fields. To me it always seemed unwise to try to settle anything so large, over a period of years so long, that no one could possibly foresee the consequences. In any case it was most unlikely that those who made these decisions would survive long enough to see the end result.

As we have seen in Chapter 15, the Council had taken the precaution of studying methods used in the United States for controlling the price of natural gas. Federal control of gas prices dating back to 1938 had been decisively affected by the Phillips Petroleum case of 1954. Our application of the cost-based formula in use by the Federal Power Commission to the early BP finds has also been discussed above. More immediately, we were also affected by clauses in the North Sea Act, which followed closely a clause in the 1934 Petroleum Act. The effect of this was that the finder must first offer gas to the appropriate Area Board (or as a result of the 1965 Gas Act, to the Gas Council), with these exceptions:

> The finder was entitled to use it for his own purposes or to sell for chemical purposes without restriction. The finder could not under any circumstances

sell it for domestic use, but could sell it to industry, if it had first been offered to the Gas Council or Area Board at a reasonable price, and refused.

There was absolutely no guidance in the Act as to what constitutes a 'reasonable' price, and the Government at no time attempted to define what was 'reasonable', or even what criteria might be used to arrive at a 'reasonable' cost. The long list of cases which had appeared before the Federal Power Commission, the long list still waiting to be heard, and the record of the time consumed in these hearings, were enough to suggest that this was not an easy task. The Ministry of Power was probably well advised not to attempt it, at least openly where it could have been challenged. Instead it was made known that the Minister would be pleased if the Gas Council could freely negotiate a price. If that price fell within the limits of what he considered 'reasonable' and in the public interest he would be pleased to indicate his approval publicly by a statement in Parliament. Nothing was said about what would happen if the figure did not fall within those limits. It is neither useful nor profitable for a nationalized industry to pursue speculations of this kind.

The Council made no secret of its plans to be first with a comprehensive transmission system by which gas could be delivered to all the Area Boards. The Boards in their turn were exceptionally well placed to deliver it to domestic and industrial consumers alike. The Council and the Boards had all the powers necessary to lay mains for the purpose. An oil company seeking to deliver gas to a customer under any of the exception clauses in the North Sea Act would first have to obtain an authorization under the 1962 Pipeline Act. Under the conditions, which existed when large quantities of gas were trying to find a market in 1966, the Gas Council and the Area Boards had pre-empted a position of great strength. They could control and manage the market. Even ICI, who as chemical industry users had the right to buy direct, preferred in the end to make a deal with the Council rather than try to organize their own supplies. As to industrial sales, no one had any idea what the Minister would consider to be a 'reasonable' price, if the matter should be referred to him. If matters went so far – and they could take a long time – it was still possible the Council would refuse to buy. Then and only then could the producer start obtaining all the permits required under the pipeline act to bring gas to the customers of his choice. The Council if it had not a complete monopoly had something almost as good – a head start on all its potential competitors.

So negotiations proceeded on the basis that the Gas Council was the single purchaser, and I do not think that any of the potential suppliers gave serious consideration to any alternative. For tax, and other reasons, each producer in a group had to negotiate, or at least appear to negotiate, independently. This gave added strength to the Council's position, providing them with the opportunity to probe the defences and detect any weak spot.

During all this everyone knew quite well that the Minister of Power and his civil servants, and the Prime Minister and his advisers were keenly interested. Lord Balogh was known to be quite involved, and has since given his views in speeches in the House of Lords and in published statements. They had all absorbed the thinking and techniques of the Federal Power Commission of the United States.

Bob Marshall, later Sir Robert Marshall, and a Permanent Secretary at the Department of Trade and Industry, had just come to the Ministry of Power as a Deputy Secretary, with a special responsibility for gas price. We had many and long discussions on the subject, and a great deal of paper passed. It was all too easy to do a great deal of arithmetic, which is a favourite phrase in the Civil Service, on the basis of premises which the history of the North Sea was far too short to establish as valid. The very large size of the early discoveries and the speed and accuracy with which they had been located were leading to extrapolations over the whole of the North Sea, about which I had, to put it mildly, very considerable reservations amounting to disbelief.

There was no certainty, not even a probability, that these early discoveries would be repeated. A true average rate of success, such as was used to establish Field Prices in the Southern (or Permian) Basin, could only be established after a long enough period of exploration and discovery. It seemed to me unreasonable to attribute to the first large field only those costs encountered up to date and calculate a price on that basis. It was as I often said, 'as if the odds on the winner of the Derby were decided after the race had been run'.

Meanwhile the Production and Supply Division, under the direction of Denis Rooke, was growing fast and would soon be fully manned to handle a programme of transmission costing £700 million. The 1965 Gas Act, which gave the Gas Council powers to buy and sell gas, had provided for the appointment of three full-time members, one of whom was Denis Rooke. Eventually the Division would also have to control the delivery of gas from the fields to the Boards on a scale of 4,000 million cubic feet a day on average over a year. They would have to be prepared to deal with variations due to the weather and the demands of 13 million consumers with all that entails in the way of control equipment and information services. An operational research team at the London Research Station was now available with its sophisticated techniques for optimizing the layout of the system. The new engineering research laboratory at Killingworth was being built up to deal with the many technical problems which would certainly arise. In short, the Gas Council had been highly successful in its first North Sea venture. That would justify the building up of an effective geological and petroleum engineering section, which more than justified its establishment later, when at Wytch Farm in Dorset, and in Morecambe Bay, it proved its own judgement sound in the face of adverse opinion from very much more experienced oil companies.

The gas industry engineers in the North Thames Gas Board and at the Gas Council had successfully pioneered the first large-scale commercial operation for liquefied natural gas. There were engineers competent to handle any extension in this direction, including the storage of gas for emergency use, to meet seasonal demand over the whole country.

The industry's sales forces had abandoned old prejudices against the heating load, which market alone offered a prospect of expansion. They had acquired an aggressive attitude towards selling and a really modern attitude to publicity.

Administratively there was still some way to go towards integrating the industry. What it might have lost in centralized efficiency it gained in the sturdy independence of the Boards. For at any one time you could be sure at least one Board was making a useful advance in administration, technology or sales technique, even though another might be doing something altogether less useful. The Chairmen were shrewd observers, quick to detect the failures and equally quick to emulate the success of others. I could see no good reason for change, but I knew there would be pressures to integrate the industry in pursuit of whatever management doctrine was in fashion at the time.

Politicians of all kinds had tinkered relentlessly with nationalized industries, driven by ideological urges, and secure in the knowledge that they were unlikely to remain long enough in that particular office to experience the full results of their efforts. The gas industry was fortunate in that during the twenty-one years after nationalization there were twelve Ministers of Power, six Permanent Secretaries, three Chairmen of the Gas Council, and only one new Gas Act. They had tinkered with coal until Harold Macmillan appointed Lord Robens, and he kept everyone quiet for the next ten years. They had centralized and de-centralized electricity, on the basis of reports by committees of enquiry, and they had taken to pieces the railway and transport industries and put them together again with all the enthusiasm of a child in charge of a box of building bricks. Lord Beeching's successful spell in charge of railways had come to an abrupt end with a change of Minister. Steel found itself in and out of the national fold with every change of government.

Alone among these industries gas escaped attention, perhaps because for the first ten years it had neither been sufficiently successful nor failed dramatically. The Select Committee in 1961 had seen the need for some change when they were examining our proposals to import liquid natural gas. They had heard Lord Robens on the merits of centralized gas production by the Lurgi process and a national grid to transmit the gas to all or most of the Area Boards. I have earlier dealt with the fate of that proposition.

We made it clear in our evidence that the importation of liquefied natural gas from Algeria, about which the Minister was at that time still undecided, would have to be an operation on a national scale if it were to succeed. We gave it as our view that the best way to achieve this result would be to give the Gas Council powers to buy, produce, distribute and sell gas in bulk. In 1961 the Select Committee had urged the Minister, then Lord Mills the Paymaster General, to make up his mind about promoting our work with LNG. They recognized the need for central powers but came down on balance in favour of a separate production board, on the same pattern as in electricity.

It was to be four years before the opportunity arose to obtain these extra powers. The Government had promised to introduce a bill to regulate storage of gas in underground structures. It followed all the furore down in Hampshire when the Gas Council promoted a Private Bill to enable it to store gas in the Chilcombe Anticline, close to Winchester. By this time we had persuaded the Government and the administration that our proposed organization was preferable, since for some time to come the Area Boards would be constructing and operating their own production plants. Meanwhile the central body could be carrying out operations such as the distribution of imported LNG and the production and transmission of North Sea gas, which by their nature could only be done effectively by a central body. The fact that all Area Boards were represented on the Council and its Production Policy

Committee ensured that there was proper co-ordination between the two sides.

Sir Dennis Proctor observed that if we would limit our requirements to such powers as were required to buy and sell gas and distribute it to our customers who were the Area Boards and if we could set out our proposals in three clauses which would precede the Government's Underground Storage (1965) Bill, for which Parliamentary time had already been allotted, we could get what we wanted. The Gas Act (1965) was the result. By 1966 the system was working well, although it involved more committee work, and more discussion than at times seemed strictly necessary, depending on the personality of those involved in any particular debate. As a form of character building it was probably first-class. Any firm of management consultants would be shocked, and no doubt one such was, when the Gas Council brought in the most fashionable of them all.

That was in the future. Meanwhile a lively and rather nostalgic round of leave-takings up and down the country left me the recipient of many delightful reminders of the good times I used to have as guest of the Boards. Finally a friendly gathering of the staff at Head Office and a drink or two led up to the presentation of a gift of books which they insisted should be of my own choosing: one observant young lady inferred that from the titles it seemed I intended to travel widely in my retirement. And so, on 30 December 1966, I retired from the Gas Council. Charles Rider, who had driven me for twenty years, urged me to let him continue as driver of whatever car I might have. I had to point out firmly that his accumulated years in the Pension Fund and his prospects with the Gas Council were worth far more than I was ever likely to be able to afford. I was driven home for the last time and said goodbye to Charles and to my official Daimler car, and that was all there was to it.

Index